WILLIAM WORDSWORTH

CRITICAL ISSUES

Published

George Eliot	*Pauline Nestor*
Virginia Woolf	*Linden Peach*
Charles Dickens	*Lyn Pykett*
Henry James	*Jeremy Tambling*
William Wordsworth	*John Williams*

In preparation

Geoffrey Chaucer	*Ruth Evans*
Jane Austen	*Darryl Jones*
Charlotte Brontë	*Carl Plasa*
James Joyce	*Kiernan Ryan*
D. H. Lawrence	*Rick Rylance*
Thomas Hardy	*Julian Wolfreys*

Critical Issues

William Wordsworth

John Williams

First published 2002 by
PALGRAVE
Houndmills, Basingstoke, Hampshire RG21 6XS
and 175 Fifth Avenue, New York, N. Y. 10010
Companies and representatives throughout the world

PALGRAVE is the new global academic imprint of
St. Martin's Press LLC Scholarly and Reference Division and
Palgrave Publishers Ltd (formerly Macmillan Press Ltd).

ISBN 0–333–68732–9 hardcover
ISBN 0–333–68733–7 paperback

This book is printed on paper suitable for recycling and
made from fully managed and sustained forest sources.

A catalogue record for this book is available
from the British Library.

A catalogue record for this book is available from
the Library of Congress

10   9   8   7   6   5   4   3   2   1
11   10   09   08   07   06   05   04   03   02

Printed in China

For Eleanor
(Better late than never)

Contents

Acknowledgements

I have received invaluable support and encouragement from colleagues at the University of Greenwich in the writing of this book. This includes not only a preparedness on the part of colleagues teaching English to listen to and discuss ideas and issues, it also involves the goodwill of the School of Humanities as a whole when it came to creating space to work on the project. I am also indebted to colleagues from other institutions who have helped shape parts of this book by their responses to conference papers over the past few years. Editors at what was then Macmillan and is now Palgrave were prepared to wait while I finished an earlier book, thus allowing me to undertake the work. I am grateful to them for that, and I owe a particular debt of thanks to Martin Coyle and John Peck, who read the initial manuscript and gave such valuable advice over the period of its subsequent revision. The responsibility for the final product, of course, rests entirely with me. Finally I should mention my own University Library, who at a time towards the end of the writing of this book, assisted me so willingly with a number of important loans, despite the fact that they were involved in a major move to a new location. The patience and willingness of staff to assist in those difficult circumstances is very much appreciated.

Note on References

References contained within the text use the following format: abbreviated form; volume number where appropriate; sonnet number in Roman numerals where appropriate; for *The Prelude* and *The Excursion*, Book number in Roman numerals where appropriate; page number; line number(s). Where the text already supplies information it will not normally be duplicated.

ABBREVIATED FORMS

Early Poems: *Early Poems and Fragments 1785–1797*, ed. Carol Landon and Jared Curtis (Ithaca, NY and London: Cornell University Press, 1997).

Excursion: quoted from *PW*, vol. 5.

LB: *Lyrical Ballads and Other Poems 1797–1800*, ed. James Butler and Karen Green (Ithaca, NY and London: Cornell University Press, 1992).

Peter Bell: *Peter Bell*, ed. John E. Jordan (Ithaca, NY and London: Cornell University Press, 1985).

Poems 1807: *Poems in Two Volumes and Other Poems 1800–1807*, ed. Jared Curtis (Ithaca, NY: Cornell University Press, 1992).

Prelude: *The Prelude 1799, 1805, 1850*, ed. Jonathan Wordsworth, M. H. Abrams, and Stephen Gill (New York and London: Norton, 1979). Unless otherwise stated, quotations are from the 1805 version.

Prose Works: *The Prose Works of William Wordsworth*, 3 vols, ed. W. J. B. Owen and Jane Worthington Smyser (Oxford: Clarendon Press, 1974).

PW: *The Poetical Works of William Wordsworth*, 5 vols, ed. Ernest de Selincourt (Oxford: Clarendon Press, 1952).

Ruined Cottage: *The Ruined Cottage and The Pedlar*, ed. James Butler (Ithaca, NY and Hassocks: Cornell University Press, 1979).

The Waggoner: *Benjamin the Waggoner*, ed. Paul F. Betz (Ithaca, NY and Brighton: Cornell University Press, 1981).

White Doe: *The White Doe of Rylstone*, ed. Kristine Dugas (Ithaca, NY and London: Cornell University Press, 1988).

Introduction

I

In *The Prelude* Book IV the poet looks out across a lake from a 'sheltered coppice'. He is alone; even his dog has gone. In the silence, it seems, he hears the breathing of Nature itself:

> Meanwhile
> The mountain heights were slowly overspread
> With darkness, and before a rippling breeze
> The long lake lengthened out its hoary line,
> And in the sheltered coppice where I sate,
> Around me, from among the hazel leaves –
> Now here, now there, stirred by the straggling wind –
> Came intermittingly a breath-like sound,
> A respiration short and quick, which oft,
> Yea, might I say, again and yet again,
> Mistaking for the panting of my dog,
> The off-and-on companion of my walk,
> I turned my head to look if he were there.
> (*Prelude* IV, 134, 168–80)

This is a familiar enough attitude for the Romantic poet to strike, and from the outset Wordsworth frequently had recourse to it:

> My Friends, restrain
> Those busy cares that would allay my pain:
> Oh! leave me to myself; nor let me feel
> The officious touch that makes me droop again.
> ('Written in very early Youth', *Poems 1807*, 146, 11–14)

The twenty-first-century reader is very familiar with this Wordsworth, but the public persona that the *Lyrical Ballads* of 1798

1

began to establish for him was rather different. The first readers of the *Ballads* were not confronted with the image of the poet as primarily a recluse, though he was clearly interested in writing about society's rejects. He was a poet involved in contemporary life. Later readers, however, have largely come to know Wordsworth primarily through *The Prelude* and a handful of anthologised lyrics, and in this guise he remains the 'daffodil poet', wandering 'lonely as a cloud'.

The image of Wordsworth as a poet who worked, and for much of the time lived, alone, has long since been recognised as a myth by literary critics of all persuasions. Jerome McGann argues that what happened over the years to Wordsworth as a poet is analogous to what happened to Romanticism as a descriptive category in literary history. 'Romanticism' is an ideological construct; in it history has been elbowed aside and replaced by a myth that evokes a unified, transcendental aesthetic; in the process what we witness, McGann argues, is 'that most secret and impalpable of all human acts: the transformation of fact into idea, and of experience into ideology'.[1] Wordsworth's solitary state is just such an 'idea'. Emphasising the initiative of the writer in this process, McGann suggests that, in the 'Ode: Intimations of Immortality', 'Wordsworth made a solitude and he called it peace'. He worked hard to create a persona for himself that, perversely, appears to oppose the publicity and approval he was bound to seek as a publishing poet:

> I am not One who much or oft delight
> To season my fireside with personal talk,
> About friends, who live within an easy walk,
> Or Neighbours, daily, weekly, in my sight...
> Better than such discourse doth silence long,
> Long, barren silence, square with my desire;
> To sit without emotion, hope, or aim,
> By my half-kitchen my half-parlour fire,
> And listen to the flapping of the flame,
> Or kettle, whispering its faint undersong.
> (*Poems 1807*, 253–4, 1–4, 9–14)

We know full well, of course, that the image created in 'I am not One who much or oft delight' is an idealised one. The poet's claim to be able to sit in silence by his 'half-kitchen...half-parlour fire' strongly implies that he sits alone. In fact, a reading of his sister's Grasmere *Journal* will suggest that in the cramped confines of the cottage in which the family was living when this poem was written, Wordsworth was unlikely ever to have been able to sit alone, or in silence, in the room he mentions. Indeed, it is very clear that, when the occasion demands, Wordsworth was all too ready to associate the voice of nature with public oratory rather than with private, solitary mediation:

> Loud is the Vale! The Voice is up
> With which she speaks when storms are gone,
> A mighty Unison of streams!
> Of all her voices, One!
> (*Poems 1807*, 265, 1–4)

These 'Lines, composed at Grasmere', Wordsworth explains at the head of the poem, were written after learning of the imminent death of the politician, Charles James Fox. The poem was placed immediately before the 'Elegiac Stanzas' in the 1807 *Poems, in Two Volumes*, a poem which commemorates the death of his brother John. Public mourning thus gives way to private grief; private feelings mingle uncertainly with public sadness.

The tensions evident here between the public and private voice of the 'Romantic' poet are encapsulated in an unpublished fragment Wordsworth wrote in 1798 (and later incorporated into *The Prelude* Book IV, ll.400–95) describing his meeting with a discharged soldier. The paradox becomes apparent in the first five lines:

> I love to walk
> Along the public way, when, for the night
> Deserted, in its silence it assumes
> A character of deeper quietness
> Than pathless solitudes.

In the unpeopled public road, with the appearance of reality dimmed by night, the poet may indulge his loneliness with visionary dreams. Yet he knows it is a public road, and his encounter there with a discharged soldier abruptly confronts the idealising tendencies he readily indulges. The soldier has been rejected by the society he has served; he directly challenges the credibility of Wordsworth's perception of a wholesome solitariness. The soldier is, compared to the poet, 'an uncouth shape':

> There was in his form
> A meagre stiffness. You might almost think
> That his bones wounded him. His legs were long,
> So long and shapeless that I looked at them
> Forgetful of the body they sustained.
> His arms were long and lean; his hands were bare;
> [His visage, wasted though it seem'd, was large
> In feature, his cheeks sunken, and his mouth]
> Shewed ghastly in the moonlight...
> (Reproduced in *LB*, 278–9, 43–51)

The soldier represents a disturbing intrusion into a social order that sought to maintain the appearance of plenitude and well-being. He steps out of a darkness that might otherwise serve to cloak uncomfortable truths laid bare by the light of day. As such this solitary figure becomes a destabilising metaphor for the poet Wordsworth is becoming, as against the poet he might wish to be; or indeed as against the poet we might wish him to be.

II

This book discusses how Wordsworth criticism has evolved since he first began to publish his work. As it does so, it will reflect on the various ways that discovering the complex identity of the Wordsworth who walked by night has increasingly become the goal of the modern critic. 'Essentially', Ralph Pite is prepared to admit, 'he was odd.'[2] While not everyone is prepared to be quite as blunt as that about Wordsworth, understanding the 'oddness' of the man is now a recurring feature in much critical engagement with the poetry.

The discharged soldier passage quoted above may be read in exactly this way, as an image of the 'odd' poet; but its fate as a fragment of unpublished poetry is equally revealing. If Wordsworth appears now to have had a personality that included enigmatic, hidden depths, much of his poetry also remained literally inaccessible for many years, hiding information about its author. The version of the passage I am using comes from a text that has only been widely available to the general reader since 1992, when it was included among other unpublished fragments in the Cornell edition of *Lyrical Ballads*. The redrafted version Wordsworth inserted into *The Prelude*, though not profoundly altered, remained unavailable to the reading public until after his death in 1850. With the appearance of *The Prelude* in that same year, Victorian readers were presented with an autobiography that told the story of the poet's formative years as Wordsworth wished it to be understood. Although its initial reception was far from enthusiastic, by the end of the century *The Prelude* had become – of all Wordsworth's writings – the text that increasingly assumed control over the way the poet's life and work came to be read.

This state of affairs lasted at least until the mid-twentieth century, by which time the appearance of unpublished drafts of the poem had thoroughly undermined any sense of there being a single, authoritative *Prelude*. From our twenty-first-century vantage point, we now find ourselves looking back across a long period during which the hegemony of *The Prelude* has been steadily eroded.

The chapters which follow investigate critical issues for the study of Wordsworth arising from circumstances such as these, circumstances which have significantly influenced the critical reception of Wordsworth's poetry since he first began to publish. In Chapter 4, for example, a discussion of Frances Furguson's widely acclaimed book, *Wordsworth: Language as Counter-Spirit* (1977), draws attention to the way later twentieth-century criticism included studies which progressively tended to marginalise all orthodox biographical criticism in favour of pursuing linguistic issues. These were concerns which clearly became dominant preoccupations for Wordsworth himself from relatively early on in his career as he began to edit and arrange, as well as compose, his poetry and prose.

In common with many other poets, the onset of middle age found Wordsworth spending an increasing amount of time revising and ordering his work, while he continued to write new pieces. Behind this constantly evolving body of published work there existed an ambition to produce a monumental philosophical poem to be known as *The Recluse*. He never completed it. The unpublished *Prelude* formed part of that project, as did *The Excursion*, a massive work in its own right that first appeared in 1814. But subsequent editions show him constantly editing that text in the same way that he was redrafting passages of *The Prelude*. We see further evidence of this complex story unfolding through his publication of a series of expanding 'Collected Poems', beginning in 1815, and running through 1820, 1827, 1832, until by 1836–7 the *Collected Works* filled six volumes. Wordsworth scholars have since published vast quantities of previously unread poetry, ranging from early drafts and brief fragments to substantial poems, much of which material was unavailable to readers until well into the twentieth century. This is the private Wordsworth treading the public road by night.

III

As I suggested at the beginning of this Introduction, the modern reader, encountering the public and the private Wordsworth, becomes aware without too much difficulty of powerful creative tensions at work. There is an abundance of autobiographical reference within the writing. Sometimes it would seem to be direct, at others it is oblique, and not infrequently it will be disguised as someone else's story. As the years pass, it is subject to revision and reinterpretation. The familiar Wordsworthian preoccupation with childhood is clearly an important ingredient in this process, as is 'Nature', but to understand how these ingredients combine is to embark on a difficult and intriguing critical journey.

This book is designed to explore the route that Wordsworth criticism has taken as the intricacies of his creative life have been progressively explored by each succeeding generation of scholars. Wordsworth studies still represent hotly contested ground, but for the most part they do so after a fashion that has come to differ significantly from the way he was discussed by the first readers of the *Lyrical Ballads* in 1798, by those who ridiculed *Poems, in Two Volumes* when it first appeared in 1807, and by those who reviewed *The Excursion* in 1814, an equally controversial text.

With this in mind, the first chapter will investigate the early years of the poet, setting Wordsworth's references to childhood in his earliest poetry alongside what evidence we have of the childhood he experienced. As we do this, we encounter one critical issue that has arguably survived in an easily recognisable form since the time of his first publications, even if the treatment has differed: analysing the relationship between Wordsworth's poetry and the political issues of the day. Behind the immediate circumstances that shaped Wordsworth's childhood, the loss of his parents and his removal from the family home at Cockermouth to his uncle's house in Penrith, lie political facts of life that reflect divisions and tensions that existed across the region, and that ran deep into the social and cultural life of the nation as a whole in this period. They were eventually to become dramatically and very obviously a part of Wordsworth's life with the coming of the French Revolution, and his decision to travel to France as a student in 1790, and even more so with his determination to return there in 1791. Chapter 1 will consider the part that Wordsworth's gradual recognition of these political issues – alongside his formal education at Hawkshead School and Cambridge – played in the evolution of his poetry through to the mid-1790s. After this, if we agree with the majority of twentieth-century critics, we begin to recognise the emergence of a mature poet increasingly in control of his voice. This is the Wordsworth who began work on a narrative poem he called *The Ruined Cottage*, the subject of Chapter 2; and who – with Coleridge – published *Lyrical Ballads* in 1798, the subject of Chapter 3.

After Wordsworth's years of engagement with radical political ideas in the mid-1790s, we shall see that *The Ruined Cottage* signals an important change in his attitude. This did not initially imply a denial of his commitment to the need for radical reform. It signalled, rather, a questioning of the means by which reform might properly come about. Subsequent chapters will discuss the critical issues which surround the poetry following *The Ruined Cottage* and *Lyrical Ballads*. This will include considering the views of critics who have resisted a reading of Wordsworth that rests heavily on biographical and political material. In *Lyrical Ballads* and in the *Poems in Two Volumes* of 1807 (Chapter 4), however, we may find continuing traces of political and autobiographical reference, and also an engagement with the issue of language as a tool for poetry. Wordsworth's commitment to a principle of 'simplicity' of language and subject (found in his Preface to the *Lyrical Ballads*), and his use of nature and natural objects in his poetry, will be considered as an integral part of the concern of so many critics to understand the relationship between Wordsworth's poetry, and the way he attempted to trace his development as a poet through childhood and youth to manhood. Chapter 5, therefore, looks at three of his longer narrative poems, where autobiography and politics, alongside the powerful evocation of the natural world, remain a central, but frequently suppressed, preoccupation. In Chapters 6 and 7, we consider *The Prelude* of 1805 as a retrospective account by Wordsworth of the way in which his relationship as a poet to the natural world had fundamentally altered in the course of the late 1790s, and of the way those changes were linked both to his experiences as a child, and as a politically engaged young man. The most important point here must be to appreciate that this was Wordsworth's analysis of how he had come to be the poet he was. Chapters 8 and 9 look at the later work, beginning with *The Excursion* of 1814.

Here we continue to consider the implications of the way Wordsworth revised, modified, and generally sought to control the presentation of his work.

The major issues raised throughout this book are those raised for the most part by influential critical voices that have written on Wordsworth since the time he first began to publish. All these critics have, in various ways, found it necessary to deal with the relationship between the poet and the poetry, which is to say the relationship of Wordsworth as biographical subject to the business of reading and interpreting his poetry. They have almost all of them in some way had to consider the relationship between political engagement and poetry, and the relationship between language and meaning as it applies to Wordsworth's choice of subject matter and style. As the twentieth century progressed, all of them have also had to weigh the public Wordsworth against the private Wordsworth, assessing a poet who spent increasing amounts of time editing, ordering, arranging and rearranging his work through a series of Collected Editions that established his reputation in the course of the last 25-years of his life. The final chapter offers a review of the evolution of Wordsworth criticism through to the current century. In the process, it is suggested that the critical issues we see dominating the study of Wordsworth may be more fully understood by placing them in the context of the debate (vigorously pursued since the 1830s) over the identity and location of the Romantic Movement in literary history.

1

The Early Years: Politics and Poetry

> Yes, I remember when the changeful earth
> And twice five seasons on my mind had stamped
> The faces of the moving year, even then,
> A child, I held unconscious intercourse
> With the eternal beauty, drinking in
> A pure organic pleasure from the lines
> Of curling mist, or from the level plain
> Of waters coloured by the steady clouds.
>
> (*Prelude* I, 58–60, 586–93)

I

Wordsworth himself ensured that after his death a steadily increasing number of readers would become convinced that the key to much of his poetry lay in the experiences of his childhood. Surprisingly, while he lived, the situation was very different. As a young poet he achieved considerable notoriety; his most formidable critic, Francis Jeffrey of the *Edinburgh Review*, portrayed him as eccentrically perverse, obsessed with 'an affectation of great simplicity and familiarity of language'. It was a critique that plainly linked a would-be revolutionary aesthetic with dangerously revolutionary political and religious ideas. In response to Wordsworth's claim of 1800 that the *Lyrical Ballads* sought to 'make the incidents of common life interesting by tracing in them ... the primary laws of our nature', and that they would do this by using 'the language of men' associated with 'the manners of rural life', Jeffrey wrote:

> The poor and vulgar may interest us, in poetry, by their *situation*; but never, we apprehend, by any sentiments that are peculiar to their condition, and still less by any language that is characteristic of it.[1]

Responses to *Lyrical Ballads* were by no means all negative, but in order to facilitate the long and painful journey towards acceptability, Wordsworth sought to remove his childhood and early manhood as far from the public gaze as possible. There were skeletons in his cupboard that needed to be kept locked away, not least among them the fact that in 1792 he had had an affair with Annette Vallon, and had become the father of their illegitimate child, Anne-Caroline.

In any case, the early Victorian Wordsworth whose epic poem of 1814, *The Excursion*, became (despite Jeffrey's initial savaging in the *Edinburgh Review*) increasingly admired as a work of humane wisdom, had little use for reference to a childhood lived in what by then seemed another age. Wordsworth was born in 1770, six years before the American War of Independence began and nineteen years before the outbreak of the French Revolution. By the time *The Excursion* appeared, the Revolution had come to be seen as a curtain raiser to England's heroic struggle with an aggressively imperialist rather than revolutionary French nation. Perspectives had shifted rapidly. Battles remained to be fought within the British political establishment for a fairer society, but the terms of reference used by liberals and radicals of a post-war generation were fundamentally changed from the 1790s. As Mary Shelley commented in a letter to Maria Gisborne in 1820, 'Thirty years ago was the era for Republics, and they all fell – This is the era for *constitutions* . . .'[2]

It is hardly surprising, therefore, that much critical work on Wordsworth throughout the twentieth century has been repeatedly drawn towards analysing the way in which so much of his poetry seems to engage in autobiographical evasion. While many Victorians were content with a Wordsworth who offered them a world of spiritual permanence glimpsed in both the magisterial forms of nature and in 'the meanest flower that blows', in the twentieth century he became an insecure, nervous poet, 'more like a man / Flying from something that he dreads, than one / Who sought the thing he loved.'[3]

It was the poem that Wordsworth chose not to publish while he lived, *The Prelude*, that significantly influenced the process of deconstructing the Victorian image of Wordsworth as a sage elder statesman of letters, replacing him with a poet of far greater complexity.[4] Revisionary criticism was initially prompted by Ernest de Selincourt's publication of a parallel text edition of the poem in 1926; this set an 1805 version of *The Prelude* alongside the one published in 1850. Another significant step forward came in 1970 with Jonathan Wordsworth's editing of an even earlier two-Part *Prelude* of 1799. All these texts were recognised as juxtaposing passages that dwelt upon the beauties of the natural world with passages concerned with personal and political turmoil. The 'new' 1799 text was a poem concerned solely with the poet's Lake District childhood, and it proved a valuable asset to the study of a poet whose childhood had long seemed to hold the key to an understanding of his creative achievement. Kenneth R. Johnston's biography of the early part of Wordsworth's life, *The Hidden Wordsworth* (first published in 1998 and revised two years later), suggests that there yet remains a good deal more to discover from both the historical and the literary account.[5]

The Wordsworth who emerges from the pages of more recent critical works such as Johnston's becomes ever more complex, both as a poet and as a man. For many years, however, it was something of a critical commonplace to emphasise the connection between the significance for Wordsworth of childhood, and his avowed commitment to 'simplicity' as a guiding principle in the poetry he wrote. The assumption tended to be that an important key to reading and understanding Wordsworth lay in what could be discussed about his own childhood. The source for such information was primarily taken to be *The Prelude*. For a number of readers at the turn of the eighteenth century confronted with Wordsworth's insistence on the virtues of simplicity, however, it had seemed that he was prepared all too often to adopt an infantile style, perversely claiming that it was a source of profundity otherwise unobtainable. This chapter will consider the early poetry as a way of appreciating that Wordsworth's understanding of simplicity became associated with another key concept for him, that of 'permanence'; and that together they formed the basis of a theory of language that constituted a very adult debate around the way language worked in relation to culture and politics. As John F. Danby observed in *The Simple Wordsworth* (1960), for Wordsworth, '"simplicity" as a literary programme involves questions of considerable sophistication'.[6]

Quite apart from anything else, there was, as Francis Jeffrey had insisted, a political agenda embedded in Wordsworth's commitment to simplicity, and this chapter is also therefore concerned with investigating the way in which the juvenilia reveals the evolution of a political motivation in Wordsworth's poetry. In *Doing Things With Texts* (1987) M. H. Abrams suggested that scholars were being tempted to over-politicise Wordsworth's work. Wordsworth's own politicisation of his poetry, however, is arguably visible in the juvenilia, and by the time he was composing his 'Salisbury Plain' poem in 1793, there can be no doubt that a political agenda was uppermost in his mind. It then becomes necessary to see what happens to that political poet when he begins work in 1796 on his play *The Borderers*, and in 1797 on *The Ruined Cottage*, and on poems that find their way into *Lyrical Ballads* of 1798. Abrams' remark was applied primarily to *Lyrical Ballads* and subsequent poetry; his views have recently been endorsed by Richard Cronin in his book *The Politics of Romantic Poetry* (Palgrave, 2001), where attention is particularly focused on readings of poems from the 1807 *Poems in Two Volumes*. In later chapters we will move on to consider that, while 'political' readings of the *Ballads* are by no means unjustified, there is indeed a danger that politically motivated readers, 'by imposing their critical ideology – have veiled, displaced, and in important aspects totally occluded' significant areas of meaning from the poems they claim to be understanding.[7]

II

Wordsworth's earliest years were lived in relative affluence in Cockermouth, but by the time he was five, family life was beginning to fragment. Pressure of work removed John Wordsworth from Cockermouth for long periods of time, and the five children were regularly boarded out with John's brother Richard at Whitehaven, and more frequently with Christopher Cookson at Penrith. With the death of their mother, Ann Wordsworth, in 1778, the Wordsworth boys (Richard b.1768, William b.1770, John b.1772 and Christopher b.1774) were sent permanently to Penrith, while Dorothy (b.1771) was dispatched to her mother's cousin at Halifax. In the same year William was sent as a boarder to Hawkshead School. His father died five years later. William soon came to loathe his uncle Christopher, and Dorothy's verdict on 'the ill nature of my Uncle' is well known: 'Many a time have William, John, Christopher and myself shed tears together, tears of bitterest sorrow.'[8]

There was an inescapably political complexion to the domestic turmoil of these years. When John Wordsworth died, his employer, Sir James Lowther, the richest and most powerful political magnate in the North West, owed him approximately £4000. It was a debt he had no intention of honouring. The responsibility for educating the children and finding them gainful employment fell to Christopher Cookson, a supporter of the Whig faction led by the Duke of Norfolk, and as such a sworn enemy of Lowther. Cookson found himself with the expense of raising the children of a brother-in-law who had worked tirelessly to further the career of a man he believed to be dishonourable, if not downright evil. At his death, that same brother-in-law was looking to build a political future for himself very much in the Lowther mould.

Of the four brothers, it was William who developed and cherished a sizeable chip on his shoulder. Hawkshead School was a place where he might enjoy a sense of liberty simply by virtue of it not being Penrith; but the situation was further influenced by the fact that in the late eighteenth century, Hawkshead was a relatively liberal institution. Its commitment to the Classical curriculum was offset by a progressive Enlightenment culture in its teaching of mathematics and science. It had long-established connections with St John's College, Cambridge, but it also sent students from Dissenting backgrounds to the prestigious Warrington and Manchester Academies. Lying outside Lowther's sphere of political influence, Hawkshead town also boasted a liberal community in which Anglican, Baptist and Quaker worthies appear to have lived and worked together with little difficulty. We also know that William Taylor, the Headmaster whom Wordsworth deeply respected, had been a close friend of the radical reformer George Dyer when at Emmanuel College. Wordsworth himself was to meet Dyer in London in the 1790s.[9] It is therefore not surprising to find that modern poetry and prose was readily available to the boys, and Wordsworth proceeded to read widely in the sentimental, picturesque works of Cowper, Beattie, Gray, Goldsmith and others, while he also discovered Langhorne, Crabbe, Charlotte Smith and Burns, writing that was beginning to transform an elegant, ornamental regret for a lost golden age, into poetry of radical Whig polemic, objecting with an ever sharper edge to contemporary materialism and greed. Whatever the source, Classical, sentimental or gothic, the surviving fragments of Wordsworth's juvenilia from this period show us a young man enjoying an eclecticism that characterised the cultural regime of the school.

In his five-volume edition of Wordsworth's poetical works Ernest de Selincourt devoted 57 pages to 'Juvenilia'. The section extends to include poetry written at the time when *Lyrical Ballads* were being compiled (though he places *An Evening Walk* and *Descriptive Sketches* – published together in 1793 – separately). Three distinct phases of poetical development are represented by this work as a whole: Wordsworth's time at Hawkshead Grammar School (1779–87), his undergraduate life at Cambridge (1787–91), and the period from the time he left Cambridge to when he moved to Alfoxden in Somerset in 1797. Each phase is marked by the poet's concern to pursue the theme of liberty as it relates to his perception of his own circumstances, circumstances he progressively politicises and projects onto a wider social order.

Through his editorial procedure, de Selincourt therefore implies that the 'mature' Wordsworth first appears in 1798 (aged 28) with *Lyrical Ballads*. It is worth reflecting that the poems thus cited as mature frequently define themselves – through Wordsworth's manipulation of various voices and his choice of subject matter – as rooted in a seemingly juvenile perception. Byron's jibe at the 'namby-pamby' Wordsworth of the 1807 *Poems in Two Volumes* should remind us that many contemporary critics believed Wordsworth was producing 'juvenilia' well on into his late thirties and beyond.[10] In fact, as the biographical record and the evidence contained in the early work suggests, *Lyrical Ballads* and the 1807 *Poems* include poetry that sought to reclaim a sense of childhood joy that in truth the poet had never really been able to lay claim to until adulthood. As a child and a young man Wordsworth was well justified in seeing himself as having been cruelly denied a secure social life; in 'The Vale of Esthwaite', for example, composed during the late 1780s, he had written: 'For I must never prove / A tender parent's guardian care' (*Early Poems*, 452, 366–7). Certain poems in *Lyrical Ballads* therefore celebrate with particular intensity the supportive love and esteem generated within the coterie that by 1798 had formed around him.

We cannot read the poetry that survives from Wordsworth's schooldays without remembering that it was a time when he had to cope with the loss of his parents, and the consequent loss of liberty that resulted from his dependence on the charity of relatives. His formal education over, he had then to cope with the loss of his political faith in the power of reason. It was upon this faith that he had pinned his hopes for the realisation of a Utopian state of universal liberty. This is the terrain across which Wordsworth's fraught journey towards poetic maturity took place; it is a journey that is charted, and begins to be defined by his juvenile work. 'Fostered alike by beauty and by fear' was how he described the experience in Book I of the 1805 *Prelude* (*Prelude* I, 44, 306), and the juvenilia illustrates how significant for the evolution of his later work were the 'fears' that haunted him in his youth.

Wordsworth's poetry appears from the first to have been a poetry of protest, born of his sense of having been denied a true home, and then denied the liberty to pursue the career of his choice because of an unjustly imposed condition of financial dependency. The juvenile poetry prior to the affirmative note present in many of the poems in *Lyrical Ballads* reveals how the experiences of youth and early manhood, from personal grief and bitterness to a political awakening in the shadow of the American War and the French Revolution, shaped a poet regarded by men like Jeffrey, Charles Burney and Byron as perpetually inclined to childishness, political subversion, and paganism. In 'The Vale of Esthwaite' Wordsworth posed the rhetorical question: 'What from the social chain can tear / This bosom link'd for ever there?' (*Early Poems*, 454, 388–9). By the time he was writing 'The Vale' in his late teens, he believed that the answer, though never directly stated in that poem, was very clear. It was first the loss of his parents, and second Sir James Lowther, who had refused to pay the orphaned children the money he owed their late father.

In *The Prelude*, Wordsworth's celebration of the freedom his schooldays brought him is presented primarily in terms of the development of an intense relationship with natural forms; but there remains also a persistent counterpoint of darker, negative forces:

> For I would walk alone
> In storm and tempest, or in starlight nights
> Beneath the quiet heavens, and at that time
> Have felt whate'er there is of power in sound
> To breath an elevated mood, by form
> Or image unprofaned, and I would stand
> Beneath some rock, listening to sounds that are
> The ghostly language of the ancient earth,
> Or make their dim abode in distant winds.
> Thence did I drink the visionary power.
> (*Prelude* II, 82, 321–30)

Accounts like these are frequently accompanied by memories of a sense of guilt, 'Low breathings coming after me', of abandonment, 'blank desertion', and in due course actual bereavement when first his father, then William Taylor, the Hawkshead Headmaster he so admired, died (*Prelude* I, 46, 330; 56, 422; X, 386, 500–14).

Reading the juvenilia composed during these years it becomes very clear that the poet's childhood was anything but a perpetual idyll. Given the persistence of a quotidian view that Wordsworth's early years were dominated by a serene communion with nature, it is important to recall the circumstances in which he began to write. As a child he cannot be expected to have understood at once the political implications that surrounded his father's death and his subsequent fostering. Divided political loyalties across the Wordsworth and Cookson families will eventually, however, have combined with a grasp of the political ambience of Hawkshead School to make it clear to him why life at Hawkshead proved preferable to the repressive atmosphere in the Penrith home of his uncle. Hawkshead was the place where Wordsworth could indulge his youthful delight in the society of other boys, and in the countryside where he was relatively free to roam and transgress. So long as he toed the line when it came to formal compositional exercises, Hawkshead encouraged him to experiment with his reading and writing to his heart's content.

III

While all biographies of Wordsworth discuss the importance of his exposure as a child to the natural world for his development as a poet, it has also long been recognised by many commentators that his reading was at the very least equally responsible for the way he described his encounters with nature, and the way he then began to relate that landscape to the social and political context in which he found himself. A landmark in this kind of critical approach came in 1954 with Robert Mayo's essay, 'The Contemporaneity of the *Lyrical Ballads*'.[11] Mayo contextualised the *Lyrical Ballads* in the light of the popular poetry of the day. Forty-eight years later, Kenneth Johnston found himself reinforcing the view that we should never lose sight of Wordsworth's literary experiences: 'when time and place and local inspiration are wholly substituted for other literary influences,' he writes, 'we have not learned all we should about the process of Wordsworth's self-creation.' This is because literary influences lie at the heart of Wordsworth's perception of his role as a poet. Referring to the formidable catalogue of poets in Wordsworth's juvenile reading, Johnston claims that it was 'Not only what they wrote and how they wrote it, but also the career conditions these poets established in order to give themselves time to write [that] were matters of keen estimation for the young Wordsworth, especially the degrees to which these writers depended on the old system of patronage or on the emerging new one of marketplace capitalism.'[12] As a critical approach, this contrasts dramatically with the opening sentence of Geoffrey Hartman's essay, 'Wordsworth Revisited' (1969):

> When Wordsworth was fourteen, the ordinary sight of boughs silhouetted against a bright evening sky left so vivid an impression on his mind that it marked the beginning of his career as a poet.[13]

The critical issues encapsulated in this comparison will need to be considered in more detail later. For the moment, however, I want to consider some of the political implications that may be associated with Wordsworth's early reading, and how they are reflected in the juvenilia.

Aged 14, Wordsworth was busily occupied in writing poetry to order for a 'School Exercise' to celebrate the bicentenary of Hawkshead school. He produced an affirmation of liberty in traditional Augustan tropes. Education, powered by science and reason, liberates 'British youth' from the dark ages of superstition and ignorance:

> The shades of night no more the soul involve,
> She sheds her beam, and, Lo! the shades dissolve;
> No jarring monks, to gloomy cell confin'd,
> With mazy rules perplex the weary mind.
> (*Early Poems*, 'School Exercise', 358, 47–50)

While there is no overt political statement in these lines, the 14-year-old boy is working in the mould of an Enlightenment taste that had fostered a rationalist, and therefore also an increasingly radical political agenda; but it was a radicalism influenced now by an injection of sentiment into the Classical models of the early eighteenth century. Wordsworth was working in the tradition of James Thomson, Oliver Goldsmith and James Beattie (and in this context it is important to appreciate Beattie's prominence in the Scottish Common Sense School of political philosophy, as well as his success as a poet); he was also reflecting the influence of John Langhorne, whose polemical poem 'The Country Justice' (1775) was widely read, admired, and duly anthologised in Vicesimus Knox's *Elegant Extracts* (used at Hawkshead) in a way that replaced its conservative 'Country Party' slant with a distinctly radical Whig, Common-wealthman flavour.[14]

Though Wordsworth has neo-classical philosophy banish uncivil-ised mediaeval superstition in his poem, it is in keeping with a modernising trend that he also ensures that sensitivity and feeling are not lost. He recommends the 'secret grotto', the 'tender tear' and the poet's 'golden lyre':

> coldly rest not here – be more that just
> Join to the rigours of the Sires of Rome
> The gentler manners of the private dome;
> When Virtue weeps in agony of woe
> Teach from the Heart the tender tear to flow.
> (*Early Poems*, 360, 88–92)

With no consciously subversive intent, Wordsworth performs an implicit critique of his country's Augustan cultural and political heri-tage: 'Join to the rigours of the sires of Rome / The gentler manners of the private dome.' This is the moral high ground from which 'Old' or 'Real Whigs' evolved their opposition politics through the 1770s. The town of Hawkshead, as we know, was no stranger to such views.[15] Comprehensively researched by Caroline Robbins in her book, *The Eighteenth-Century Commonwealthman* (first published in 1959), this loosely knit group of influential writers and publicists traced the immediate origins on their political beliefs back to the English Civil War of the seventeenth century, and the so-called Commonwealth that preceded the restoration of Charles II as king in 1660.

Eighteenth-century Commonwealthmen (otherwise dubbed 'real', 'true', or 'revolution' Whigs) were the forerunners of the political radicals who emerged in the final decades of the century, people like Thomas Hardy of the London Corresponding Society, William Godwin, and Thomas Paine. Godwin and Paine in particu-lar moved revolution Whig thinking on towards a radical political ideology that identified closely with the revolutionaries in France in 1789, and continued to maintain that sense of fraternity as the French Revolution shifted from its middle-class artisan origins to become an increasingly working-class, populist movement. As chil-dren of the Enlightenment, both Godwin and Paine were using rationalist, 'Common Sense' principles as the basis for their critique of the political establishments in England and Europe. Godwin's avowed aim to temper sentimentality with rationalism and object-ivity was to prove a particularly powerful influence over Words-worth's political thinking in the mid-1790s, when he met Godwin on several occasions in London.[16] From the time that Wordsworth became an undergraduate at Cambridge, he was increasingly con-vinced by the Godwinian view that society stood in need of radical reform conducted along rationalist lines.

As a schoolboy, Wordsworth was clearly eager to experiment with sentimental, gothic and bardic literary forms. None of this, however, shows a desire to address political issues directly at this early stage in his poetic career. Rather, his enthusiasm for a liberation from Clas-sical form and subject matter facilitates the exploration of extreme emotional states. The 'Dirge Song by a Minstrel' weaves borrowings from Thomas Chatterton's pseudo-mediaeval 'Rowley' poems (pub-lished in 1777) into a morbidity also heavily dependent on Thomas Gray's 'Elegy in a Country Churchyard' (1750):

> Dumb is the ploughman's whistle shrill
> The milkmaid at her pail is dumb
> The schoolboys' laughing game is still
> And mute all evening's mingl'd hum.
> (*Early Poems*, 572, 9–12)

Political implications are arguably present in Wordsworth's first published poem, however. This was the sonnet of 1787, 'On Seeing Miss Helen Maria Williams Weep at a Tale of Distress'. Words-worth proclaims himself a kindred spirit to a woman not afraid to criticise her country's involvement in the slave trade, who was eager to proclaim the moral depravity of the Government's imperialist policies overseas, and ready to attack its lack of commitment to the pursuance of social justice at home. All were themes dealt with in Williams's *Peru*, which had been published in 1784. The appropri-ate, empathising response is the tear of sensibility:

> Dim were my swimming eyes – my pulse beat slow,
> And my heart was swell'd to dear delicious pain.
> (*Early Poems*, 396, 3–4)

Though Wordsworth's poem leaves us to imagine what the nature of the 'distress' might have been, we do know what tended to upset

Helen Maria Williams most: the cynical disregard of the British Government for the liberties of its subjects, and its preparedness to deprive men, women, and children from other countries of their liberties through the practice of slave trading. Although the sonnet is clearly the product of a young, immature poet, it illustrates a sensitivity to issues that were to inform much of the later poetry.

IV

While at Hawkshead School Wordsworth began to write what became a long, semi-autobiographical poem called 'The Vale of Esthwaite'. It went with him from Hawkshead to Cambridge in 1787, where he continued to add to it. Written in relentless tetrameter couplets, the poem exhibits his continuing determination to be free from Augustan decorum in order that he might explore the vagaries of his own emotions. It also provides valuable evidence of the way in which Wordsworth was beginning to develop a process of composition that involved a cumulative process of referring back to his own previous writing. When we think of Wordsworth as the poet of memory, he is as likely to be found remembering an earlier poetic account of an experience, as the experience itself. 'The Vale of Esthwaite' contains raw material that Wordsworth was to return to for his later accounts of bird's-nesting in the Lake District as a child, his visionary experiences at Stonehenge, and his accounts of the deaths of his father and of William Taylor, all of which are included in *The Prelude*. There is also a tribute to Dorothy in 'The Vale' that helps prepare the way for the latter section of 'Tintern Abbey'.

In the bird's-nesting episode in *The Prelude* Book I, the dramatic effect of the moment is supplied by nature:

> Oh, when I have hung
> Above the raven's nest, by knots of grass
> And half-inch fissures in the slippery rocks
> But ill sustained, and almost, as it seemed,
> Suspended by the blast which blew amain,
> Shouldering the naked crag, oh, at that time
> While on the perilous ridge I hung alone,
> With what strange utterance did the loud dry wind
> Blow through my ears; the sky seemed not a sky
> Of earth, and with what motion moved the clouds!
> (*Prelude* I, 46, 341–50)

In 'The Vale', however, where we have an early version of the same *Prelude* memory, the whirlwind is described as a nightmare of gothic ghosts, and the whole literary machinery of horror (which seems to derive in part from a memory of the first scene of Act IV of Shakespeare's *King Lear*) induces a strain of aggressive prophetic verse to which, no doubt, the young poet aspired:

> I lov'd to haunt the giddy steep
> That hung loose trembling o'er the deep
> While Ghosts of Murtherers mounted fast
> And grimly glar'd upon the blast
> With the dark whirlwind rob'd, unseen
> With black arm rear'd the clouds between
> Alone [?high] Heaven's terrific Sire
> Struck prophetic like the mighty Lyre
> Of Nature...
> (*Early Poems*, 524, 61–9)

Evil rises up, confronts the young poet, and is duly vanquished by God's poetry played out upon the 'Lyre of Nature', the model for the young bard's own defiant poetry. Derivative as this may be, the poet performs his role of the heroic harbinger of revolt against the forces of evil to the full, and it would be wrong to dismiss such an energetic execution of the clichés of the day as merely imitative.

The passage in 'The Vale' where Wordsworth reflects on the death of his father is important for several reasons in addition to the way it anticipates later writing for *The Prelude*. This is how he recalls waiting to return home from Hawkshead just a few days before his father died, in 'The Vale':

> One Evening when the wintry blast
> Through the sharp Hawthorn whistling pass'd
> And the poor flocks all pinch'd with cold
> Sad drooping sought the mountain fold
> Long Long upon yon steepy rock
> Alone I bore the bitter shock
> Long long my swimming eyes did roam
> For little Horse to bear me home
> To bear me what avails my tear
> To sorrow o'er a Father's bier.
> (*Early Poems*, 446, 276–85)

These lines have been preceded by a lengthy gothic fantasy in which a ghost beckons the poet to follow him; the similarity with Hamlet's encounter with the ghost of his father is unmistakable. The progression from this into his recollection of bereavement is indicative of Wordsworth's developing preference while at Cambridge for a plainer style, and for the imaginative use of his own biography in his poetry. Several points of detail remain very close when Wordsworth comes to describe the same experience for *The Prelude* Book XI (the 'sharp Hawthorn' becomes the 'whistling hawthorn', and the 'naked rock' is replaced by a 'naked wall'):

> One Christmas-time,
> The day before the holidays began,
> Feverish, and tired, and restless, I went forth
> Into the fields, impatient for the sight
> Of those two horses which should bear us home,
> My brothers and myself. There was a crag,
> An eminence, which from the meeting-point
> Of two highways ascending overlooked
> At least a long half-mile of those two roads,
> By each of which the expected steeds might come –
> The choice uncertain. Thither I repaired
> Up to the highest summit. 'Twas a day
> Stormy, and rough, and wild, and on the grass
> I sate half sheltered by a naked wall.
> Upon my right hand was a single sheep,
> A whistling hawthorn on my left, and there,
> With those companions at my side, I watched,
> Straining my eyes intensely as the mist
> Gave intermitting prospect of the wood
> And plain beneath. Ere I to school returned
> That dreary time, ere I had been ten days
> A dweller in my father's house, he died,
> And I and my two brothers, orphans then,
> Followed his body to the grave.
>
> *(Prelude* XI, 434, 344–67)

The comparison shows how Wordsworth was prepared to make creative use of his earlier poetry, and of the extent to which he considered it a trustworthy guide to the emotions he experienced as a child.

In this respect 'The Vale of Esthwaite' draws our attention to the fact that reminiscences in *The Prelude* are shaped to a significant degree by the poet's literary growth (his earlier writing and reading), and the form they therefore take will owe as much to his concern to describe himself as a particular kind of poet in the making, as they will to his memory of the events themselves. This point is further illustrated by the fact that there are passages in 'The Vale' in memory of his father, which appear to have found their way into the eulogy of William Taylor included in *The Prelude* Book X. Indeed, it is possible that Taylor's words quoted in *The Prelude*, 'My head will soon lie low', were in his mind when writing 'The Vale' passage for his father:

> A still Voice whispers to my breast
> I soon shall be with them at rest . . .
> So dearly shall man buy a shed
> To hide but for an hour his head . . .
> (*Early Poems*, 448, 302–4; 310–11)

Wordsworth's developing preference for direct autobiographical writing as against sensationalist melodrama is illustrated further by the absorption of 'The Vale of Esthwaite' into a new poem, *An Evening Walk*. The Gothic tropes of 'The Vale' were abandoned in favour of a sentimental mood and a picturesque style of nature description cast in heroic couplets. The autobiography that begins to emerge in 'The Vale', and that was subsequently developed further in *An Evening Walk*, tells of a young, abandoned, victimised wanderer, very much in keeping with the fashionable late eighteenth-century perception of the poet; in consequence there would seem to be very little to distinguish the poet of *An Evening Walk* from countless other imaginary poetic personae who are more or less intended to resemble their creators:

> Alas! The idle tale of man is found
> Depicted in the dial's moral round;
> With Hope Reflexion blends her social rays
> To gild the total tablet of his days;
> Yet still, the sport of some malignant Pow'r,
> He knows but from its shade the present hour.

> While, Memory at my side, I wander here,
> Starts at the simplest sight th'unbidden tear,
> A form discover'd at the well-known seat,
> A spot, that angles at the riv'let's feet,
> The ray the cot of morning trav'ling nigh,
> And sail that glides the well-known elders by.[17]

Lines such as these call to mind the chapter in Thomas R. Edwards's *Imagination and Power* (1971) where he dispatched eighteenth-century poetry to the minor leagues of the English literary canon:

> the dominant poetic mood of the middle of the eighteenth century was anything but active and violent, as is well known to the reluctant readers of period anthologies, which leave you with the depressing picture of a rural landscape crowded with lugubrious figures, none of them seeming to know the others are there too, busily writing poems called 'A Hymn on Solitude', 'Ode to Evening', or 'The Pleasures of Melancholy'. By the testimony of their verses, at least, these poets never read newspapers, went to parties, or held a steady job, and it is hard to think of an age whose literature...shows less contact with public experience.[18]

Thirty years after that was written, current readers of eighteenth-century poetry have no excuse for arriving at such a sweepingly uninformed conclusion. Edwards deserves our sympathy, however, if only because the 'period anthologies' available to him then would for the most part have supported his prejudices. John Sitter's *Literary Loneliness in Mid-Eighteenth Century England* illustrates how much better informed scholars had become by 1982. What Edwards would have written had he had to hand, for example, Robert Demaria Jnr's anthology of 1996, *British Literature: 1640–1789*, we can only guess, but we can be reasonably sure that it would have been more complimentary, if, perhaps, less amusing.[19]

V

Although the image of the poet in *An Evening Walk* is, then, characteristic of the sentimental poetry of the period, when we look back to its precursor, 'The Vale of Esthwaite', we find important evidence that Wordsworth was thinking about his melancholy poet in a way that was already significantly different from the narrator of Gray's *Elegy*, Akenside's *The Pleasures of Imagination* or Goldsmith's *The Deserted Village*. In the dark gothic world invoked in 'The Vale' the author of all misery and woe is predictably type-cast as a tyrannical baron. Wordsworth's description of him immediately precedes his account of the beckoning ghost/ father already referred to; but the Shakespearean point of reference implies also that the father's death has been brought about by foul play, and suggests that we have a combination of Claudius and Lowther in the evil Baron. Equally interesting is Wordsworth's inclusion of a passing reference to the fate of the patriot Gloucester in *King Lear*, the inference of which is that the poet has much in common with the man unjustly blinded by the treacherous Cornwall:

> together are we hurled
> Far Far amid the shadowy world –
> [And since that hour the world unknown
> The world of shades is all my own]
> (*Early Poems*, 444, 268–71)

Wordsworth's reference to Gloucester's son, Edmund (who connives at Cornwall's brutal assault on the old man), suggests that he is interested in him as a tragic father figure in addition to the fact that he is a victim of political duplicity.

Wallowing in a state of self-pity may be characteristic of many late-eighteenth-century poets of sensibility, but the sense of victimisation Wordsworth repeatedly expresses in 'The Vale' ('Why fix on me for sacrifice?') signals an important aspect of how his work was to develop, conditioned as it was by the knowledge that Lowther was denying him the economic liberty he should have had, and that his Uncle Christopher was denying him the benefits of a caring home life in the absence of his true parents:

> Nor did my little heart forsee
> – She lost a home in losing thee
> Nor did it know – of thee bereft
> That little more than Heav'n was left.
> (*Early Poems*, 446–7, 292–5)

When it was time to discard the gothic fantasies of 'The Vale of Esthwaite' in favour of the picturesque imagery of *An Evening Walk*, Wordsworth lost none of his interest in the connections between his personal circumstances and the wider political context that the Lowther debt (not to mention the vexed question of his father's relationship with Lowther) presented him with; in fact, for all its picturesque predictability, the poem marks a further stage in the politicisation of Wordsworth's aesthetics. At Cambridge, we know that he began to study John Scott's *Critical Essays on Some of the Poems of Several English Poets* (1785). Scott was a Quaker, and his literary criticism clearly reflected the views he held as a political reformer of the Common Sense school. It is in Scott that we find a critical argument pointing towards what became in Wordsworth's thinking a commitment to simplicity: a rejection of poetic diction applied for superficial, decorative effect, reflecting the decadence of a privileged readership rather than a quest for truth. Scott's book aligns aesthetic simplicity with the severe honesty of political dissent; he demanded 'precision' from the poet, and the exploration of 'real existence' rather than 'fictions'.[20] This was very much in keeping aesthetically with what we have seen Godwin and Paine arguing for politically, a tempering of sentimentality with Enlightenment rationalism when it came to exposing the dishonest conduct of the British political establishment. The welter of real place names at the start of An Evening Walk are immediate evidence of Scott's influence. To his loco-descriptive account of the Lake District, Wordsworth went on to add an overtly political section on the fate of a war widow and her children. John Langhorne's popular poem The Country Justice (1775) (mentioned earlier) provided a model for this, but Wordsworth updated it – significantly altering the political slant in the process – by having the woman left to fend for herself and her children when her husband is killed in the American War.

Conditions at Cambridge, despite its reputation for Whiggery, reflected the injustices and corrupt practices found in society at large; and to this experience was added Wordworth's first visit to France in 1790, and then his second visit in 1791–2 after graduating. In An Evening Walk we observe a growing tension between the received notion of the poet as a retired, reflective individual, and the poet who wishes to set the life of enforced marginalisation on the broader stage of political and social events. This is the poet we began with in this chapter, walking the 'public road' by night. With Thomas Edwards's suggestions in mind, we should appreciate that such poets not only went to parties, but they also became interested in joining them. Wordsworth's trip to France in the summer vacation of 1790 was a calculated act of rebellion. He refused to accept the well-prepared route that would have taken him from Hawkshead through Cambridge and into the Church of England. The Wordsworth/Cookson tribe had all the required connections to ensure Wordsworth's future prosperity, but he would have none of it, and with his Cambridge friend, Robert Jones, he took his own carefully planned route across France and into Switzerland, mingling with parties of French citizens celebrating the Revolution. After gaining an undistinguished degree early in 1791, he negotiated a return trip to France, ostensibly to perfect his French with a view to taking employment as a private tutor.

Two important relationships mark this period of Wordsworth's life. He met and fell in love with Annette Vallon. She belonged to a Roman Catholic family, and was thus no friend of the Revolution, though initially sympathetic to some degree of reform. She was sufficiently friendly to the young English poet to have his child, born soon after his return to England towards the end of 1792. Wordsworth was also befriended by Michel Beaupuy, an aristocrat who had wholeheartedly embraced the Revolutionary cause, and who seems (from Wordsworth's later account of him in *The Prelude*) never to have tired explaining what was going on and why to his new friend.

An Evening Walk had been written by the time Wordsworth set out for France in 1791. Once arrived, he set about writing *Descriptive Sketches*, a poem intended to memorialise his long vacation journey of 1790, and provide marketable copy on his return to England. We can only imagine the frame of mind that resulted from living in a Revolutionary France that was already so different from the country he had seen a year or so previously. The celebrations were now replaced by an atmosphere of crisis, rumour and conspiracy. While he tried to write his verse travelogue of 1790 he was making physical love to a reactionary agent, and having what appears to have been an intense intellectual affair with a staunch defender of the Revolution and all its works. Inevitably, *Descriptive Sketches* became a poem infiltrated by the ambience of 1792; but equally it remained a poem that was intended to launch Wordsworth on his career as a professional poet, and its radical politics are muted. In the final lines of the poem, the poet seems to have settled for retreat into a literary landscape: 'To night, my friend, within this humble cot / Be the dead load of mortal ills forgot.'[21]

In reality Wordsworth returned from Paris to London to become engrossed in radical political circles, and, as his abortive *Letter to the Bishop of Llandaff* of 1793 shows, it was now that he made a wholehearted commitment to Painite radicalism, Godwinian rationalism, and to the open expression of these ideas in his poetry. The consequences for his poetry were dramatic. His imitation of Juvenal's eighth satire (written around 1795) involves the poet in direct, unambiguous political statement:

> Ye Kings, in wisdom, sense and power, supreme,
> These freaks are worse than any sick man's dream.

> To hated worth no Tyrant ere design'd
> Malice so subtle, vengeance so refin'd.
> Even he who yoked the living to the dead,
> Rivall'd by you, hides the diminish'd head...
> Must honour still to Lonsdale's tail be bound?
> – Then execration is an empty sound.
> Is Common-sense asleep? Has she no wand
> From this curst Pharoah plague to rid the land?
> (*Early Poems*, 814–15, 1–6, 13–16)

The gothic baron of 'The Vale of Esthwaite' unequivocally becomes Lowther (now Lord Lonsdale), and Paine's attack on Edmund Burke in *Rights of Man*, 'I am contending for the rights of the *living*, and against their being willed away, and controlled and contracted for, by the manuscript assumed authority of the dead', is referred to by way of the poet's assault on the 'Pharoah-plague' of political injustice that Lowther and his ilk perpetuate.[22] Where the young poet had previously looked to the picturesque for comfort and a way forward in his art, he now displays a tangible political agenda.

Throughout the juvenilia, nature exists in an essentially literary form; in *An Evening Walk*, specific as the location of the Lake District is, it is realised in highly self-conscious literary terms that include quotations from other poems. The completeness with which the Godwinian political programme now took hold of Wordsworth's mind suggests that the visionary poet of nature had not yet come into being, a fact easily forgotten if discussion of the early years relies too heavily on *The Prelude*. Godwin offered a precise, practical way forward against which the healing qualities of landscape beauty as expressed by other poets seemed at best insubstantial, at worst misleading.

In the Godwinian verse narrative he began to compose in 1793, *Salisbury Plain*, the setting is unremittingly barren:

> On as he passed more wild and more forlorn
> And vacant the huge plain around him spread;
> Ah me! the wet cold ground must be his only bed.[23]

Here we find once more the war widow from *An Evening Walk*. She was joined by other outcast wanderers as the poem went through a series of revisions. For all these people the promise of rest in the pastoral landscape of a picturesque literary tradition seems as irrelevant as it is unattainable. Wordsworth began the poem as he was walking over Salisbury Plain in 1793, carrying with him the weight of failure, personal guilt (he had left Annette behind him in France to have their child), and a sense of the grinding personal injustice done to him in particular. What this poem illustrates is Wordsworth's continued attachment – whatever the political intent – to the confessional process of retelling his own story and analysing the moods of his own mind. Godwinian and Painite as he now presumably felt himself to be, he clung with equal firmness to the idea of the poet encapsulated in the confessional poem that had provided him with a model for his own work, James Beattie's *The Minstrel* (1771–4).

Wordsworth had returned to London from France in late November or early December 1792, when he lodged with his brother Richard. In late June 1793 he set out on a tour of the west of England with William Calvert, a one-time fellow pupil at Hawkshead. The partnership terminated abruptly on Salisbury Plain when their carriage ended up in a ditch. Calvert returned to civilisation on the horse while Wordsworth walked on alone across the Plain and up into Wales to stay with his companion on the French walking tour of 1790, Robert Jones. Back in London, he was offered a place where both he and Dorothy could stay on the Dorset–Somerset border, Racedown Lodge. This was in 1795, and the pair moved there in late September of that year. The house belonged to the Pinney family. John and Azariah were the sons of John Pretor Pinney, a wealthy and influential Bristol merchant; they were members of the liberal set that Wordsworth was associating with in London. As this section of the biographical narrative draws to a close in 1796, we see Wordsworth having second thoughts about the credibility of Godwin's political philosophy. It was this shift in his thinking that led in due course to his abandonment of the Salisbury Plain poem and the beginning of work on a verse drama in Shakespearean style set in the Middle Ages, *The Borderers* (1796–7), which became a major preoccupation while at Racedown.

The Borderers is a key transitional work which takes Wordsworth from juvenilia towards the poetry of his creative maturity. Even while he was working on a poetry of direct political satire, and at narrative poetry intended to dramatise the integrity of a Godwinian programme of reform, the evidence is that he retained a fascination for the way in which the experience of injustice could warp and pervert the individual mind. In the end, it seems, fear of

psychological damage was what touched Wordsworth most profoundly. After years spent brooding on his fate as an outcast, he
himself was discovering that the chronic depression he was experiencing at Racedown could only be alleviated through a rediscovery
of love and domestic commitment. It had been the influence of such
sentimentally perceived commodities that Godwin had sought to
purge through reasoned argument in the first edition of his *Enquiry
Concerning Political Justice* (1793).

In *The Borderers* it is proposed that Godwinian principles have
been responsible for creating a cynical villain, 'a young Man of
great intellectual powers, yet without any solid principles of genuine benevolence. His master passions are pride and the love of
distinction'.[24] Still writing from a sense of fear rather than beauty
at this time, Wordsworth's political agenda is moving into a new
relationship with what had always been his determination to live as
a poet. Nowhere is this shift more dramatically apparent than in
two fragments dating from around 1797 that appear at the end of
de Selincourt's Juvenilia section. In 'The Baker's Cart' the social
consequences of prolonged neglect are described in terms of its
effect on an impoverished mother; she has 'a mind / Which being
long neglected, and denied / The common food of hope, was now
become / Sick and extravagant.' In the second fragment, 'Incipient
Madness' we read:

> There is a mood
> A settled temper of the heart, when grief,
> Become an instinct, fastening on all things
> That promise food, doth like a sucking babe
> Create it where it is not.
> (Reproduced in *Ruined Cottage*, 461–5)

Both passages are concerned with food, but the subject they have in
common is the health of the mind, and it was at Racedown and
subsequently Alfoxden that Wordsworth came to believe (with
Dorothy and Coleridge's help) that he could write poetry capable
of addressing the issue of minds 'long neglected, and denied / The
common food of hope.' His poetry would provide food for a
nation's damaged psyche, where Godwinian rationalism had previously promised to create food 'where it is not'. Out of this process
of discovering anew his vocation as a poet, grew a commitment to
seek a way of writing that would of necessity distance itself from
much contemporary poetry. Coleridge had already met Words-

worth; he now made his way to Racedown from where he lived at Nether Stowey, arriving in June 1797. He enthused about Wordsworth's poetic powers, and about a new piece he was working on, *The Ruined Cottage*. It was his companionship and conversation that moved Wordsworth forward to develop a theory of poetry that addressed both his own personal needs, and those of society at large. Central to that theory was the ideal of 'simplicity'.

VI

Wordsworth's juvenilia charts a course from the formal classical school exercise through gothic balladry and picturesque scene painting, to melodramatic narrative and political satire, finishing with his attempt to construct a full-scale Shakespearean drama. He sought a voice to articulate his own story of loss and isolation. He developed a growing sense of the location of that story in the wider context of a corrupt political world, and gradually and painfully came to realise that the solution for him as a committed poet was to be found in the delicate process of building sound human relationships, rather than laying plans for political reform founded on abstract formulae.

The catalyst that moved Wordsworth on into his maturity as a poet was his discovery of a visionary perception of nature. The infectious enthusiasm of Coleridge for pantheism, a fundamentally organic, equalitarian description of the world and its creator, answered to the political needs of the disenchanted disciple of Godwin. Here was a notion of beauty that counteracted the anxiety and fear to be found stalking through so much of the immature work. An example of this latter is to be found in de Selincourt's Juvenilia section. He pieced together from fragments (certainly written before 1793) what appears to be a possible model for the narrative of *Salisbury Plain*. In this 'Gothic Tale' we find the characteristically barren landscape of an outcast poet's life:

> The road extended o'er a heath
> Weary and bleak; no cottager had there
> Won from the waste a rood of ground, no hearth
> Of Traveller's half-way house with its turf smoke
> Scented the air through which the plover wings
> His solitary flight.
>
> (*PW* I, 292–5, 1–6)

He attempts to escape his fate:

> Me from the public way the common hope
> Of shorter path seduced, and led me on
> Where smooth-green sheep-tracks thridded the sharp furze
> And kept the choice suspended, having chosen ...
>
> (ll.9–12)

And there, in the final line, we glimpse the means by which the mature poet is eventually to escape from a 'public way' that appears unremittingly 'weary and bleak'. The way forward is not to take the short cut; it is rather to be able to reflect on the matter of there being a choice, and that when the choice is made, even then the outcome remains a mystery; as such it is held within the paradox of an iambic pentameter line which allows the extra, musical syllable in 'chosen'. This signifies recognition of a truth 'suspended', a 'something far more deeply interfused' that was duly to be celebrated in 'Tintern Abbey'. In this early fragment, however, such a realisation is at best only briefly glimpsed; the poet proceeds to follow his 'shorter path' with increasing anxiety:

> Now fast against my cheek and whistling ears
> My loose wet hair and tattered bonnet flapped
> With thought-perplexing noise, that seemed to make
> The universal darkness that ensued
> More dark and desolate.
>
> (ll.19–23)

A more familiar version of this story of taking what appears to be a short cut and getting lost occurs in *Peter Bell*, written in 1798, after the move from Racedown to Alfoxden:

> Quoth Peter, 'here's a nearer cut;
> 'Twill save a mile, as sure as day.'
> He took the path, the path did lead
> Across a smooth and grassy mead
> And a tall wood before him lay.
>
> And now he to the wood is come
> And Peter there in whole cart loads
> Is heaping curses on them all,
> Commissioners both great and small,
> Who made the zig-zag roads.

For while he drives among the boughs
With head and hands and cheeks that burn
With downright fury and with wrath,
There's little sign that Peter's path
Will to the road return.
                    (*Peter Bell*, 70–2, 321–35)

The poet of 1798 is confidently able to watch Peter (his former self) make the mistake he once had made. *Peter Bell* is in this sense yet another slice of autobiography, and again the juvenilia reveals a Wordsworth who habitually reached back to his earlier writing, linking his poetry together as a collective expression of how he perceived his evolution as a poet through to 1798 when his creative partnership with Coleridge took fire.

VII

In 1797 Wordsworth began a new narrative poem, *The Ruined Cottage*. It was a project that further endorsed the altered direction his work was taking after the effective abandonment of *Salisbury Plain*. In 1798 he eventually wrote the lines that he would use to introduce it:

'Twas summer and the sun was mounted high.
Along the south the uplands feebly glared
Through a pale steam, and all the northern downs
In clearer air ascending, shewed far off
Their surfaces with shadows appled o'er
Of deep embattled clouds. Far as the sight
Could reach those many shadows lay in spots
Determined and unmoved, with steady beams
Of clear and pleasant sunshine interposed –
Pleasant to him who on the soft cool moss
Extends his careless limbs beside the root
Of some huge oak whose aged branches make
A twilight of their own, a dewy shade
Where the wren warbles while the dreaming man,
Half-conscious of that soothing melody,
With side-long eye looks out upon the scene,
By those impending branches made more soft,
More soft and distant.
                    (*Ruined Cottage*, 43, 1–18)

The choice is made, the transition from the juvenile to the mature poet has taken place, and what is most immediately apparent is the cessation of movement. The barren landscape of a difficult, restless youth has been replaced by a verdant landscape which is now the poet's own to rest in. Reminiscent as it might be of other landscapes in other poems, this we know to be Wordsworth's own. He is so confident of it that he need hardly look at it ('With side-long eye' he 'looks out upon the scene'). It is a Wordsworthian landscape because even as we look upon it with him, it becomes 'More soft and distant', as its purpose is gradually defined. This landscape feeds the mind, not the eye.

Wordsworth's mature poetry becomes a celebration of what he felt he had never, until Racedown and Alfoxden, possessed: a loving, close-knit family of friends and relations. It was from within this context that he could now express his political convictions; and his discovery of a natural world no longer controlled by literary convention, but by his own powers of perception, meant that he experienced a tangible sense of healing after years spent writing and brooding over the deprivations of his youth. It was at this point that Wordsworth began to imbue his early life with traces of the benediction that nature now seemed to be offering him. They become ghostly presences of beauty offsetting the threat of more fearful powers; and what he wrote he believed. The 'simplicity' that so annoyed his critics was to a significant extent the product of a childhood he had missed; but it was described with a mature grasp of the social and political issues that had then beset him. Wordsworth had found his way to a point on the interface between the individual and society, from where he felt it was possible to understand why the relationship between language and ideas invested the permanent truths he so craved with an inevitable degree of mystery. We can see this illustrated in the interface of his juvenilia and his mature poetry.

'Septimi Gades' is a poem based on Horace dating from around 1794. It is in part still manifestly juvenilia in its clichéd picturesque descriptions of the natural world; but from 'finny myriads' that 'twinkle bright' in the streams as milkmaids pass by with 'brimming pails', and from 'parting Phoebus' which leaves the landscape in a 'purple gloom', we suddenly pass into a world which we recognise as Wordsworth's own, poised between material reality and vision, between thought and expression. The truth is 'unobvious', 'veiled', but 'not unseen'. 'Septimi Gades' is no 'Tintern Abbey', and the poet still has much to learn – or unlearn – before he will be able to achieve the serenity of lyrics such as 'A slumber did my spirit seal'; but for all that, this is the juvenilia of transition where 'the breath of this corporeal frame' is, for a brief moment, 'almost suspended' in advance of 'Tintern Abbey':

> No spot does parting Phoebus greet
> With farewell smile more fond and sweet
> Than those sequestered hills
> While as composing shades invest
> With purple gloom the water's breast
> The grove its music stills.
>
> When shouts and sheepfold bells and sound
> Of flocks and herds and streams rebound
> Along the ringing dale
> How beauteous, round the gleaming tide
> The silvery morning vapours glide
> And half the landscape veil
>
> Methinks that morning scene displays
> A lovely emblem of our days
> Unobvious and serene
> So shall our still lives half betrayed
> Shew charms more touching from their shade
> Though veiled yet not unseen.
>
> (*Early Poems*, 764–6, 49–66)

2

New Directions: *The Ruined Cottage*

> My Friend, enough to sorrow you have given,
> The purposes of wisdom ask no more;
> Be wise and chearful, and no longer read
> The forms of things with an unworthy eye...
> (*Ruined Cottage*, 73–5, 508–11)

I

The next two chapters consider a collection of poems, the *Lyrical Ballads*, first published in 1798, and a single poem, *The Ruined Cottage*, that remained in fragmentary form from 1797 until 1814, when it was published under another name as the first Book of *The Excursion*. *Lyrical Ballads* is universally recognised as Wordsworth's first major poetic achievement; *The Ruined Cottage* is by comparison a ghost text. The discussion in both chapters will be guided in part by speculation on the significance of each for Wordsworth, and by considering how literary criticism subsequently came to regard them. In their introduction to the Cornell edition of *Lyrical Ballads* (1992), James Butler and Karen Green make the point (in common with a good many other recent Wordsworth scholars) that the *Ballads* were not a carefully planned aesthetic experiment. The lengthy Preface which Wordsworth added to the second augmented edition of 1800 (and then proceeded to expand for subsequent printings) most certainly did elevate the collection to the level of a coherently organised anthology, one which has now been recognised as a defining document for the study of English Romanticism. In addition to the Preface, Coleridge's reminiscences of the origins of *Lyrical Ballads* in his *Biographia Literaria* (1817) are often referred to as confirmation of the fact that there was a carefully worked out plan for putting together a collection of contrasting poems.[1]

Looking back across a selection of critical texts, however, it turns out to be difficult to find anyone, including Coleridge, actually making the overt claim that the *Lyrical Ballads* were a thoughtfully premeditated assault on the literary orthodoxy of the day. Critics such as George McLean Harper in the 1920s, Roger Sharrock in the 1960s, and Heather Glen in the early 1980s are all characteristically concerned to draw attention to what *Lyrical Ballads* indisputably became as the reputation of the collection gathered momentum on into the early nineteenth century. It is reasonable, therefore, to ask whether it really matters that the origin of the 1798 volume was a haphazard business, and that what carried the venture forward was not a long-term plan to kick-start the Romantic Movement, so much as a short-term scheme aimed at providing the poets with some much needed cash. I think it probably does.

Revolutionary literary schemes were certainly a topic for discussion at Racedown, but the plan that was gradually taking shape as Wordsworth and Coleridge began to talk in 1797, and particularly once Wordsworth had moved to Alfoxden to become Coleridge's near neighbour in July of that year, had little to do with *Lyrical Ballads*. Wordsworth and Coleridge belonged to a generation that had been encouraged to believe that society could be fundamentally changed for the better, and swiftly. They played host on more than one occasion to a leading campaigner for radical reform, John Thelwall, who purchased Liswyn Farm across the Bristol Channel in Wales. While Thelwall was to pursue his radical political career for some years to come, he visited Somerset to seek relief from a world of political intrigue that had already threatened his life, and might do so again at any time. Fear of a French invasion somewhere along the coast of Devon and Somerset, or possibly South Wales, was at its height at this time, and the arrival of an experienced Government agent, James Walsh, to assess the threat to public order that the Alfoxden coterie might represent is not at all surprising in the circumstances.[2]

Wordsworth had abandoned the Godwinian belief that change might be brought about by an appeal to the rationally argued principles of political justice. The move to Alfoxden signalled what in effect became a new chapter in his literary life, marked by a resurgence of optimism about the regeneration of society that overtly challenged Godwinian teaching. But the poetry through which Wordsworth sought to facilitate this regeneration was most emphatically not planned as a series of ballads. With *The Borderers* finished, he turned his attention to an extended narrative in blank verse. His idea of the way forward (now eagerly encouraged by Coleridge) was to work on from what he had already been able to do, refashioning it to suit the poetic vocation he now envisaged for himself with increasing determination. As we have seen, in 'The Vale of Esthwaite' he had begun to narrate his own story, looking for his own voice and personality among the literary voices that surrounded him; *An Evening Walk* and *Descriptive Sketches* had taken him further with the same project to a point where, in 1793, the politically explicit narrative of the female vagrant in *Salisbury Plain* became his major preoccupation. *The Borderers*, however, makes it clear why *Salisbury Plain* was no longer a viable way forward, no matter how he then attempted to revise and augment the poem to trim its Godwinian rhetoric. The poem that mattered, as Coleridge was quick to affirm when he heard it at Racedown in 1797, was the draft of a sombre narrative work of about 400 lines called *The Ruined Cottage*.[3]

The story was no doubt prompted by Wordsworth's first-hand encounters with rural poverty in the vicinity of Racedown; he and Dorothy – though not in a comparable situation – were themselves finding it difficult to make ends meet. This would explain the writing of fragments dwelling on the hardships of rural life; what then happened was that they began to come together as a connected narrative. The central figure of *The Ruined Cottage* is Margaret, a victim in the eighteenth-century 'female vagrant' literary tradition which Wordsworth had already taken up in *An Evening Walk*, and then used in a way that was pivotal to the narrative of *Salisbury Plain*.[4]

The new poem begins by describing the meeting of the poet with a pedlar who is resting in the doorway of a ruined cottage. The pedlar is already known to him, and in the 1798 version of the manuscript the poet describes his background and beliefs before allowing him to assume the role of narrator and tell the story of Margaret and Robert, the couple who once lived in the cottage. Robert was an industrious weaver, providing for his wife and two children. Two years of poor harvests coupled with the impact on the rural economy of warfare are sufficient to destroy the family's precarious livelihood. In desperation, Robert enlists, leaving the money used to entice people like himself into the army on the windowsill of the cottage for Margaret to find. The pedlar then describes how, at each visit, he finds the cottage increasingly dilapidated, and Margaret's health – both mental and physical – in decline. The eldest child is taken from her by the Parish to become a 'serving-boy' (*Ruined Cottage*, 64, 404–5); the youngest, presumably because no profit is to be had from him, is left with her. He dies, leaving Margaret to survive only a short while longer. The 1798 text ends with her death:

>   Yet still
> She loved this wretched spot, nor would for worlds
> Have parted hence; and still that length of road
> And this rude bench one torturing hope endeared,
> Fast rooted at her heart, and here, my friend,
> In sickness she remained, and here she died,
> Last human tenant of these ruined walls.
>   (*Ruined Cottage*, 72, 522–8)

The 1799 manuscript adds a further 45 lines giving the poet's reactions and the pedlar's thoughts. Understandably, at a tale of such unredeemed misery, the poet is saddened, but he finds some relief in a quintessentially Wordsworthian act of simplicity; he leans on the gate:

> I stood, and leaning o'er the garden-gate
> Reviewed that Woman's suff'rings, and it seemed
> To comfort me while with a brother's love
> I blessed her in the impotence of grief.
>   (*Ruined Cottage*, 73, 497–500)

A spontaneous blessing is wrung from the heart as the poet clings to a solid object in the midst of ungovernable circumstances and overwhelming sadness. It is inevitable that Coleridge's Ancient Mariner should come to mind here, leaning over the side of his cursed vessel and blessing the water-snakes in a similarly unpremeditated moment. Awful as the human story is, we are intended to understand that there is something in 'the calm oblivious tendencies / Of nature', if we can but appreciate them, which has the power to reconcile us to the situation. It is the pedlar's job to explain what the poet has begun to discover:

'My Friend, enough to sorrow have you given,
The purposes of wisdom ask no more;
Be wise and chearful, and no longer read
The forms of things with an unworthy eye.
She sleeps in the calm earth, and peace is here.
I well remember that those very plumes,
Those weeds, and the high spear-grass on that wall,
By mist and silent rain-drops silver'd o'er,
As once I passed did to my heart convey
So still an image of tranquillity,
So calm and still, and looked so beautiful
Amid the uneasy thoughts which filled my mind,
That what we feel of sorrow and despair
From ruin and from change, and all the grief
The passing shews of being leave behind,
Appeared an idle dream that could not live
Where meditation was. I turned away
And walked along my road in happiness.'
(*Ruined Cottage*, 73–5, 508–25)

Throughout the story the gradual decay of the cottage, matching the decay and ruin of Margaret's life, has been accompanied by a narration of growth. Nature, in the form of grass, weeds, and cultivated plants run wild, has been reclaiming the cottage and its ground. This in itself is hardly a convincing antidote to Margaret's fate, particularly since we hear of no one in the vicinity taking practical steps to help her. Such objections were made early on in the poem's life as a published text, where, as Book I of *The Excursion* (1814), it was called 'The Wanderer'. De Quincey claimed that Wordsworth's lack of realism when it came to the manner of Margaret's death 'vitiates and nullifies the very basis of the story'.[5] Certainly we are left wanting to know a great deal more about what 'meditation' might mean in these circumstances, although it is not difficult to see what Wordsworth is trying to achieve by setting this story in the context of the 'tendencies / Of nature' which unlock 'that secret spirit of humanity' (*Ruined Cottage*, 73, 503–5). Nature, in a mysterious fashion, is able to convey so powerful 'an image of tranquillity' to the observer, that Margaret's death is somehow absorbed into a greater scheme of things. The 'calm earth' she sleeps in will calm our sorrow at the manner of her death, should we cultivate the appropriate manner of meditation as we reflect on her story, 'and no longer read / The forms of things with an unworthy eye' (ll.75–6).

II

The Ruined Cottage was not responsible for Wordsworth abandoning the *Salisbury Plain* poem entirely, despite the fact that the 1794 manuscript had ended with an unequivocally Painite call for the overthrow of 'Th'Oppressor's dungeon' using 'the herculean mace / Of Reason'.[6] The poet whose work was now (in Kenneth Johnston's words) beginning to 'reflect the universalizing, *un*specifying direction his imagination was . . . beginning to take at the time', set about revising *Salisbury Plain* in an attempt to render it politically correct according to his own changed opinions.[7] But it was Margaret's story in *The Ruined Cottage* that enabled him to do what was necessary: start again. The new direction is clearly discernible in a fragment written at this time, and already referred to towards the end of the previous chapter, 'The Baker's Cart'.

'The Baker's Cart' is a discarded sketch based on a scene most probably witnessed at this time. There is no indication as to whether Wordsworth intended to find a place for it in *The Ruined Cottage*. A baker's cart stops at the door of a cottage because the horse drawing it is in the habit of doing so. The driver whips the horse into motion even as the inhabitants of the 'wretched hut' appear. The distribution of food (bread most particularly) is a natural right; the horse's instinctive halting implies a recognition of this, but it is unnaturally forced to move on:

> and you were left, as if
> You were not born to live, or there had been
> No bread in all the land. [8]

What matters here is how Wordsworth responds to the woman who watches the cart move away. Her mood is bitter and angry, and the poet can sympathise and even identify with her 'rebellious heart'; but as he describes it, he also rejects it as a response that is 'sick and extravagant'. She is one of many who in these times have been

> driv'n to that state
> In which all past experience melts away
> And the rebellious heart to its own will
> Fashions the laws of nature.

Wordsworth is beginning to think about social and political injustice in a way that is quite distinct from the political credo that had fired his initial *Salisbury Plain* stanzas. In *The Ruined Cottage* he is reflecting not only on how the relationship of humanity to nature has been perverted in a society where war and famine threaten human existence, but equally on the perverse belief on the part of man that he can regain control of his destiny through his own perfected rationality of mind. When in 'The Market Cart' he observes that 'the rebellious heart to its own will / Fashions the laws of nature', he means us to understand that the rebellious (revolutionary) heart has misguidedly sought to refashion nature to its own inferior will. He is proposing that there has been a general failure to recognise the need for a power greater than the imperfect human mind to exert its healing influence. In *The Ruined Cottage* the natural world – appropriately represented and interpreted – is there to offer us a glimpse of this redeeming power: 'an image of tranquility, / So calm and still ... so beautiful / Amid the uneasy thoughts which filled my mind...' (*Ruined Cottage*, 75, 517–19). This idea is encapsulated in an untitled fragment Wordsworth composed in 1798. It describes the poet resting in an idyllic summer landscape, and was quoted towards the end of the previous chapter. In due course it was used to provide the opening lines for *The Ruined Cottage*:

> Pleasant to him who on the soft cool moss
> Extends his careless limbs beside the root
> Of some huge oak whose aged branches make
> A twilight of their own, a dewy shade
> Where the wren warbles while the dreaming man,
> Half-conscious of that soothing melody,
> With side-long eye looks out upon the scene...
> (*Ruined Cottage*, 43, 10–16)

From this idyll the reader is then abruptly thrown back to the bleak and unforgiving location (physical and mental) in which the poem originally began, and where the rest of the action takes place:

> Across a bare wide Common I had toiled
> With languid feet which by the slipp'ry ground
> Were baffled still, and when I stretched myself
> On the brown earth my limbs from very heat
> Could find no rest...
> (*Ruined Cottage*, 43–5, 19–23)

The poem therefore begins prophetically with a description of the reward the poet will receive for having learnt from the narrative of

Margaret's story, that even here, in the face of cruel, unmerited hardship and death, there is reason to believe in the working of a power for good that we can only as yet dimly perceive. That reward is symbolised by the gift of repose in a welcoming summer landscape.

Jonathan Wordsworth's study of *The Ruined Cottage* (incorporating the manuscript sources from 1799–1800) was published in 1969; James Butler's Cornell edition of the poem and its attendant fragments appeared in 1979.[9] By the early 1980s *The Ruined Cottage* of 1796–8, now clearly distinguished from Book I of *The Excursion* (1814), had achieved celebrity status as the text which illustrated Wordsworth's emergence as a poet in command of his own distinctive voice. Though a number of critics had already praised it (in 1936 F. R. Leavis had described it as 'the finest thing Wordsworth wrote'[10]), it was now perceived as the text which revealed the mature Wordsworth as the poet of unresolved tensions, a poet whose very greatness lay in his struggle to bring the disparate parts of human experience and the natural world into a unified vision of the human soul. This was the poet already comprehensively described in Geoffrey Hartman's *Wordsworth's Poetry* of 1964. Hartman summarised the subject of *The Ruined Cottage* as 'the perfected mind of man facing a still imperfect world', and his criticism becomes an extension of Wordsworth's attempt to formulate a resolution of what must, it would seem, remain in some respects for ever unresolved: 'a spectrum bounded at one side by the apocalyptic imagination and at the other by an alien nature'.[11]

This Wordsworth is not Leavis's Wordsworth; rather, he is the poet of fragments: fragments of poetry, fragments of ideas, fragments that he will continually be seeking to unite. He seeks an elusive organicism that stretches his inventiveness to the limit and beyond. William H. Galperin, writing in 1989, lists three 'opposed doctrines' that the poem finds itself struggling to resolve: 'Calvinism, pantheism and humanism'.[12] Recalling the observations of the first chapter on how a growing political sense was important to Wordsworth's poetry, we need to remember that in *The Ruined Cottage*, while human suffering remains a political issue, Godwin's mechanistic solutions are replaced by a pedlar addicted to the Bible, pantheism, and the poetry of Robert Burns. For Galperin, and also for David Pirie in *The Poetry of Grandeur and Tenderness* (1982), struggling with such contradictory forces is what makes Wordsworth an interesting, and a great, poet. Pirie argues that *The Ruined Cottage* confronts a language of 'real things' with a language of 'the abstract and the generalised'. He goes on: 'Wordsworth is trying to maintain a balance between his two voices, is often threatened by the limits of language operating more harshly on one than the other.' He suggests there are 'moments' (they can only be moments) when the balance is achieved; here lies the 'greatness of The Ruined Cottage'.[13]

But for Wordsworth in 1798, an overall lack of resolution punctuated by only transient moments 'when the balance is achieved' was a measure of failure, not of success. His intentions were to make it clear that in completing The Ruined Cottage he had moved on. This was the function of the opening lines; they claim that for the poet the difficulties of The Ruined Cottage already lie in the past. The main body of the work describes the poet then; the poet now is in possession of his idyllic repose, the 'good hope that soon / Under a shade as grateful I should find / Rest . . .' has been fulfilled.

Prior to The Ruined Cottage, Wordsworth's poetry had been peopled by social outcasts more or less in a state of decline. The figure of the poet/narrator appeared as an observer scarcely less traumatised by the circumstances that were destroying those he described around him. In The Ruined Cottage his chief narrator, though no less marginalised from society, acts as the purveyor of a positive philosophy of redemption. This is the 'Pedlar', the epitome of the principle of Wordsworthian simplicity:

> He from his native hills
> Had wandered far: much had he seen of men,
> Their manners, their enjoyments and pursuits,
> Their passions and their feelings, chiefly those
> Essential and eternal in the heart,
> Which 'mid the simpler forms of rural life
> Exist more simple in their elements
> And speak a plainer language.
>
> (Ruined Cottage, 46, 58–65)

The style of Wordsworth's verse was taken primarily from the blank verse of John Milton's Paradise Lost (1667). Translated into a late-eighteenth-century context, the solemn Latinate cadences of Milton's religious epic – which in the seventeenth century constituted a veiled lament for the collapse of the Puritan Revolution – became the means by which a man of humble origins expressed a knowledge and a wisdom unavailable to those of a higher social standing:

He was a chosen son:
To him was given an ear which deeply felt
The voice of Nature in the obscure wind,
The sounding mountain and the running stream.
To every natural form, rock, fruit, and flower,
Even the loose stones that cover the highway,
He gave a moral life; he saw them feel
Or linked them to some feeling.
                    (*Ruined Cottage*, 46, 76–83)

The epigraph quoted at the beginning of the poem is by a fellow republican, but in a very different style; Robert Burns is one of the Pedlar's favourite poets, and Wordsworth's slightly misquoted lines from Burns's 'Epistle to J. Lapraik' establish a republican simplicity as the guiding principle of the poem at the outset:

Give me a spark of nature's fire,
Tis the best learning I desire.
                . . . . .
My muse though homely in attire
May touch the heart.
                    (*Ruined Cottage*, Epigraph, 42)

At the centre of the 'simple' Pedlar's philosophy of life is his capacity to view the world around him pantheistically. Pantheism held that God was present in all things, and thus the Pedlar, a thoughtful observer of 'every natural form', could find, even in 'the loose stones that cover the highway', 'a moral life'. While this might be seen as an extreme form of democratisation, a view of life where all things counted equally, it was also, of course, a corrective to the Godwinian privileging of people and their rationally perceived opinions. Pantheism proposed that there was an all-embracing principle governing society that was far superior to anything which might be found in rational human thought. It was a doctrine, as Wordsworth wrote, of 'one life':

From nature & her overflowing soul
He had received so much, that all his thoughts
Were steeped in feeling...
                              ... Wonder not

If such his transports were; for in all things
He saw one life, & felt that it was joy.
One song they sang, & it was audible,

> Most audible, then, when, the fleshly ear
> Oer come by grosser prelude of that strain
> Forgot its functions, & slept undisturbed.
> (*Ruined Cottage*, 173 & 177)

These lines were not included in any published version of *The Ruined Cottage*, but they were written into the first version of *The Prelude*, completed in 1799 as a poem in two parts:

> Wonder not
> If such my transports were, for in all things
> I saw one life, and felt that it was joy...
> (*Prelude*, 25, 458–60)

In a letter to James Tobin of 6 March 1798, Wordsworth reported having written '1300 lines of a poem in which I continue to convey most of the knowledge of which I am possessed'.[14] It was, then, *The Ruined Cottage*, not the *Lyrical Ballads*, that Wordsworth believed would be the genesis of the great work that would herald a new age of poetry in a nation that had lost its way both aesthetically and politically. It is therefore to *The Ruined Cottage* that we should turn if we are properly to understand Wordsworth's perception of the literary revolution he planned to bring about. In 1959 Stephen Parrish included *The Ruined Cottage* alongside *Salisbury Plain* and *The Borderers* in a list of poems to be considered as merely 'forerunners of the *Lyrical Ballads*'.[15] By the 1980s, however, *The Ruined Cottage* was firmly established as a major work of the late 1790s, while Lyrical *Ballads*, important as they were to become for the poet after 1800, may be considered at the point of their publication in 1798 as an offcut from the more serious work in hand.

3

New Directions: *Lyrical Ballads*

> Books! 'tis a dull and endless strife,
> Come, hear the woodland linnet,
> How sweet his music; on my life
> There's more of wisdom in it.
> ('The Tables Turned', *LB*, 109, 9–12)

I

If *The Ruined Cottage* reveals where Wordsworth believed his vocation as a poet was taking him in 1798, the *Lyrical Ballads* volumes were undoubtedly to become a major influence on the shaping of English Romanticism in later years. The first edition of the *Ballads* contained a brief 'Advertisement' which refers to critical issues that were as much germane to *The Ruined Cottage* as to the poetry of the *Ballads*. The general tone is dismissive, and assumes that most readers will find the poetry unsatisfactory. Wordsworth peremptorily suggests that the problem lies with the faulty taste of the reader, not the poet. The impression given is that he really can't be bothered to take the time to argue the case fully. This is not a poet prepared to linger; he has other things on his mind. We are thus presented with a critical issue to savour, and it is one that has long been with us. Bernard Groom, writing in 1966, describes the first edition of the *Ballads* as evidence of 'a vital phase in Wordsworth's poetic life', 'phase' being the operative word. He suggests that it would be wrong to see the volume as a quintessential expression of the poet's 'romanticism': 'Many of these early poems [those included in the first 1798 volume] ... are of a transitional character.'[1]

The 1798 *Ballads* do, indeed, indicate that this was a transitional period in Wordsworth's development, one where we find him taking up and testing themes central to the composition of *The Ruined Cottage*. But in marked contrast to the tone of *The Ruined Cottage*, he frequently examines his political beliefs along with his commitment to simplicity and pantheism from an ironic distance. One reason for this was suggested by Stephen Parrish in 1959 (Parrish was in turn referring back to an essay of 1914 by Charles Stork) when he claimed that 'Wordsworth lacked natural feeling for the ballad'.[2] Over against the seriousness of *The Ruined Cottage*, we find a Wordsworth in *Lyrical Ballads* whose lack of full commitment to the ballad form freed him to experiment more playfully with what in *The Ruined Cottage* are seriously investigated issues of the function of the poet and the location of the narrative voice. In *The Ruined Cottage* the poetic persona becomes little more than a cipher, having relinquished control of the narrative to the Pedlar. The wise, philosophical poet of the eighteenth century gives way to the humble Pedlar, and the Pedlar in turn gives way to the even humbler Margaret. In consequence we witness the 'modern' poet formally declaring his need to be instructed. In *Lyrical Ballads*, by contrast, though similar shifts take place in the location of the narrative voice, these are executed in such a way that the consequences tend to be far more problematic for the assumed credibility of the poems and their author.

II

The *Lyrical Ballads* were planned as a jointly authored volume. Coleridge supplied four poems for the 1798 edition, including the first two, 'The Rime of the Ancyent Marinere' and 'The Foster-Mother's Tale'. For his ballads, Wordsworth experimented with a range of narrative voices, including himself as a younger poet in 'Lines left upon a Seat in a Yew-tree which stands near the Lake of Esthwaite', revised from a poem composed in the late 1780s. This was the first poem by Wordsworth in the volume. Other work from an earlier period included 'The Female Vagrant', an extract from the *Salisbury Plain* manuscript, 'Old Man Travelling', 'Lines written near Richmond, upon the Thames, at Evening', and 'The Convict'. The first poem in the volume which Wordsworth wrote specifically for the collection was 'Goody Blake and Harry Gill'. Coming after his 'Lines left upon a Yew-tree Seat' and 'The Female Vagrant', the contrast between the old and the new Wordsworth could not have been more marked. 'Lines left upon a Yew-tree Seat' is not in ballad form; it describes the disenchantment of the Rev. William Braithwaite, a Hawkshead worthy:

> he to the world
> Went forth, pure in his heart, against the taint
> Of dissolute tongues, 'gainst jealousy, and hate,
> And scorn, against all enemies prepared,
> All but neglect: and so, his spirit damped
> At once, with rash disdain he turned away,
> And with the food of pride sustained his soul
> In solitude.
>   (*LB*, 48–9, 14–21)

Wordsworth's use of the Spenserian stanza in the following poem, 'The Female Vagrant', creates a very different frame for a narrative he had been experimenting with since Hawkshead days. From Braithwaite, a man whose goodness is ignored by society and who sinks into melancholy, we turn to a woman whose life is destroyed by a rapacious, nouveau riche landowner, and a war which her husband is forced, for want of money, to fight. Raw anger and despair are communicated in the woman's narration, and we are left with a poet in need of a pedlar to reconcile him to the cruel injustice of the woman's fate:

> – She ceased, and weeping turned away,
> As if because her tale was at an end
> She wept; – because she had no more to say
> Of that perpetual weight which on her spirit lay.
>   (*LB*, 58, 267–70)

By contrast, the opening lines of 'Goody Blake and Harry Gill' strike a jovial, near comic note. This is Wordsworth writing up a story of social injustice, of the strong persecuting the weak, as the kind of ballad that had interested him most. In 1796, *The Monthly Magazine* began to publish William Taylor's translations of ballads by the German poet, Gottfried Bürger. Bürger was praised for the energy of his driving rhythms, and for his use of 'popular forms of expression'.[3] Now, through Wordsworth's experimental use of ballad form, a new vista begins to open on the possible meaning of 'simplicity':

> Oh! What's the matter? what's the matter?
> What is't that ails young Harry Gill?
> That evermore his teeth they chatter,
> Chatter, chatter, chatter still.
> Of waistcoats Harry has no lack,
> Good duffle grey, and flannel fine;
> He has a blanket on his back,
> And coats enough to smother nine.
>
> (*LB*, 59, 1–8)

The solemnity of *The Ruined Cottage* is cast aside for a subject no less important. Goody Blake, old, poor and alone, steals wood for her fire from the wealthy Harry Gill. By the letter of the law she is therefore 'bad', and Harry Gill catches her at it:

> And fiercely by the arm he took her,
> And by the arm he held her fast,
> And fiercely by the arm he shook her,
> And cried, 'I've caught you then at last!'
>
> (ll.89–92)

But Goody proves that she is 'good' by appealing to a higher form of justice:

> She pray'd, her wither'd hand uprearing,
> While Harry held her by the arm –
> 'God! Who art never out of hearing,
> 'O may he never more be warm!'
>
> (ll.97–100)

And true justice is done; Harry Gill will never feel warm again.

The political point remains the same as that which had concerned Wordsworth throughout *Salisbury Plain*. The responsibility for crime in a situation such as this does not belong with the perpetrator, but with the individual or the society inhumane enough to drive people to such a pitch of desperation. 'Goody Blake and Harry Gill', like *The Ruined Cottage*, explores the 'simplicity' of serious subject matter, and Goody, like the Pedlar, appeals to an authority beyond humanity. For the Pedlar this constitutes the 'one life'; for Goody Blake it is more traditionally '"God! Who art never out of hearing"'. What now begins to complement the simplicity of the subject matter is the simplicity of the form. Wordsworth was composing in a style that promised to produce marketable copy;

Bürger was popular, Thomas Percy's *Reliques of Ancient English Poetry* of 1765 had encouraged a vogue for English ballads, and Robert Southey's 'Ballads and Metrical Tales' of 1797 were making money for him. Though Parrish's point about Wordsworth's aptitude for writing ballads in the popular style remains to a degree an important one, the evidence here suggests that Wordsworth had discovered a vein of poetry he enjoyed working, and that he found it increasingly interesting to do so.

It is, however, in 'Simon Lee, the old Huntsman' that we first sense Wordsworth appraising the lyrical ballad style as he writes, and beginning to manipulate it for his own specific purposes. In 'Simon Lee' the 'simplicity' of the style he was adopting is pushed to the limit with predictable rhythms, repetition, and a concentration on banal detail:

> And he is lean and he is sick,
> His little body's half awry,
> His ancles they are swoln and thick;
> His legs are thin and dry.
> When he was young he little knew
> Of husbandry or tillage;
> And now he's forced to work, though weak,
> – The weakest in the village.
> (*LB*, 66, 33–40)

You could hardly ask to find a less poetical subject, but the point here, as it is with that other ballad destined to be frequently criticised for its banality, 'The Thorn', is that the authority of the narrative voice is being questioned. Where in *The Ruined Cottage* we have the poet reduced to the status of a walk-on part, and a culturally destabilising shift to the Pedlar as the source of all wisdom, in 'Simon Lee' the poet's voice continues to dominate, but it is a poet who admits to being insensitive to the serious issues involved in the 'tale' until almost the end of the poem (something also true of 'Anecdote for Fathers').

Behind the jingling lines of 'Simon Lee' we learn of a huntsman too old to work, left with his wife to fend for himself, the victim of an uncaring society. Wordsworth engineers a dramatic change of voice halfway through the ninth verse. From the balladeer he becomes the teacher:

> My gentle reader, I perceive
> How patiently you've waited,

> And I'm afraid that you expect
> Some tale will be related.
>
> O reader! Had you in your mind
> Such stores as silent thought can bring,
> O gentle reader! You would find
> A tale in every thing.
> What more I have to say is short,
> I hope you'll kindly take it;
> It is no tale; but should you think,
> Perhaps a tale you'll make it.
>   (ll.69–80)

In the next verse it becomes impossible to read the poem with the galloping rhythm that has abetted the trivialising level of narration:

> One summer-day I chanced to see
> This old man doing all he could
> About the root of an old tree...
>   (ll.81–3)

The point is clear: the story alone signifies nothing. What matters is thought; it is only when 'you think' that you make 'the tale' that matters. The final verses expose this poet as one who has tended not to 'think'. He helps Simon chop out the root of the old tree; for him it is easy, but for Simon it represents a Herculean task. Simon's disproportionate gratitude forces the thoughtless poet to think about the true meaning of the act, and thus of the true meaning of the poem:

> – I've heard of hearts unkind, kind deeds
> With coldness still returning.
> Alas! The gratitude of men
> Has oftner left me mourning.
>   (ll.101–4)

The ballad, where it constitutes no more than a sentimental tale, is taken to task. Wordsworth is writing modern ballads; they are becoming self-conscious exercises in simplicity of style as well as subject matter, and though they therefore differ profoundly from *The Ruined Cottage* in form, their function is to explore the same issues.

In 'Anecdote for Fathers' and 'We are Seven' we learn that if the Pedlar happens not to be there to advise the poet, then a child – in all its innocence – may do as well. In 'Anecdote for Fathers' the father figure 'in very idleness' asks the child which of two places he prefers, Kilve or Liswyn, knowing himself that he prefers Liswyn and assuming that the child will share his preference. But the child opts for Kilve, and can offer no rational explanation for his choice. The father insists on hearing the reason, and in desperation the child (being physically held by the arm throughout the ordeal, and like Goody Blake given a good shaking) manifestly lies to rid himself of his persecutor. Too late, the father realises his mistake:

> Oh dearest, dearest boy! My heart
> For better lore would seldom yearn,
> Could I but teach the hundredth part
> Of what from thee I learn.
> (*LB*, 73, 57–60)

'We are Seven', which follows, explores the same theme. The child's simple, instinctive knowledge is a corrective to the adult's insistence on rational logic. No matter how many of her brothers or sisters have died, the little girl in 'We are Seven' knows herself to be one of a family of seven.

These, then, are ballads which seem designed to suggest an insufficiency on the part of the poet, a poet that we know had sought to live by, and found wanting, the virtues of Godwinian rationalism. The 'simple' child, not the knowledgeable poet, is revealed as the true source of wisdom. In this respect, what is true of 'We are Seven' is true also of *The Ruined Cottage*. In both cases we learn that death is not a closure, but a doorway that opens onto a more profound sense of being. The main difference between *Lyrical Ballads* and *The Ruined Cottage*, however, is that this revelation in *Lyrical Ballads* is frequently accompanied by an apparent tendency to call into question the validity of the poem as an appropriate vehicle for truth. From the time of their initial publication, there have always been readers of the *Ballads* who have felt uncomfortable with Wordsworth's decision to write some of the narrative ballads as though they were the product of ill-informed gossip (two notable examples being 'The Thorn' and 'The Idiot Boy'). In such instances, it may seem that Wordsworth is abnegating his responsibility: the work of finding the 'tale' is left to the reader, and it is a tale which must consequently exist somewhere beyond the poem as it appears on the page.

Even where we have every reason to respect and trust the narrator, as in 'The Last of the Flock', and 'The Complaint of a Forsaken Indian Woman', these are people who do not control the process of interpretation as the Pedlar does in *The Ruined Cottage*. In the *Lyrical Ballads*, then, the reliability of the poet and the poem seem frequently to be threatened by the poet's engagement with 'simplicity' as a deceptively complex phenomena.

III

The poems in *Lyrical Ballads* have been read to this point as explorations of the by-ways branching off from Wordsworth's central project, encapsulated in *The Ruined Cottage*. It has been a critical approach designed to present the poems as working a number of frequently playful variations on Wordsworth's central theme: human suffering resolved through the ministrations of nature. There is, of course, a good deal more to the *Ballads* than this. The focus of much Wordsworth criticism in the wake of Geoffrey Hartman's work has been to emphasise the extent to which his mature poetry enters a shadowy world of uncertainty, what David Pirie has described as the 'unconvincingly vague'.[4] This reminds us that there remains a very different critical route into the *Ballads*, one that concentrates on Wordsworth's tendency to conceal as much as he reveals about his subject. Marjorie Levinson's 'new historicist' reading of Wordsworth in 1986, *Wordsworth's Great Period Poems*, has become a key text for setting this agenda. She described her approach as 'a self-consciously belated criticism that sees in its necessary ignorance – its expulsion from the heaven of Romantic sympathy – a critical advantage: the capacity to know a work as neither it, nor its original readers, nor its author could know it.'[5]

Levinson argues that in the poems she intends to discuss, Wordsworth's object was 'to replace the picture of the place with "the picture of the mind", such as it might be at any time and in any place'.[6] If we accept what is in effect her invitation to psychoanalyse the poet through his work, to tap into his subconscious agenda, or indeed to reveal a story that has been knowingly concealed, we would not expect to travel far before encountering Annette and her daughter Caroline. If we consider the poetry Wordsworth composed after returning to England in 1793, leaving behind him the woman he loved and her child, their spectral presences are not hard to locate; but of course the matter will be dealt with clandestinely. The abandoned, heart-broken soldier's widow of *Salisbury Plain* cries out for retribution; as Margaret, she is there in *The Ruined Cottage* watched by males who seem incapable of rendering her any practical assistance, and she haunts *Lyrical Ballads* in 'The Female Vagrant', 'The Thorn', 'The Mad Mother', and 'The Complaint of a Forsaken Indian Woman'.

Levinson chose to apply her new historicist method to what is probably the least characteristic poem of *Lyrical Ballads*, 'Lines written a few miles above Tintern Abbey'. She begins by reminding us of the full title of the poem: 'Lines Written a Few Miles Above Tintern Abbey, on revisiting the Banks of the Wye during a tour, July 13, 1798'. She then builds a psychoanalytic, politicised reading of the poem on the basis of what she maintains are the poem's allusive tendencies. These include the fact that the date in the title suggests the signalling of four anniversaries: Bastille Day, Wordsworth's first visit to France, the murder of Marat, and the poet's first visit to Tintern Abbey. She notes also as symptomatic of the poem as a whole the fact that, having mentioned Tintern Abbey in the title of the poem, the poem itself contains no specific reference to the Abbey. The poem's 'absences' are thus read to reveal the presence of a public 'history' informing its structure, while within that public history lies an even more illusive personal history that Levinson understands Wordsworth to be in some way attempting to exorcise.

The controversy that built up around Levinson's interpretation of this poem has taken many forms. One of the most sustained attacks came in 1992 when Thomas McFarland devoted the first chapter of his book, *William Wordsworth: Intensity and Achievement*, to decapitating what he called Levinson's 'bizarre reading'.[7] At one level the problem for McFarland appears to be the '*decorum*' of a criticism that seems to place more value on 'what Wordsworth chooses not to put into the poem compared to what he does put in'. At another level he clearly deeply distrusts Levinson's politics, spawned by 'recent theoretical currents flowing from France':

> Levinson charges 'Tintern Abbey' with escapism – calls it 'this great escape'. She implies that it should be blamed for suppressing the awareness of the poor; as she says, 'mixing metaphors, the "still, sad music of humanity" drowns out the noise produced by real people in real distress'. Even at the outset we must surely find the contention

ironic in light of John Keble's tribute to Wordsworth as the poet of the poor, as 'the one among all poets who has set forth the manners, the pursuits, and the religion of the poor'.[8]

The ability of *Lyrical Ballads* to stir up controversy remains undiminished. There are critical issues involved here to which we shall return later, not least the way in which critical debate may divert attention from the text in question.

The inclusion of 'Tintern Abbey' in *Lyrical Ballads* was characteristically fortuitous. The poem was prompted by a walking tour of the Wye valley with Dorothy in July 1798. They had left Alfoxden for good, and planned to travel to Germany that Autumn. The poem became a reflection on the changes that had taken place in the poet's life, specifically because he had travelled that way five years before, following his traumatic trip to France. For a number of reasons, therefore, it was an appropriate poem with which to round off a collection of occasional pieces all of which reflected his changing ideas, although none of them (up until that point) presented the poet in the persona of the serious, philosophical poet he now aspired to be. 'Tintern Abbey' reaffirms his identity as a poet (after so many ballads that seemed to question it), and claims the Pedlar's identity as his own, a wanderer who returns to a specific place and finds that his meditative nature removes him to a higher plane of being:

> that serene and blessed mood,
> In which the affections gently lead us on,
> Until, the breath of this corporeal frame,
> And even the motion of our human blood
> Almost suspended, we are laid asleep
> In body, and become a living soul:
> While with an eye made quiet with the power
> Of harmony, and the deep power of joy,
> We see into the life of things.
>
> (*LB*, 117, 42–50)

The unifying language of pantheism, of the 'one life', recognises the precise location of the poem (made indelibly precise by the detail in the full title, 'On revisiting the banks of the Wye during a tour, July 13, 1798'), only to dissolve it (as the Pedlar would dissolve the fact of Margaret's miserable death) into a 'something far more deeply interfused' with the workings of nature:

And I have felt
A presence that disturbs me with the joy
Of elevated thoughts; a sense sublime
Of something far more deeply interfused,
Whose dwelling is the light of setting suns,
And the round ocean, and the living air,
And the blue sky, and in the mind of man,
A mfotion and a spirit, that impels
All thinking things, all objects of all thought,
And rolls through all things.
(*LB*, 118–19, 94–103)

'Tintern Abbey' restores the chameleon poet of *Lyrical Ballads* to the role he claimed as the poet of *The Ruined Cottage*. In the final section of the poem, his tribute to Dorothy, we find him – in what may well be a conscious act of writing with the intention of summing up the *Lyrical Ballads* collection as a whole – drawing a clear distinction between the embittered, reclusive Braithwaite described in his first poem, 'Lines left upon a Yew-tree seat', and the poet who has learnt

that neither evil tongues,
Rash judgments, nor the sneers of selfish men,
Nor greetings where no kindness is, nor all
The dreary intercourse of daily life,
Shall e'er prevail against us, or disturb
Our chearful faith that all which we behold
Is full of blessings.
(*LB*, 119, 129–35)

In the Advertisement written for the 1798 edition, the reader is initially assured that most of the poems included should not be considered as anything more than 'experiments': 'They were written chiefly with a view to ascertain how far the language of conversation in the middle and lower classes of society is adapted to the purposes of poetic pleasure' (*LB*, 738). Wordsworth allows that the contents may well not strike the reader as poetry at all. Popular poetry (especially of the ballad genre) was marked by its 'gaudiness and inane phraseology', and for many 'poetry' had thus become very narrowly defined. Wordsworth's response is to say that if the reader can agree that the pieces contain 'a natural delineation of human passions, human characters, and human incidents', then that should be sufficient recommendation, regardless of whether they satisfy this or that definition of 'poetry'. The use of 'expressions' which are 'too familiar, and not of sufficient dignity' will offend polite taste, but polite taste is not the same as an 'accurate taste', and here what matters is 'painting manners and persons' in a 'natural way' (*LB*, 738–9). Taking the simplicity advocated in *The Ruined Cottage*, the same principles, then, are here being applied to a collection of very different poems, producing a considerably radicalised theoretical position that in little more than a thumbnail sketch advocates a comprehensive redefinition of poetry, its language and its function. This is why, regardless of the nature of their initial composition, the *Lyrical Ballads* were soon to become axiomatic to the development of Wordsworth's subsequent poetry.

IV

Though Wordsworth did not see writing *Lyrical Ballads* as central to his main poetical task, their composition extended and deepened his thinking about poetry, and he continued to write in lyric style while in Goslar (1789–99). When he returned, it became clear that *Lyrical Ballads* had occasioned sufficient interest to merit their republication in revised and extended form. It was from this point that they became of sufficient importance to merit the introductory essay, the 'Preface' that subsequently earned Wordsworth the reputation of being the first major theoretician of the Romantic Movement in English literature. Needless to say, critics have been debating the appropriateness of that claim ever since, but it does alert us to the fact that the second, two-volume edition of *Lyrical Ballads* of 1800 is a substantially different production from the 1798 collection.

Having discovered an important (not to mention potentially lucrative) way forward for his poetry, Wordsworth now began to shape, reshape and revise the material around him. His first task was to reorder the poetry in Volume One, initiating the process of marginalising the presence of Coleridge, who would eventually disappear altogether. The authorship reverted increasingly to Wordsworth; not only did his choice of poem to begin the new Volume One, 'Expostulation and Reply', place the central principle of 'a wise passiveness' (l.24) at the head of the collection, it began by naming the poet:

> 'Why, William, on that old grey stone,
> 'Thus for the length of half a day,

'Why, William, sit you this alone,
'And dream your time away?'
(*LB*, 107, 1–4)

The poet reflects on the nature of his art. Poetry is knowledge, and knowledge is no longer what it once was for him: that is, rationally perceived, clearly understood truths. In the Advertisement he described 'Expostulation and Reply' as a poem designed to debunk 'modern books of moral philosophy'; he had, as ever, Godwin in mind. Knowledge is the fruit of meditation, and its substance will be mysterious, its meaning frequently a matter of feeling rather than the fruit of 'Our meddling intellect'. This statement is made in the second poem, 'The Tables Turned' (*LB*, 109, 26). Knowledge will seek us out if we learn how to make ourselves available (and the reclining poet at the beginning of *The Ruined Cottage* is doing just that). We should not chase it:

'Nor less I deem that there are powers,
'Which of themselves our mind impress,
'That we can feed this mind of ours,
'In a wise passiveness.'
('Expostulation and Reply', *LB*, 108, 21–4)

The third poem of the revised Volume One then offers an example of this 'wise passiveness' in 'Old Man Travelling', where the central figure is 'insensibly subdued / To settled quiet':

He is by nature led
To peace so perfect, that the young behold
With envy, what the old man hardly feels.
(*LB*, 110, 6–7, 12–14)

The *Lyrical Ballads* collection was being redesigned around an evolving perception of simplicity; in the process Wordsworth was redefining the scope and nature of poetry as a means of redefining our perception of knowledge. Each poem becomes a counter in that argument, and each counter needs to be placed in the best position for the reader. The wise passiveness of the old man is followed by the wise passiveness of the forsaken Indian woman (which came near the end of the 1798 volume), and the shepherd in 'The Last of the Flock' (similarly brought forward); we then hear of the fate of William Braithwaite, a cautionary tale about those who fail to achieve sufficient levels of wise passiveness.

Coleridge's 'The Foster-Mother's Tale' is moved from its original place in the 1798 volume as the second poem, to function as an interval before a series of Wordsworthian narratives. Here we now find 'Goody Blake and Harry Gill', 'The Thorn', 'We are Seven', 'Anecdote for Fathers' and 'The Female Vagrant', with 'Lines written at a small distance from my House' inserted among them to remind us of the vantage point from which we should be reading this group of poems:

> There is a blessing in the air,
> Which seems a sense of joy to yield
> To the bare trees, and mountains bare,
> And grass in the green field.
> (*LB*, 63, 5–8)

Coleridge again supplies an interval with 'The Dungeon', before 'Simon Lee' poses a problem the careful reader can begin to solve from 'Lines written in early Spring' that follows it: 'And much it griev'd my heart to think / What man has made of man' (*LB*, 76, 6–7). 'The Idiot Boy', a particular favourite of Wordsworth's, but a poem he knew caused his readers considerable difficulty, is held over until almost last, coupled (with an intervening Coleridge poem reflecting on how love can bring about madness) with 'The Mad Mother'. This left 'The Ancient Mariner', followed by 'Tintern Abbey' still providing the final word.

The second volume extends the range of the 'lyrical ballad' significantly. Indeed, Wordsworth's perception that he had moved on from that initial venture to produce a two-volume set of new poetry of a far more comprehensive nature than the 1798 collection is reflected in his wish to rename the set as a whole 'Poems in Two Volumes'. The publishers (Longmans) retained *Lyrical Ballads*; but although the ballad continued to dominate ('Hart-leap Well' which begins the second volume is just such a poem), Wordsworth included an increasingly varied style of story telling, adding poems where the narrative is far less significant, and poems that are effectively meditative fragments ('There was a Boy', 'A slumber did my spirit seal'). In a number of cases ballad metre is replaced by a style that belongs to his *Ruined Cottage* oeuvre. This category includes 'The Brothers', 'The Old Cumberland Beggar', 'Poems on the Naming of Places', and 'Michael'.

These are all poems which now systematically illustrate and explore the theory of poetry that Wordsworth discussed in his

Preface to the 1800 edition. To turn to the Preface is to turn to a well-worn battlefield. The point is frequently made that it was the Preface of 1800 rather than the poetry that escalated the critical controversy over Wordsworth's poetry towards something approaching hysteria in the Reviews. Wordsworth begins by portraying himself as a somewhat diffident but evidently scholarly poet, a man who wishes to distance himself at once from certain tendencies in modern thought: 'I was unwilling to undertake the task [of writing a Preface]...since I might be suspected of having been principally influenced by the selfish and foolish hope of *reasoning* him [the reader] into an approbation of these particular poems' (*LB*, 742, 25–30). He is not to be mistaken for a peasant poet, justifying bad poetry because he knows no better; the names of the great flow from his pen: Catullus, Terence, Lucretius, Statius, Shakespeare, Donne, Dryden and Pope (*LB*, 742–3, 48–51). His aim is to challenge 'certain known habits of association' (*LB*, 742, 43) – meaning narrow prejudicial views – as to what a poem is and what a poet should be doing.

There is nothing here not already covered by the 1798 Advertisement. It is in the sixth paragraph that the first reference to 'simplicity' is made (the word was not used in the Advertisement), and from then on it becomes a key point of reference, and, of course, the stick by which Wordsworth was to be regularly beaten by contemporary critics. Wordsworth's 'principal object' was 'to make incidents of common life interesting' by showing how they revealed fundamental truths about human nature (a statement that might be seen as revealing a dangerously levelling agenda). Therefore 'Low and rustic life' tends to provide the subject matter, and 'the essential passions of the heart' thus exposed will be found speaking 'a plainer and more emphatic language' (*LB*, 743, 64–89). He does not initially suggest the direct reproduction of rustic speech; the 'plainer...language' is the language of 'the passions of the heart'. The movement from that to the actual adoption of 'the very language of men' (*LB*, 747, 186) for poetry is the subject of the latter part of the paragraph. Before that, while still concerned with 'the essential passions of the heart', he further defends his use of 'Low and rustic life' by claiming that 'in that situation our elementary feelings exist in a state of greater simplicity...' (*LB*, 743, 70–1).

Latterly the 1800 Preface debate has revolved in part around just how 'modern' the theories contained in it are. Marilyn Butler has written of the *Ballads* and its Preface as an unexceptional example 'of the culture of the Enlightenment'. Had the poems appeared ten years earlier, she claims, 'they would hardly have attracted attention'.[9] It was the volatile political complexion of the late 1790s that encouraged a controversy around a set of poems claiming that they were modern, different, and that they challenged established views. By contrast, in 1825, Hazlitt, while hinting at a politically subversive agenda for *Lyrical Ballads* ('His muse...is a levelling one'), was concerned to describe the poems as difficult, and in the process he reminded his readers of a point Wordsworth makes relatively early on in the Preface:

> He takes a subject or a story merely as pegs or loops to hang thought and feeling on; the incidents are trifling, in proportion to his contempt for imposing appearances; the reflections are profound, according to the gravity and aspiring pretensions of his mind.[10]

Hazlitt was remembering the way Wordsworth had outlined the distinctive nature of his poems. First, he reaffirmed his determination to take as his subject 'the great and simple affections of our nature', that is to say, the most profound area of human experience 'belonging rather to nature than to manners'. As an illustration of this, he proposes a reading of 'Old Man Travelling', '...of which the elements are simple' (*LB*, 745–6, 118–47). This led him to distinguish between 'action and situation':

> it is proper that I should mention one other circumstance which distinguishes these Poems from the popular Poetry of the day; it is this, that the feeling therein developed gives importance to the action and situation, and not the action and situation to the feeling.
>
> (*LB*, 746, 141–4)

We are directed to 'Poor Susan' and 'The Childless Father' as instances of this principle.

'The Childless Father' begins with the poet urging Timothy, an elderly, bereaved parent, to follow the hunt as he always has done in the past. The scene is an active, happy, social one; the metre creates a childishly enthusiastic atmosphere:

> – Of coats and of jackets grey, scarlet and green,
> On the slopes of the pastures all colours were seen,
> With their comely blue aprons and caps white as snow
> The girls on the hills made a holiday show.
>
> (*LB*, 227, 5–8)

As in so many of these poems, we now see the poet's insensitivity corrected. His urging on of Timothy to the frenetic activity of hunt in the first verse is put in its place by the old man shutting 'With a leisurely motion the door of his hut' (l.16). The last of Timothy's children has died six months before, and the poet seems to be responding by urging the father to go and have a good time. He seems to fail to understand how Timothy may feel, and in the first line of the final verse goes on to admit that a part of what he is writing is necessarily his own invented version of the father's state of mind; Timothy is by no means telling him everything. The final line introduces sorrow into what should be a joyous event, and does so against the grain of the tale the poet would write. With the poet unable to grasp the point, we are left (as in 'Simon Lee') to make a tale of it ourselves:

> Perhaps to himself at that moment he said,
> 'The key must I take, for my Ellen is dead,'
> But of this in my ears not a word did he speak,
> And he went to the chace with a tear on his cheek.
> (ll.17–20)

In the eighteenth century the hunt was a trope frequently used to represent the hectic excitement of social life, and even more specifically the rough and tumble of an active political life. 'The Childless Father' depicts just such an 'action and situation' in the distance. We can imagine the poet insensitively recommending it to Timothy as a means of cheering himself up. In other words, it is an invitation to avoid thought and reflection, to avoid 'feeling'. What we have, in a poem controlled by its subject in defiance of the poet, is minimal action and situation: essentially we see the old man close his cottage door and walk steadily towards the hills 'with a tear on his cheek'. But because of the feeling involved (in this case bereavement), the action and situation become charged with significance.

This is a call to 'wise passiveness', a call to pause and reflect specifically in relation to political activity, as Wordsworth was himself doing at this time, in the process beginning to plan a philosophical poem designed to heal the wounds of contemporaries who had given themselves to the 'chace' of radical, reforming politics, only to be horrified by the disasters that followed, specifically in France. He returns to a strain of traditional eighteenth-century radical Whig, Commonwealthman political thinking, where 'retirement' from the corrupt political world was praised, frequently in the form of hill-top poems like William Crowe's *Lewesdon Hill*, a poem he read and admired at Racedown.[11]

Wordsworth's enthusiasm for tranquil reflection is not hard to understand given the restlessness of his own life since Cambridge. The years of constant travel and temporary homes reached its climax in the visit to Germany of 1798–99, and seemed to be finally terminated by the renting of Dove Cottage in the Lake District at the end of 1799. During this time he had found, and lost, a political creed, and likewise found and lost a role model, William Godwin. He had found and lost two great loves: Annette was one, and must now be counted dead to him; the other was Michel Beaupuy, his political and moral mentor who died fighting in the French Revolutionary wars. It is hardly surprising, then, to find that death and bereavement inform so much of the poetry, or that a theme central to many poems is that of the need for a 'wise passiveness' in the face of adversity.

V

The theme of the abandoned, doomed female, important in the first collection, runs on through the new poems that appear in the two-volume *Lyrical Ballads* of 1800. These later poems are frequently linked to the more general problem of becoming reconciled to death. In 'Lucy Gray' the child sets off to the town to fetch her mother home, and is lost in the snow. Her death can never quite be accepted:

> Yet some maintain that to this day
> She is a living Child,
> That you may see sweet Lucy Gray
> Upon the lonesome Wild.
> (*LB*, 172, 57–60)

In 'Strange fits of passion I have known' the death of Lucy is suggested to the poet's mind as the moon drops behind the roof of her cottage. The unresolved fear is confirmed by the two poems that follow, both of which are meditations on bereavement. Lucy dies in 'Three years she grew in sun and shower', and in ''Tis said that some have died for love' the poet frightens himself with the thought that experiencing the death of a loved one can bring on irredeemable madness.

Wordsworth's treatment of death in *Lyrical Ballads* focuses throughout on the issue of what constitutes knowledge. In his discussion of death in the 'Lucy poems', David P. Haney suggests that Wordsworth presents knowledge as a form of not knowing: 'the anticipatory certainty of death is way ahead of and incompatible with our usual sense of experimental knowledge'.[12] Haney perceives Wordsworth's underlying concern to be an investigation of the complexities of the relationship between words and meaning.

The fourth poem in the 'Poems on the Naming of Places' group (the penultimate poetry in Volume Two) offers a particularly clear statement of the untrustworthy nature of words, linking the problem specifically to the rhetoric of picturesque scene painting. A privileged, carefree party walk on the shore of Grasmere lake:

> And in our vacant mood
> Not seldom did we stop to watch some tuft
> Of dandelion seed or thistle's beard,
> Which, seeming lifeless half, and half impell'd
> By some internal feeling, skimm'd along
> Close to the surface of the lake that lay
> Asleep in a dead calm...
> (*LB*, 248, 16–22)

To this idyllic scene is added the sound of harvesters. The labour being unseen, the sound encourages an artistic construction of an idealised image, but the sight of a man fishing then intrudes onto their view, and all are quick to judge him:

> We all cried out, that he must be indeed
> An idle man, who thus could lose a day
> Of the mid-harvest, when the labourer's hire
> Is ample, and some little might be stor'd
> Wherewith to chear him in the winter time.
> (ll.56–60)

They in turn are then judged when they come close enough to see that he is 'worn down / By sickness... with sunken cheeks / And wasted limbs':

> The man was using his best skill to gain
> A pittance from the dead unfeeling lake
> That knew not of his wants. I will not say
> What thoughts immediately were ours, nor how

> The happy idleness of that sweet morn,
> With all its lovely images, was chang'd
> To serious musing and to self reproach.
> (ll.70–6)

'I will not say...'. It is not, of course, an impossible task to render this experience into words. This is what the poem does; but we are asked to imagine a situation where words are abandoned in the face of an 'admonishment' (l.82) that has been delivered by what was seen, not by what was said. What has been 'said' has been at best a poetically imprecise, at worst a poetically false construction.

Critical readings of this kind draw attention to the fact that the poetry of *Lyrical Ballads* explores and validates concerns that threaten to undermine the credibility of Wordsworth's aim in his intended great work of philosophical poetry. *The Recluse* was to be an epic poem of reassurance and healing; it would provide meaning and give direction to lives cut adrift from the mainstream of society. In the Preface to *Lyrical Ballads*, however, Wordsworth found himself exploring a seemingly irresolvable crisis of meaning when it came to writing for the healing of a stricken nation. He describes the situation as an identity crisis on the part of the literary culture in which he is placed, triggered by the social, political and demographic changes of the day:

> The invaluable works of our elder writers...are driven into neglect by frantic novels, sickly and stupid German Tragedies, and deluges of idle and extravagant stories in verse....I should be oppressed with no dishonourable melancholy, had I not a deep impression of certain inherent and indestructible qualities of the human mind, and likewise of certain powers in the great and permanent objects that act upon it which are equally inherent and indestructible...
> (*LB*, 746–7, 166–76)

The final poem of the two-volume *Lyrical Ballads* is 'Michael, a Pastoral', not infrequently read now as a window into the changing nature of the times, and as a mark of Wordsworth's conservative instincts. Roger Sales takes Wordsworth to task for presenting an idealised representation of eighteenth-century rural life:

> Wordsworth is deliberately vague about economic agency because he is trying to play the oldest trick in the crooked pastoralist's cooked book. He wants to suggest that early eighteenth century rural society was a pre-capitalist utopia.[13]

This reading challenges Hartman's interpretation of the poem as an attack on the effects that industrialisation was having on the liveli- hood of the Lakeland hill farmers. John Lucas is equally dissatisfied with Hartman, and suggests that Wordsworth knew himself to be part of the problem that was bringing about the demise of people like Michael. He draws attention to the relationship that developed between the poet and Sir George Beaumont after 1803 as highlight- ing the problematical nature of Hartman's interpretation:

> Beaumont himself was a large, wealthy landowner, although much of his money came from coal which was mined close to his estate, Coleorton, in Leicestershire. Guests at the house were spared the sight of workers and workings. Beaumont so landscaped the estate as to screen off the colliery. He was helped in this by Wordsworth.[14]

We may be sure that Wordsworth's decision to end the *Lyrical Ballads* with this poem signified his belief in its importance. Given the debate about its politics (described by Wordsworth as his con- cern for 'the encreasing disproportion between the price of labour and that of the necessaries of life'[15]), it is worth revisiting the poem to observe how Wordsworth set about his task, rather than consider- ing what he chose to ignore (according to Sales), or to discuss (as Lucas does) the strategies by which the poet managed to 'conceal feelings of contradiction, or discomposure, which cannot be brought into the open'.[16] As Kenneth Johnston has reminded us, this was a poem written to order; it was composed specifically to supply the need for an appropriate conclusion to the *Ballads* as a whole, and as such, whatever it might have to tell us from the analyst's couch, it constitutes a carefully planned work with a very public agenda.[17]

'Michael' returns the reader of *Lyrical Ballads* to the blank verse style of *The Ruined Cottage*. The principle of simplicity is re- instated in its original guise:

> Therefore, although it be a history
> Homely and rude, I will relate the same
> For the delight of a few natural hearts...
> (*LB*, 253, 34–6)

At 491 lines, 'Michael' is far longer than the 'tale to be related' requires; the formula of 'Simon Lee' is turned around, and while the undue length recalls the proportions of 'The Idiot Boy', the tone is solemn; and where 'The Idiot Boy' has a happy ending which leaves the reader to reflect on the truth revealed (the wisdom of the 'idiot'), 'Michael', like *The Ruined Cottage*, ends in a human disaster that needs nature to help us become reconciled to it.

The poem begins with an invitation to turn aside 'from the public way'; it echoes what 'Lines written at a small distance from my house', 'Expostulation and Reply' and 'The Tables Turned' have already said. We turn from public life towards a form of 'retirement', towards a different kind of narrative poetry, away from the 'chace' of 'The Childless Father' and 'Hart-leap Well' towards a wise passiveness that contains a turbulence of its own born of nature, the 'boisterous Brook' with which the poem begins and ends:

> If from the public way you turn your steps
> Up the tumultuous brook of Green-head Gill,
> You will suppose that with an upright path
> Your feet must struggle; in such bold ascent
> The pastoral Mountains front you, face to face.
> But, courage! For beside that boisterous Brook
> The Mountains have all open'd out themselves,
> And made a hidden valley of their own.
>
> (*LB*, 252–3, 1–8)

Here once more we encounter the 'rocks and stones and trees' of 'A slumber did my spirit seal'. 'Michael' is written as a summation of all the previous poems in the collection, and in its method of meditative narration it seeks to establish a way forward for *The Recluse*; or more specifically for that part of *The Recluse* that was to achieve publication, *The Excursion*, where Wordsworth linked together stories of this kind to follow on from the *Ruined Cottage* narrative.

Like the Pedlar, we find in the character of Michael a very specific emphasis on a life those of us travelling on the 'public way' have ceased to value. Considerable emphasis is placed on the way in which inanimate nature responds to Michael's presence; it is a reciprocal relationship:

> these fields, these hills
> Which were his living Being even more
> Than his own Blood – what could they less? had lay'd
> Strong hold on his Affections, were to him
> A pleasurable feeling of blind love,
> The pleasure which there is in life itself.
>
> (ll.74–9)

Michael, with his wife Isabel and son Luke, form an idealised community within their larger, rural community: 'they were as a proverb in the vale / For endless industry' (ll.96–7), a fact symbolised by the lamp which burns late into the night as they work:

> And from this constant light so regular
> And so far seen, the House itself by all
> Who dwelt within the limits of the Vale,
> Both old and young, was nam'd The Evening Star.
> (ll.143–6)

That such a family should be destroyed through no fault of their own presents the reader with the same scenario of injustice around which *The Ruined Cottage* revolved. It is the poet's task once more to seek to reconcile us to the human tragedy. Michael is duty bound to honour a debt incurred by his nephew; thus the world of modern commerce enters the rural world and wreaks havoc. Michael cannot relinquish his hold on the land; Wordsworth emphasises the strength of the relationship that existed between the farmer and his territory. That and his wish that it should be there for his son Luke to inherit explains his decision not to solve the problem by selling up (we should be thinking back to 'The Last of the Flock' at this point). Luke is sent to the city to earn the money to pay the debt, but is himself then seduced into its wicked ways. The sheepfold that father and son had begun to build before the boy departs remains a ruin, a symbol of their lost retreat and shelter, as is the now extinguished lamp.

VI

Wordsworth subtitled 'Michael' 'A Pastoral Poem', and here this means a poem that describes the actual, intimate relationship of people with the land. It is Wordsworth's riposte to the spectre of uncertainty, to the 'perhaps' of 'The Childless Father' ('Perhaps to himself at that moment he said...'); it is a powerful statement of his major preoccupations. The land marks the presence of Michael and his family in tangible forms: the cottage with its lamp, the garden and the sheepfold. We are meant to register the decay of these things as both catastrophic, and as inevitable. Catastrophic because of their intimate, organic relationship to the people in the story; inevitable because Wordsworth is duty bound to make the situation as hopeless as possible in order to show how hope may still be found in the worst of all possible situations. The same might be said of this story as De Quincey and others said of Margaret's demise in *The Ruined Cottage*; if the story were told with due regard for what in reality was likely to have happened, somebody in the community, noticing that the 'Evening Star' had gone out, would have made their way up there and set about helping the family in their difficulties (John Lucas is one of several late-twentieth-century readers who express scepticism about the implied inevitability of Michael's fate).

Wordsworth himself, of course, did indeed solicit help for the victims described in the poem. While it was clearly not the poet's task to rescue the family, it lay within the politician's power to guard against a repetition of the circumstances, and Wordsworth thought they might be encouraged to take action by reading *Lyrical Ballads*, and in particular 'Michael'. In January 1801 he wrote to Charles James Fox, urging him to read 'The Brothers' and 'Michael':

> It appears to me that the most calamitous effect, which has followed the measures which have lately been pursued in this country, is a rapid decay of the domestic affections among the lower orders of society. This effect the present Rulers of this country are not conscious of, or they disregard it.[18]

Specifically to blame are 'the spreading of manufactures...heavy taxes upon postage...workhouses, Houses of Industry, and the invention of Soup-shops...superadded to the encreasing disproportion between the price of labour and that of the necessaries of life'. He might usefully have sent 'The Baker's Cart' fragment to Fox to round off his appeal for legislation aimed at restoring 'the bonds of domestic feeling among the poor'. That was the politician's job. The poet's job, by comparison, is to reconcile us to the tragedy and give us hope for the future. *Lyrical Ballads* brings us to a point of closure very much in keeping with the closure of *The Ruined Cottage*, a closure fraught with tensions and contradictions that were already beginning to emerge as critical issues destined to accompany the study of Wordsworth for as long as he continues to be read:

> Three years, or little more, did Isabel
> Survive her Husband: at death the estate
> Was sold, and went into a Stranger's hand.

The Cottage which was nam'd The Evening Star
Is gone, the ploughshare has been through the ground
On which it stood; great changes have been wrought
In all the neighbourhood, yet the Oak is left
That grew beside their Door; and the remains
Of the unfinished Sheep-fold may be seen
Beside the boisterous brook of Green-head Gill.

(*LB*, 268, 482–91)

4

Putting the Poetry in Order: *Poems in Two Volumes* (1807)

> My apprehensions come in crowds;
> I dread the rustling of the grass;
> The very shadows of the clouds
> Have power to shake me as they pass...
> ('The Affliction of Margaret' *Poems 1807*, 91, 64–7)

I

In the course of the last four chapters Wordsworth has become a poet of divided aims. *Lyrical Ballads* sets him in the public eye as a gifted but awkward poet. He is the author of short, unusual lyric pieces, of curiously obtuse narrative poetry like 'The Idiot Boy' and 'The Thorn', a poet who could excite sympathy and even admiration with 'Tintern Abbey', and after 1800 a poet on his way to becoming a laughing-stock in the reviews for his commitment to an eccentrically 'simple' style of poetry. While this is happening, and taking his career as a poet with it, he is also striving to compose *The Recluse*, an epic philosophical poem intended to stand alongside Milton's *Paradise Lost* as a work of universal significance.

The Recluse was to be a monumental rebuttal of Godwinian rationalism that would revive the spirit of the Nation through its appeal to the power of a pantheistically conceived wholeness. The only part of this work to be published in Wordsworth's lifetime was *The Excursion* (1814). Other projects, most notably *The Prelude*, 'Home at Grasmere', 'The Tuft of Primroses', 'To the Clouds' and

'St. Paul's', remained on the workbench, and only ever found their way into print after the poet's death.[1] But in the meantime, the aspiring author of *The Recluse* had stumbled, almost by accident it seemed, upon the device of short lyric pieces and upon the verse narrative that parodied as much as it paid tribute to the contemporary ballad. Different as the poetry within the two projects appears at times to be, therefore, it is possible to see *Lyrical Ballads* exploring the same issues as those central to *The Recluse*, while *The Recluse*, as it began to take poetic form in *The Ruined Cottage*, reveals an affinity to the *Ballads*. But for all that, the differences remain very real, and what Wordsworth required of himself was the ability to see all his work as an integrated statement.

In the 1800 Preface to *Lyrical Ballads* Wordsworth aimed to deflect any temptation there might be to define his literary personality in terms of that particular collection. Between the *Lyrical Ballads* Preface and the publication of *The Excursion* in 1814, he proceeded to develop an argument for the coherence of his entire output. Using the image of a 'gothic church' in the Preface to *The Excursion*, he was able to place *Lyrical Ballads*, *Poems in Two Volumes* (1807), and the as yet unnamed 'biographical' 'preparatory poem', *The Prelude*, in their appropriate relationship to *The Excursion*, which in turn 'belongs to the second part of a long and laborious Work', *The Recluse*:

> The preparatory poem is biographical, and conducts the history of the Author's mind to the point when he was emboldened to hope that his faculties were sufficiently mature for entering upon the arduous labour which he had proposed to himself; and the two Works [*The Prelude* and *The Recluse*] have the same kind of relation to each other, if he may so express himself, as the ante-chapel has to the body of a gothic church. Continuing this allusion, he may be permitted to add, that his minor Pieces [brought together in *Lyrical Ballads* and *Poems in Two Volumes*], which have been long before the Public, when they shall be properly arranged, will be found by the attentive Reader to have such connection with the main Work as may give them claim to be likened to the little cells, oratories, and sepulchral recesses, ordinarily included in these edifices.
>
> (*Prose Works* 3, 5–6)

Wordsworth insists that he is not prepared to be judged on the merits of any single poem he has written. He is engaged in building a body of work that ultimately should be viewed (by a necessarily 'attentive reader') as an inclusive statement; he claims a comprehensive unity for his poetry. 'Michael' had been written (and Coleridge edged out) specifically to confirm the unity of the *Lyrical Ballads* collection. The 'Ode' (written 1802–4 and later subtitled 'Intimations of Immortality from Recollections of Early Childhood') would do the same for the *Poems in Two Volumes* of 1807. Wordsworth's representation of his work in this light, as a huge, seemingly random but ultimately coherent building, was reaffirmed in the years following publication of *Lyrical Ballads* by prose statements asserting the fundamental principles which he claimed underpinned all his work. In 1810, in *Essays Upon Epitaphs*, he described what poets should strive for as 'the general language of humanity', 'a species of composition' which 'will be found to lie in a due proportion of the common or universal feeling of humanity to sensations excited by a distinct and clear conception...' (*Prose Works* 2, 57). The stress, as ever, falls on universality (a 'general language' to present 'the common or universal feeling of humanity'), though by 1810 Wordsworth is avoiding referring to 'simplicity' as a key term, such was the bruising ridicule it had attracted. For simplicity we now have 'distinct and clear conception'. However, as we read through the poetry of *Lyrical Ballads*, through the Goslar lyrics and then on to the poems brought together for the 1807 collection, we recognise that the task of finding words to convey a 'distinct and clear conception' was far from easy, and progressively preoccupied Wordsworth's treatment of his various subjects. In the discussion of *Poems in Two Volumes* that follows, a recurring point of reference will be Wordsworth's engagement with the space he increasingly perceived as existing between language and meaning.

II

'Resolution and Independence' is a poem in which Wordsworth engaged as directly as any he wrote with the problematic of the relationship between words and meaning. It was written in 1804, and was published in Volume I of *Poems in Two Volumes*:

> The Old Man still stood talking by my side;
> But now his voice to me was like a stream
> Scarce heard; nor word from word could I divide;
> And the whole Body of the man did seem
> Like one whom I had met with in a dream;
> Or like a man from some far region sent,
> To give me human strength, and strong admonishment.
> (*Poems 1807*, 128, 113–19)

A stable state of mind is retrieved as the spoken word fades away to be replaced by a transcendental experience. The process points towards a situation where poetry itself must ultimately become redundant. The same proposition had been rehearsed in 'Tintern Abbey' where it is conceded that Dorothy's presence may not always be available to inform Wordsworth's mature poetic voice: 'Nor, perchance, / If I should be, where I no more can hear / Thy voice, nor catch from thy wild eyes these gleams / Of past existence...' (LB, 120, 147–9). In the third of his *Essays on Epitaphs* Wordsworth confronts the issue bluntly:

> Words are too awful an instrument for good and evil to be trifled with; they hold above all other external powers a dominion over thoughts. If words be not...an incarnation of the thought but only a clothing for it, then surely will they prove an ill gift.... Language, if it do not uphold, and feed, and leave in quiet, like the power of gravitation or the air we breathe, is a counter-spirit, unremittingly and noiselessly at work to derange, to subvert, to lay waste, to vitiate, and to dissolve.
>
> (*Prose Works* 2, 84–5, 178–88)

In 'The Solitary Reaper' (again from *Poems in Two Volumes*) Wordsworth seeks to rescue language from its manifestation as an 'ill gift', as he does in 'Tintern Abbey' and 'Resolution and Independence'. Listening to a language he does not understand, the poet claims to be aware of it as 'an incarnation of the thought'. Meaning, in its mundane form, has been by-passed; language has been transformed to the condition of music: 'Will no one tell me what she sings?' No one does, and not only does it not matter, we are to understand that not knowing the literal 'meaning' of the words purifies and immortalises the experience:

> Whate'er the theme, the Maiden sang
> As if her song could have no ending;
> I saw her singing at her work,
> And o'er the sickle bending;
> I listen'd till I had my fill:
> And, as I mounted up the hill,
> The music in my heart I bore,
> Long after it was heard no more.
>
> (*Poems 1807*, 185, 25–32)

A less frequently discussed poem, but one that is considerably enriched when read in this context, is 'The Blind Highland Boy'. The child in this poem has been blind from birth:

> And yet he neither drooped nor pined,
> Nor had a melancholy mind;
> For God took pity on the Boy,
> And was his friend; and gave him joy
>   Of which we nothing know.
>   (*Poems 1807*, 222, 21–5)

He lives by a sea loch, and it is his deepest longing to sail upon it. Eventually he finds a wash tub by the water, climbs into it and, delighted with his adventure, floats out into the loch. Soon he is being swept away by the tide, while the panicstricken villagers launch a boat and attempt to rescue him:

> With sound the least that can be made
> They follow, more and more afraid,
> More cautious as they draw more near;
> But in his darkness he can hear,
>   And guesses their intent.
>
> '*Lei-gha* – *Lei-gha*' – then did he cry
> '*Lei-gha* – *Lei-gha*' – most eagerly;
> Thus did he cry, and thus did pray,
> And what he meant was, 'Keep away,
>   And leave me to myself!'
>
> Alas! And when he felt their hands –
> You've often heard of magic Wands,
> That with a motion overthrow
> A palace of the proudest shew,
>   Or melt it into air.
>
> So all his dreams, that inward light
> With which his soul had shone so bright,
> All vanish'd; – 'twas a heartfelt cross
> To him, a heavy, bitter loss,
>   As he had ever known.
>   (ll.156–75)

The villagers, celebrating the saving of the child, have no idea of the way they have destroyed his dream. His world, deprived of sight, is an inward one of visionary intensity. Although the villagers will have understood his cry of 'Lei-gha', the fact that the reader requires a translation only confirms the existence of a gulf between what Wordsworth (in the first of the *Essays upon Epitaphs*) calls a 'universal feeling of humanity' (*Prose Works* 2, 57, 316), and the linguistic medium through which we attempt to perceive it (and in this particular poem, also sight). At the end of the poem, the child comes to understand that he did need to be saved from 'The perilous Deep' (l. 202); he learns to live with the lesser reality that translates his dreams into the world in which he is constrained to live. The fact remains that appearances, whether couched in words or presented to the sight, prove fickle, no matter how reliable they may at first seem.

This point is reinforced by the poem placed after 'The Blind Highland Boy', 'The Green Linnet'. A very different poem in many ways, this unassuming piece of observation tells the same tale as its predecessor. The bird is praised for its quiet self-effacement, spending its time hidden among the leaves:

> When in a moment forth he teems
>   His little song in gushes:
> As if it pleas'd him to disdain
> And mock the Form which he did feign,
> While he was dancing with the train
>   Of Leaves among the bushes.
>   (*Poems 1807*, 230, 35–40)

All things 'mock the Form' they 'feign'. And in the 1807 *Poems* often the most apparently unassuming, simple poems – the children's ballad (which is how 'The Blind Highland Boy' is described), the short lyric with the 'traveller's tale' flavour such as 'The Solitary Reaper', or 'The Green Linnet' manifestly displaying a commitment to 'simplicity' – all contribute to the profoundly serious issue of how language relates to its subject, to the 'form' it 'feigns'. As the next section will show, this issue has been an important preoccupation for much recent criticism.

III

It is important not to forget that in his brief 'Advertisement' to the 1807 *Poems*, Wordsworth appears to be dismissively brief about the value of the contents. They were poems written, he explains, 'to refresh my mind', and were the source of 'much pleasure', but they are not to be considered as anything more than incidental pieces made available to pass the reader's time while waiting for the completion of 'my larger work' (*Poems 1807*, 527). We know very well that he set far more store by these poems than this would suggest, but we also know that he was striving to construct a literary life for himself that saw *The Recluse* as its crowning achievement. The twentieth-century critic, sensitive to the anxieties Wordsworth betrays about the properties of language, and alive to the way in which biography feeds off the notion of a narrative that is expected in some way to 'make sense' of what is going on, has tended increasingly to question, and duly deconstruct, Wordsworth's self-presentation (along with the way he tended to be described by later nineteenth-century commentators) in order to be able to read his poetry satisfactorily.

For many years now, despite the continuing appearance of biographical studies, the key to understanding Wordsworth has been represented as necessarily recognising the insecurities and contradictions of what John Powell Ward has recently described as the 'liquid and elusive' poetry of Wordsworth. Ward's description of the poet's voice is a helpful summary of a characteristic late-twentieth-century reading of Wordsworth (it was published in 1991):

> It is very hard to describe Wordsworth's poetry. The extraordinary haunting voice, so moralistic and yet so eerie, so stern yet so guiltily vulnerable, so ghostly and so dull at once, at times so firm while elsewhere, or even in the same passage, so liquid and elusive.[2]

Ward's next move is to discuss an incident from childhood described in *The Prelude*, and he does so to illustrate the complexity of the poet's way of seeing: 'It was, in truth, / An ordinary sight', wrote Wordsworth; Ward continues, 'An ordinary sight, yet somehow otherworldly at the same moment, uncanny and strange'.[3] The subject is the poetry. Relating the incident being described in *The Prelude* to a time and place in Wordsworth's childhood (the story he would seem to be telling in the poem) has very little place in the discussion.

Wordsworth's determination to establish an appropriate narrative framework for his life and work is encapsulated in *The Prelude*, but the undeniably 'liquid and elusive' nature of the poetry explains why that poem has long since been abandoned as a trustworthy biographical guide. Mary Jacobus describes *The Prelude* as 'a site of historical repression', quoting with approval Jerome McGann's view that the poem is 'exemplary of the tendency of Romantic poems "to develop different sorts of artistic means with which to occlude and disguise their own involvement in a certain nexus of historical relations"'.[4] Wordsworth's commitment to the task of writing his literary life into what he perceived as a satisfactory order through *The Prelude* extended into a general preoccupation with the ordering of all his output. Hence the order he progressively imposed on *Lyrical Ballads*, marginalising and eventually extinguishing Coleridge's voice, while composing 'Michael' as a summative narrative.

The 1807 *Poems* were subject to an even greater degree of scrutiny when it came to their arrangement across the two volumes. If Wordsworth could not yet publish his major work, *The Recluse* (or any part of it), at least he could try to present a collection of his shorter poems so that they might be seen as parts of a larger whole. They exist, therefore, as sequences, marked out by the circumstances of composition (various tours), by their type and theme (miscellaneous sonnets and sonnets dedicated to Liberty), by a category designated 'Moods of My Own Mind', and otherwise by an apparently miscellaneous group at the beginning (originally to be called 'The Orchard Pathway'), and a similar group ('The Blind Highland Boy; with other Poems') at the end.[5] At the end of Volume 2 he placed, as a final statement, the Ode the title of which was subsequently extended to 'Ode. Intimations of Immortality from Recollections of Early Childhood'. Relationships between individual poems are not hard to identify; and the whole effect is indicative of the ordering he undertook with increasing seriousness as he worked alongside his writing of *The Excursion* to assemble the Collected Edition of his poems that eventually appeared in 1815.

In 1977 Frances Ferguson published *Wordsworth: Language as Counter-Spirit*. The book is premised on an investigation of the relationship between Wordsworth's poetic language and the system of classification he developed for his poems in the collected editions. Ferguson discussed the way Wordsworth strove to establish an order of events with respect to the stated aim of *The Prelude*: to record 'the growth of a poet's mind'; but as she did so, she directed the reader's attention away from the familiar biographical detail, focusing instead on a narrative that traces the growth of the poet's engagement with language. As we have seen, Wordsworth had described language as potentially a 'counter-spirit' in the *Essays Upon Epitaphs*, expressing his anxieties over the consequences of language failing to fulfil the demands placed on it by the writer.

The 'life' of Wordsworth that Ferguson investigated was a poetic life increasingly structured by the need the poet felt to guard against failure by building a system of classification for his poetry. She considered the way that the categories into which he grouped his poems increased as Wordsworth moved on from the *Poems in Two Volumes* to produce his Collected Editions (beginning in 1815). Informing that process at every step lay the poet's engagement with language. It is not hard to see how the traditional narrative of a biographical cycle of events is recycled by Ferguson as a linguistic 'narrative':

> Looking back to the earlier categories, one might hazard the suggestion that the 'Poems founded on the Affections' [used in the Collected Editions] portray a full life cycle of language, in which passion produces analogies which can only fall into nothingness when the central object of the affections passes out of existence. The passions are generative but restricted, in each manifestation, to one central objection which is the sole locus of meaning from which the correspondences can derive their value. Language appears most intensely tied to the human and, specifically, to the living human form in the 'Poems founded on the Affections'; and the human deaths of these poems seem to necessitate, almost oppressively, an end to speech – as when Leonard in 'The Brothers' can no longer tell who he is after learning of the death of his brother.[6]

'Language', therefore, 'becomes object':

> In such a system of analogy, language must inevitably become a 'counter-spirit' – or something counter to the spirit, because it can only exist in correspondence with the external forms of beloved humans, so that the human spirit seems inconceivable without the human form.[7]

This is the penultimate paragraph of this section of Ferguson's book and it delivers her thesis on language as 'counter-spirit' in Wordsworth. Words themselves threaten a creative impasse so frequently noted now by critics as a feature of Wordsworth's writing; this is the mismatch between language and meaning where Wordworth's spiritual yearnings (to be 'laid asleep / In body, and become a living soul') are compromised by the 'counter-spirit' of the medium he is bound to use, the written word.

Ferguson's final paragraph of Chapter 2 completes her critical narrative with a discussion of Wordsworth's attempt to escape to a happy (or at least happier) ending by way of reference to two of the categories used in the 1815 Collected Edition: 'Poems of the Fancy', and 'Poems of the Imagination'. Fancy and Imagination work to free language from a closely prescribed relationship with specific, transient forms; the mind, no longer rigidly tethered to the realisation of specific objects, can therefore undergo a process of 'regeneration'. The price to be paid for this injection of 'playfulness' is the recognition that the words do not exist 'with which to capture the "whole soul summarised"'. The end of this particular narrative of a creative journey lies in the conclusion that 'words seem finally most available precisely because they are most dispensable'.[8]

Ferguson's extensive use of the *Essays Upon Epitaphs* is indicative of a shift in critical emphasis in Wordsworth studies in recent years. The Preface to *Lyrical Ballads* remains a seminal text, but the retrieval of the *Essays* (D. D. Devlin published a book length study of them in 1980[9]) along with other prose, denotes a tendency to investigate not Wordsworth as he would have us read him (nor yet as nineteenth-century critics from Arnold to Pater would have us read him), but Wordsworth as he appears to us to have been, now that we can take advantage of increasingly sophisticated modern editions of the poetry and prose (many of which create 'new' poems for us). Ferguson acknowledges the influence on her work of (among others) Geoffrey Hartman, Paul de Man and Stanley Fish; this is to identify a Wordsworth who has passed through Hartman's philosophically rooted criticism to become a case study for post-structuralist, reception, and reader-response theory. The Wordsworth described by these critics is a divided Wordsworth, beset on the one hand with a 'nature consciousness', and on the other with 'an answering self-consciousness', and the poetry reflects this '"incumbent mystery"'.[10] De Man explores this duality by way of discussing the division inherent in grammatical and rhetorical construction, a duality which echoes Hartman's idea that Wordsworth's attempt to reconcile 'nature' and 'self' renders meaning permanently undecidable. Fish's work in reader-response theory, along with Levinson, Liu and Simpson writing as new historicists, introduces a series of related, increasingly deconstructionist proposals relating to the knowability of the text and its context. They all affirm the constant play of meaning that the process of interpretation initiates and sustains.[11]

From studying these critics, we can see that a marginalisation of a biographically-grounded criticism has taken place not just because it fails to address issues that are understood to be most worthwhile, but because compelling arguments have appeared to challenge the assumption that the biography is retrievable in a form that can yield what the contextual reader is looking for. It is worth repeating Levinson's new historicist dictum:

> This is a criticism that seeks to take hold of the conditions of literary production in a profounder way than historical enquiry into manifest theme is capable of. It is a self-consciously belated criticism that sees in its necessary ignorance – its expulsion from the heaven of Romantic sympathy – a critical advantage: the capacity to know a work as neither it, nor its original readers, nor its author could know it.[12]

The *Poems in Two Volumes* of 1807 may therefore be read in a way that delivers a deconstructionist, new historicist 'narrative'. This is to say that the poems are ordered in a way that means the collection progressively explores the relationship between words and meaning. It is further to suggest that attention to this aspect of the 1807 *Poems* is our most fruitful line of critical enquiry. However, we should not lose sight of the fact that the claim may still be made that the 1807 *Poems* reveal significant traces of a more traditional biographical project. This is one example of the 'contested ground' referred to in Chapter 1 of this book with respect to contemporary Wordsworth studies, and it applies in equal measure to the 1807 *Poems*, the editing and reordering of the *Lyrical Ballads* from 1800 onward, to *The Prelude*, to the attempt to write *The Recluse*, and to Wordsworth's editing of the Collected Editions of his poetry in later life. In the following section I shall suggest ways in which, while traditional biographical matter may be seen insinuating itself into the poetry, the relationship between language and meaning remains to problematise a biographical reading of the more predictable kind.

IV

Wordsworth chose to begin the 1807 collection with a poem whose opening lines refer us back to the final poem of *Lyrical Ballads*, Volume One. In 'Tintern Abbey' we read:

> Though changed, no doubt, from what I was, when first
> I came among these hills; when like a roe

> I bounded o'er the mountains, by the sides
> Of the deep rivers, and the lonely streams,
> Wherever nature led; more like a man
> Flying from something that he dreads, than one
> Who sought the thing he loved.
> (LB, 118, 67–73)

The opening lines of 'To The Daisy' read:

> In youth from rock to rock I went,
> From hill to hill, in discontent
> Of pleasure high and turbulent,
>   Most pleas'd when most uneasy...
> (Poems 1807, 65, 1–4)

The poem was written in 1802, and describes a poet confirmed in the poetic persona described in 'Tintern Abbey' four years earlier; an older and wiser man:

> If stately passions in me burn,
> And one chance look to Thee should turn,
> I drink out of an humbler urn
>   A lowlier pleasure;
> The homely sympathy that heeds
> The common life, our nature breeds;
> A wisdom fitted to the needs
>   Of hearts at leisure.
> (Poems 1807, 67, 49–56)

'To The Daisy' establishes a continuity with, and continues the story of, his life. The flower encapsulates all the qualities he would possess, including that of being immune to ridicule:

> Nor car'st if thou be set at naught;
> And oft alone in nooks remote
> We meet thee, like a pleasant thought,
>   When such are wanted.
> (ll.21–4)

The poem draws on lines already written in *The Prelude* to identify the daisy with himself:

> Child of the Year! That round dost run
> Thy course, bold lover of the sun,

> And chearful when the day's begun
> As the morning Leveret...
>   (ll.73–6)

In Part Two of the first version of *The Prelude* he had written: 'already I began / To love the sun, a boy I loved the sun' (*Prelude*, 19, 217–18).

'To The Daisy', then, is a poem with an underlying autobiographical agenda; it celebrates the profundity of simplicity, a lesson learned from nature by a poet who aspires to live and work in a way that emulates 'The homely sympathy' that marks the daisy's existence. It is also a poem that exhibits the unresolved tension within Wordsworth's writing diagnosed by Hartman as an attempt by the poet to sublimate 'self-consciousness' in 'nature consciousness'. Verse 8 describes the flower's loss of self in its participation with the rhythms of the natural world:

> When, smitten by the morning ray,
> I see thee rise alert and gay,
> Then, chearful Flower! My spirits play
>   With kindred motion:
> At dusk, I've seldom mark'd thee press
> The ground, as if in thankfulness,
> Without some feeling, more or less,
>   Of true devotion.
>   (*Poems 1807*, 68, 57–64)

The final two lines are strategically ambiguous: the flower exhibits devotion, while the poet is inspired by the sight to feel devotion. In the latter instance, though, it is a devotion inspired by nature, not 'naturally' experienced. And so the following, penultimate verse suggests there is something more the poet has gained from observing the flower. But at this point the sense becomes characteristically vague. This is what in 'Tintern Abbey' is described as 'a something':

> And all day long I number yet,
> All seasons through, another debt,
> Which I wherever thou art met,
>   To thee am owing;
> An instinct call it, a blind sense;
> A happy, genial influence,
> Coming one knows not how nor whence,
>   Nor whither going.
>   (ll.65–72)

The 'debt' he owes the flower is an 'instinct', an 'influence', at once 'happy' and 'genial'; no one knows how it is transmitted or where it comes from (it does not come *from* the daisy; rather it is the same 'sense' that infuses the life of the flower). It is the experience described in *The Ruined Cottage* as the 'one life', and there it remains equally vague, but intensely experienced. With reference to the reading already offered of 'The Blind Highland Boy', we note that the debt is described as a 'blind sense'. This is a stanza where, though words fail the poet (as we have seen them do in 'Resolution and Independence'), he manages to keep the poem afloat on the back of a rhetorical impetus, and to conclude by means of a promise of future clarity:

> Thou wilt be more belov'd by men
> In times to come; thou not in vain
> Art Nature's Favourite.
> (ll.78–80)

The story that rides on the surface of this poem, a narrative that leads on from 'Tintern Abbey' to supply the next chapter in the tale of the maturing poet – thus paralleling the narrative of *The Prelude* – holds beneath its surface ('suppresses' if you adopt structuralist, new historicist terminology) an unresolved crisis of relationship between the poet and his subject, between the language and its meaning.

In *Wordsworth and the Enlightenment* (1989), Alan Bewell suggests that a very specific cultural and intellectual context for Wordsworth's articulation of this 'crisis' exists in the Enlightenment debate around the condition of deafness. Bewell draws attention to the repeated references throughout Wordsworth's poetry to sensory deprivation, and the link that is explored between that and a tendency to assume idiocy. Wordsworth's problem – about communication and its origins, and ultimately, about death – is also shown to be an issue much discussed throughout the eighteenth century. Bewell shows that the debate over deafness sprang from a far more comprehensive controversy relating to the attempt to gauge the significance of language over against what appeared to be the existence of innate ideas. Poems like 'The Blind Highland Boy', and in particular the 'Intimations' Ode, he argues, drew upon a lively contemporary discourse around primitivism and the behaviour and beliefs of so-called savages. In the process of looking for the source of humanity's ability to conceptualise and reflect on experience (in particular death), Wordsworth appears to be endorsing a point of view favoured by the more advanced theorists. Language was seen as generally less significant than what was perceived to be innately present in the human mind. Language strove – by no means always adequately – to record knowledge; it was not the means whereby knowledge might be created.[13]

The poem that follows 'To The Daisy', 'Louisa', describes a girl who fulfils what the daisy teaches by example, and the words used to tell us this reinforce the view that knowledge is innate; words can only reflect the unearthly mystery of her state. Louisa lives as an integral part of nature, and in consequence she is unknowable, enigmatic, contradictory, not human:

> And she hath smiles to earth unknown;
> Smiles, that with motion of their own
> Do spread, and sink, and rise;
> That come and go with endless play,
> And ever, as they pass away,
> Are hidden in her eyes.
>   (*Poems 1807*, 69–70, 7–12)

Once more, the blindness of the Highland Boy comes to mind; the eyes Wordsworth requires are not for seeing in the mundane sense, and the poet remains estranged from the communion with nature with which Louisa is credited. The final verse (however Wordsworth intended it to be read) illustrates this only too clearly:

> Take all that's mine 'beneath the moon',
> If I with her but half a noon
> May sit beneath the walls
> Of some old cave, or mossy nook,
> When up she winds along the brook,
> To hunt the waterfalls.
>   (ll.19–24)

The quotation within the verse invites an association with either Shakespeare's *King Lear* or *Antony and Cleopatra* (the former, with its theme of kindness, would seem more appropriate); but it also suggests 'The Idiot Boy', a narrative that inverts traditional notions of wisdom, order and propriety. In this poem, the child, who has been riding his pony through the moonlit night proclaims: 'And the sun did shine so cold' (*LB*, 104, 461). What the poet asks for in

'Louisa', if he is to understand the girl's mystery, is to be able to sit quietly with her in a picturesque retreat; yet this is contradicted by his description of her restless, endless motion: 'When up she winds along the brook, / To hunt the waterfalls.' It is a mismatch: he either has not been listening, not paying attention to his own poem, or he simply doesn't understand. To be at one with her – and with nature – he must forget his book-learnt tendency to picturesque dreaming and roam the countryside in her company.

The relationship the poet would seek with Louisa prompts a comparison with the relationship between the traveller and his dog narrated in 'Fidelity', the poem which follows. In 'Louisa' the poet would 'kiss the mountain rains / That sparkle on her cheek' when she strains against the wind in her mountain walks. This sounds like self-indulgent worship of the beloved, a piece of contrived poetic rhetoric. By comparison, in 'Fidelity' we learn that words may perform a very different function; here they are 'A lasting monument' that tell a true story of the profound devotion of a dog to its master:

> But hear a wonder now, for sake
> Of which this mournful Tale I tell!
> A lasting monument of words
> This wonder merits well.
> The Dog, which still was hovering nigh,
> Repeating the same timid cry,
> This Dog had been through three month's space
> A Dweller in that Savage place.
> (*Poems 1807*, 73, 50–7)

It is a tale of 'love sublime', and of 'strength of feeling' that is, significantly, 'Above all human estimate' (ll.63–5).

Arguing for the precise appropriateness of the sequence of these poems is less important than the fact that, when the poems are read together, certain issues begin to assume prominence. The poems that come later will inevitably tend to be interpreted in an increasingly conditioned way. 'She was a Phantom of delight' is a tribute to Mary Hutchinson whom Wordsworth married in 1802; the poem strives to describe the enigma of a pure, unearthly soul perceived in human form, while 'The Redbreast and the Butterfly' confronts the idealised image of the robin with the real bird, as it darts upon a butterfly to destroy it; once more we encounter a beautiful but unreal idea, and if (as with 'Simon Lee') we choose to make a tale of it, we might find ourselves reflecting on how the bird's behaviour mirrors the nature of those who watch him: 'The Chearer Thou of our in-door sadness, / He is the Friend of our summer gladness' (*1807 76*, 32–3).

There is, then, a constant movement from abstract thoughts which have no root in specific objects, to concrete reality, setting up the dualism that twentieth-century critics have found so compelling. Thus, after being shown the imaginary robin of folk-lore and the real robin observed destroying butterflies, the next poem, 'The Sailor's Mother', introduces us to a woman who is clothed in the language of imagination, of patriotic tradition and Augustan culture:

> A Woman in the road I met,
> Not old, though something past her prime:
> Majestic in her person, tall and straight;
> And like a Roman matron's was her mien and gait.
> (*Poems 1807*, 77, 3–6)

There is then a shift within the poem that anticipates 'Resolution and Independence' as Wordsworth moves to an encounter with the real:

> When from these lofty thoughts I woke,
> With the first word I had to spare
> I said to her, 'Beneath your Cloak
> What's that which on your arm you bear?'
> (ll.13–16)

It is a bird in a cage that belonged to her son, now dead. The pedestrian reality – as she gives an unvarnished account of her trip to Hull to recover his possessions – challenges the romanticised idealism of the opening of the poem.

In the next two poems, 'To the Small Celandine' and 'To the Same Flower', Wordsworth attempts to use the simple, earthy spirituality of nature to describe his own materialistic (and frequently 'slighted') existence as a poet, where he is thought of, perhaps, as the leader of a 'band' of like-minded poets, a 'joyous train':

> Prophet of delight and mirth,
> Scorn'd and slighted upon earth!
> Herald of a mighty band,
> Of a joyous train ensuing,

Singing at my heart's command,
In the lanes my thoughts pursuing,
I will sing, as doth behove,
Hymns in praise of what I love!
(*Poems 1807*, 81, 57–64)

Implicit here is a description of Wordsworth as the kind of poet who would write 'The Sailor's Mother', and an explanation of how we should try to read it.

The two 'Celandine' poems are followed by 'Character of the Happy Warrior'. This appears at first sight to be very different from any of the preceding poems. It moves into the public sphere, and an endnote suggests that it is a tribute to Nelson, following his death at Trafalgar in 1805. What the poem in fact does is to project into public life the persona Wordsworth had been recommending for himself through the flower poetry. Before considering the poem itself and the extent to which it is an idealised self-portrait, however, it will be helpful to consider briefly a few more ways in which that persona has been perceived by others, and the reasons why perceptions have changed.

V

To the reviewers of the 1807 *Poems in Two Volumes*, in particular to the editor of the *Edinburgh Review* and declared enemy of Wordsworth's Jacobin Lake coterie, Francis Jeffrey, the new publication revealed a poet still perversely obsessed with simplicity, and inclined (with specific reference to the 'Intimations' Ode) to a fatal combination of illegibility and unintelligibilty.[14] Byron delivered much the same verdict in July 1807 in *Monthly Literary Recreations*. Readers of later generations, however, making their way through the first set of poems, then reading on into the sonnet sequences, 'Resolution and Independence', 'Peele Castle', and eventually arriving at the 'Intimations' Ode, began to discover a poet in many respects much changed, even from the later poetry of the two-volume *Lyrical Ballads*. A glance at the biographical details helps to explain why this was so.

Against the background of increasing domestic responsibilities (his marriage to Mary Hutchinson in October 1802), Wordsworth had acquired two wealthy patrons, Sir George Beaumont and Sir William Lowther, the cousin of his father's employer who succeeded Sir James – and settled his debts – in May 1802. In February

1805 John Wordsworth was drowned, a tragedy that prostrated the entire family. By May 1805 *The Prelude* had been completed, an event which will have signalled the completion of an important chapter in the poet's life. With a family now too large to fit comfortably into their Grasmere cottage, the Wordsworths removed temporarily to a farmhouse on Beaumont's Coleorton estate in Leicestershire. It was here that *Poems in Two Volumes* was finally prepared and sent to the press. Before the year was out the contents had been savaged by Jeffrey:

> Their peculiarities of diction alone, are enough, perhaps, to render them ridiculous; but the author before us really seems anxious to court this literary martyrdom by a device still more infallible, – we mean, that of connecting his most lofty, tender, or impassioned conceptions, with objects and incidents, which the greater part of his readers will probably persist in thinking low, silly, or uninteresting.[15]

Certain poems in the collection do very clearly reflect Wordsworth's response both to the shifting political sand on which he found himself standing, and to the changes in his domestic life. Loyalty and integrity, along with bereavement, become recurrent themes, and 'Character of the Happy Warrior', a poem of 85 lines written in heroic couplets, unambiguously places those themes in a political context. It was composed at the end of 1805, and the note on Nelson at the end should be read with care. We are told that 'the death of Lord Nelson...directed the Author's thoughts to the subject'. Wordsworth carefully avoids saying that the 'Happy Warrior' is a portrait of Nelson; this is not surprising when we investigate what his attitude towards this national hero was. In a letter to Beaumont on February 1806 Wordsworth describes Nelson as a sick man before the battle, who would probably have died anyway. In the event, the manner of his death has distorted an objective, balanced assessment of the man's qualities: 'The loss of such men...is indeed great and real; but surely not for the reason which makes most people grieve, a supposition that no other such man is in the Country...'. From Nelson he then turns his attention to the Prime Minister, William Pitt, who died in 1806. Again, he runs stubbornly against the grain, attempting to hold firm to his principles, 'I believe him, however, to have been as disinterested a Man, and as true a lover of his Country as it was possible for so ambitious a man to be...'[16] Pitt is damned with faint praise; at the very least this severely qualifies Wordsworth's enthusiasm for the war effort in which Nelson had played so prominent a part. What he actually celebrates in 'Character of the Happy Warrior' is the self-effacing yet steadfast patriot hero (the daisy and the celandine of the political world), whoever that might be. The poem never alludes to Nelson; what it does is eulogise the classical republican hero type Wordsworth had learnt to admire as a young radical. In a period when most biographers and critics agree that Wordsworth was clearly trimming his radicalism and adapting to changed circumstances and new friends, he seeks to describe himself as still essentially loyal to his political beliefs. He is an enthusiast, however, who must paradoxically hold back, whose natural instinct it is to retire, whose motive is honest consistency:

> – Who, if he rise to station of command,
> Rises by open means; and there will stand
> On honourable terms, or else retire,
> And in himself possess his own desire;
> Who comprehends his trust, and to the same
> Keeps faithful with a singleness of aim;
> And therefore does not stoop, nor lie in wait
> For wealth, or honors, or for worldly state;
> Whom they must follow; on whose head must fall,
> Like showers of manna, if they come at all...
> (*Poems 1807*, 85, 35–44)

This is Michel Beaupuy, but it is also Wordsworth's ideal for himself, and it can also be read as drawing on the example of his brother John.

The poem that follows 'The Happy Warrior' is 'The Horn of Egremont Castle', a historical ballad about two brothers. The eldest is the epitome of the happy warrior, while his younger brother seeks to have him killed so that he can lay claim to the family estate. Like 'The Affliction of Margaret', the next poem, the themes are loyalty, guilt and nemesis. These are poems (written between 1805 and 1807) that answer directly to Wordsworth's own recurring preoccupations:

> And I will have my careless season
> Spite of melancholy reason,
> Will walk through life in such a way
> That, when time brings on decay,

> Now and then I may possess
> Hours of perfect gladsomeness.
> (*Poems 1807*, 97, 111–16)

This is from 'The Kitten and the Falling Leaves' (the poem following 'The Affliction of Margaret'). It is a meditation (in 'simple' mode) on the innocent joy that the poet of the 'Happy Warrior', 'The Horn of Egremont Castle' and 'The Affliction of Margaret' can no longer enjoy, despite his determination to make it once more possible. 'The Seven Sisters' is another ballad that tells of desertion that leads to tragedy; it is in turn followed by three restorative poems that describe domestic love and commitment: 'To H. C. Six Years Old', 'Among all lovely things my Love had been', and 'I travell'd among unknown Men'. The section concludes with a poem intended to reflect on the character of the poet whose life is refracted through the poetry: 'Ode to Duty'.

'Ode to Duty' refers to the poetry he should be writing and isn't; it is a formal vow that he will write in future as an act of duty, not as a means of selfish pleasure. Jonathan Wordsworth is one of very few critics prepared to defend the poem, describing it as a 'beautiful and very personal lyric poem ... which because of its proto-Victorian title, and opening, so few people read with sympathy'.[17] Wordsworth himself reported to Isabella Fenwick in 1843 that Mary and Dorothy reacted unfavourably to the poem, and, Jonathan Wordsworth notwithstanding, the contrast between the prayerbook rhetoric of the 'Ode to Duty' and the lyricism of the three poems which immediately precede it makes it very hard to love:

> Oh! Let my weakness have an end!
> Give unto me, made lowly wise,
> The spirit of self-sacrifice;
> The confidence of reason give;
> And in the light of truth thy Bondman let me live!
> (*Poems 1807*, 107, 60–4)

Unlike so much of Wordsworth's best poetry, the Ode does not enact, and in the process problematise, the thought contained within it; and critics of all persuasions from Hartman to Bewell, including Jonathan Wordsworth, as well as those as far removed from each other as Levinson and McFarland, broadly agree on the significance and power of a 'humanising' strand in Wordsworth's poetry that the 'Ode to Duty' clearly lacks.

VI

Wordsworth originally intended to group the first set of miscellaneous poems in *Poems in Two Volumes* (up to and including 'Ode to Duty') under the heading 'The Orchard Pathway', with a brief verse to introduce it:

> Orchard Pathway, to and fro,
> Ever with thee, did I go,
> Weaving Verses, a huge store!
> These, and many hundreds more,
> And, in memory of the same,
> This little lot shall bear *Thy Name!*
> (*Poems 1807*, 63)

In the event, he withdrew this part of his plan. What this nevertheless shows is that he wanted the poems in this first section to be considered as a group defined by the way a reader might imagine a meandering orchard pathway. We learn also, of course, that he suffered a crisis of confidence over the wisdom of the idea. After a set of four poems grouped together as 'Composed During a Tour', the remainder of Volume One is taken up with two sonnet sequences, 'Miscellaneous Sonnets', and 'Sonnets Dedicated to Liberty'. In the case of every section, the final poem is carefully chosen to act as in some way summative. 'Poems Composed During a Tour' concludes with 'Resolution and Independence', and here, as we know, despite the 'Ode to Duty', the crisis of confidence persists:

> My former thought return'd: the fear that kills;
> The hope that is unwilling to be fed;
> Cold, pain, and labour, and all fleshly ills;
> And mighty Poets in their misery dead.
> (*Poems 1807*, 128, 120–3)

There is an answer within the poem itself; it is embodied in the old leech gatherer's stoical 'resolution and independence'. In the prefatory sonnet that introduces the remainder of the volume, 'Nuns fret not at their Convent's narrow room', there is another answer. The sonnet form itself offers the poet (the poet of the 'Ode to Duty' indulged by 'uncharter'd freedom', l.37) a prison that in truth is 'no prison'. Having 'felt the weight of too much liberty', 'solace' is to be won from the rigours of sonnet form (*Poems 1807*, 133, 13–14). In the process the reader discovers that here is a poet successfully able to combine heart and head in one of the most technically demanding poetic disciplines.

The first set of sonnets are reflective; their general theme is the mysterious power of nature and the degree to which man has become estranged from the spiritual side of his nature. The final sonnet is a tribute to Raisley Calvert, whose money enabled Wordsworth to be free and choose poetry as his career. Freedom, projected onto the screen of public events in time of war, then becomes the theme of 'Sonnets Dedicated to Liberty'. Again the grouping raises questions around an important set of critical issues. Alan Liu has discussed the 1807 *Poems* as evidence of the way Wordsworth discriminates between 'history', 'nature', and the self. In *The Prelude* he observes history being absorbed by 'the mind', otherwise described as the 'I' of the poet (a creatively ambiguous statement when read aloud). A specific case in point, he maintains, occurs in the 1807 *Poems* with Wordsworth's misdating of the famous 'Westminster Bridge' sonnet of 1803. In removing it by a year from its actual location alongside his visit in 1802 to Calais to meet Annette and Caroline, Wordsworth buries a series of painful historical events beneath the poetic self observing the calmness of the great city, and reflecting on the blessings of peace.[18] This argument will be returned to later in general terms in conjunction with 'history' and *The Prelude*.

What is very clear from the decision to create two sonnet sequences is that a partition has indeed been introduced between the business of poems that express personal reflection, and poems on national topics. In the latter category, the enemy is poised across the channel ready to strike:

> I shrunk, for verily the barrier flood
> Was like a Lake, or River bright and fair,
> A span of waters...
>   (*Poems 1807*, 163, 5–7)

Here there can be no hesitation, no uncertainty:

> We must be free or die, who speak the tongue
> That Shakespeare spake; the faith and morals hold
> Which Milton held.
>   (*Poems 1807*, 167, 11–13)

Ferguson's Wordsworth, who experiences language as 'counter-spirit', is removed to 'Miscellaneous Sonnets' where clouds may do as well, if not better, than manmade monuments:

The western sky did recompense us well
With Grecian Temple, Minaret, and Bower;
And, in one part, a Minster with its Tower
Substantially distinct, a place for Bell
Or Clock to toll from. Many a glorious pile
Did we behold, sights that may well repay
All disappointment!
                    (*Poems 1807*, 138–9, 5–11)

The opinion stated here is immediately revoked in the sonnet that follows: 'But now upon this thought I cannot brood: / It is unstable, and deserts me quite' (*Poems 1807*, 139, 5–6).

We should not forget the arguments put forward by Liu and the new historicists here; behind the strident rhetoric of the political sonnets on liberty is the hidden history of Annette and her child, left (after 1802 doubly left) in France. Alongside them is the ghost of Wordsworth's younger, radical self, still striving for recognition, still refusing to accept the identity of a turncoat, turning aside the thought of betrayal as he writes 'Character of the Happy Warrior', *Benjamin the Waggoner* and *The White Doe of Rylstone* (see Chapter 5). This is the Wordsworth whose poetry, we are told, acts to sublimate the frame of mind inscribed in the letter to Beaumont on Nelson and Pitt.

The rhetoric of the political sonnets is taken to task on more than one occasion elsewhere in the collection. For example, in the final section of Volume 2 of the 1807 *Poems*, 'The Blind Highland Boy; With Other Poems', there are verses dedicated to a Quaker friend, Thomas Wilkinson. Wilkinson's own note on the occasion is important: 'I had promised Lord Lonsdale to take William Wordsworth to Lowther when he came to see me, but when we arrived at the castle he was gone to shoot moor-game with Judge Sutton. William and I then returned, and wrought together at a walk I was then forming; this gave birth to his verses' (*Poems 1807*, 424). Wordsworth, denied his meeting with the great and the good (who have gone off in pursuit of their own particular pleasures), ends up doing some gardening with the friend who is there for him, the Quaker pacifist; and so he celebrates 'The Spade of a Friend' rather than the grouse of Lord Lonsdale:

Health, quiet, meekness, ardour, hope secure,
And industry of body and of mind;

> And elegant enjoyments, that are pure
> As Nature is; too pure to be refined.
> *(Poems 1807*, 257, 9–12)

Wilkinson's spade represents an alternative to the weapons of war, and we can see how this frequently underrated poem articulates an ironic challenge to the patriotic rhetoric of Sonnet 16 from 'Sonnets Dedicated to Liberty', Volume 1. In that sonnet (already quoted above) we read:

> In our Halls is hung
> Armoury of the invincible Knights of old:
> We must be free or die, who speak the tongue
> That Shakespeare spake...

In 'To The Spade of a Friend' the spade becomes the 'Armoury' hung in the hall of the hero:

> Who shall inherit Thee when Death hath laid
> Low in the darksome Cell thine own dear Lord?
> That Man will have a trophy, humble Spade!
> More noble than the noblest Warrior's sword.
> (ll.17–20)

'Song, At the Feast of Brougham Castle', which follows 'To the Spade of a Friend', takes up, in the form of an historical ballad, the theme of the 'Happy Warrior' in the guise of Lord Clifford, 'The Shepherd Lord':

> Love had he found in huts where poor Men lie,
> His daily Teachers had been Woods and Rills,
> The silence that is in the starry sky,
> The sleep that is among the lonely hills.
>
> In him the savage Virtue of the Race,
> Revenge, and all ferocious thoughts were dead:
> Nor did he change; but kept in lofty place
> The wisdom which adversity had bred.
> *(Poems 1807*, 264, 165–72)

VII

Taken together, as Wordsworth intended them to be, the 1807 *Poems* thus reveal a poet of complex emotions and beliefs, shifting illusively between the personal and the political. Nowhere is this situation clearer than in the final poem of Volume 2, the 'Ode: Intimations of Immortality'. This is certainly how Frances Ferguson reads it in *Language as Counter-Spirit*, but she does not discuss the poem in its 1807 context. The 'Ode' is of interest to her with respect to the categories used by Wordsworth for his Collected Editions from 1815 on. She describes the poem as it appears in these later collections as 'left conspicuously unconnected to any categories of his classification.... As such, it does not merely replace or refute the other poems. Rather, it appears both as a rehearsal and a fulfilment of the poems preceding it and as a meditation of them.'[19] The biographical record can provide a narrative that underpins this perception.

The poem began life as a four-stanza Pindaric Ode in 1802; as such it offers a melancholy reflection on the poet's loss of vision, and it enacts a rediscovery of joy:

> Ye blessed Creatures, I have heard the call
>   Ye to each other make; I see
> The heavens laugh with you in your jubilee;
>   My heart is at your festival,
>   My head hath its coronal,
> The fullness of your bliss, I feel – I feel it all.
>   (*Poems 1807*, 272, 36–41)

It then sinks into despondency with the fading (once more) of that joy:

>   – But there's a Tree, of many one,
> A single Field which I have look'd upon,
> Both of them speak of something that is gone:
>   The Pansy at my feet
>   Doth the same tale repeat:
> Whither is fled the visionary gleam?
> Where is it now, the glory and the dream?
>   (ll.51–7)

Coleridge, suffering from an unrequited passion for Wordsworth's sister-in-law, Sara Hutchinson, responded to these lines with a verse letter to Sara (the poem that became known as the 'Dejection Ode') in which all hope of an imaginative life is abandoned; the tortured human soul is isolated and alienated. 'Resolution and Independence' was Wordsworth's response. There has been a loss, 'The things which I have seen I now can see no more' ('Intimations Ode', l.9), but the mystery is still there. It draws us to it, and the poet, 'whether it were by peculiar grace, / A leading from above, a something given' ('Resolution and Independence', ll.50–1), may still glimpse a promise of redemption, a 'something far more deeply interfused' ('Tintern Abbey', l.97) in his existence that links his own redemption to the redeeming powers of the natural world. In much the same way the old leech gatherer, near to death in this life, is, in fleeting moments, also recognised as constituting a life-giving vision.

In 1804, Wordsworth returned to the 'Intimations' Ode with the intention of constructing a poem that would explore and resolve these issues in a more comprehensive form. The 'Ode' does indeed therefore feed off the matter of the poems that precede it (including poems from *Lyrical Ballads*), attempting to complete the 'narrative' of what had already been composed, while reflecting on the progress of thought delineated by the collection. The renewed 'Ode' begins with a reference to the Platonic idea of birth as a descent into generation from a previous existence:

> Our birth is but a sleep and a forgetting:
> The Soul that rises with us, our life's Star,
> Hath had elsewhere its setting,
> And cometh from afar...
> (*Poems 1807*, 273, 58–62)

The stanza as a whole maps out a life. At birth we retain for a moment the perfection from which we came; at birth, of course, we are helpless and inarticulate. 'Nature' provides us with a visionary awareness of our lost glory while childhood lasts, but 'At length the Man perceives it die away, / And fade into the light of common day' (ll.75–6). The following stanza refers to 'Earth' (not Nature) as attempting to compensate for the loss 'with pleasures of her own'; the intention of Earth, a 'homely Nurse', is to make us 'Forget' (ll.76–84).

The progress of forgetfulness is then described: a 'Child among his new-born blisses' (l.85) loses his individuality and spontaneity as he learns to speak and draw, discovering that what he must do is be like other human beings, 'As if his whole vocation / Were endless imitation' (ll.106–7). This calls forth an agonised lament: why should the child so perversely yearn for adulthood when it enjoys such privileges as a child?

> Why with such earnest pains dost thou provoke
> The Years to bring the inevitable yoke,
> Thus blindly with thy blessedness at strife?
> (ll.126–8)

As we read the 'Ode', it is important to remember that while Wordsworth was producing stanzas that several times rehearse the course of a 'life' from the 'Soul's immensity' (l.109) of childhood to the 'frost' of adulthood (l.131), he was also writing up the details of his own life in *The Prelude*. In the latter poem his entry into adulthood was portrayed as a maturing of his poetic powers; it was designed to establish the basis upon which his career as a poet had been built following his arrival at Racedown. In this later section of the 'Ode' Wordsworth seeks to move forward in time, basing his argument on the experience of his attempt to salvage a sense of joy from the past (what Coleridge now confessed to having failed to do). The intention is to confirm the victory implied in *The Prelude*. New historicists like McGann and Liu would argue, however, that Wordsworth is doing far more in the process than just rescuing something of the childhood power of vision for comfort in the face of encroaching old age. He is attempting to exorcise a great many personal ghosts that have haunted him through an insecure childhood and a turbulent adolescence and youth. The memories that haunt him, including, of course, his phase of extreme political radicalism, his affair with Annette, and the death of his brother John, go on the new historicist's list of 'absences', things which give the poem as much (if not more) meaning than that which is explicitly stated in the text.

Whatever we may feel about being encouraged to supply, and then 'read' absences, however, in the opening of the eighth stanza there is clearly an appeal to Coleridge to believe that the 'Joy' he mourns lives on, but not in the poet. It lives in 'Nature'. To know of its existence must be sufficient; add this to the fact that we can remember 'our past years' when such joy was known, and you have the basis of Wordsworth's argument. Our loss of childhood gives rise to

> obstinate questionings
> Of sense and outward things,
> Fallings from us, vanishings;
> Blank misgivings of a Creature
> Moving about in worlds not realiz'd,
> High instincts, before which our mortal Nature
> Did tremble like a guilty Thing surpriz'd...
> (ll.144–50)

And it is for these 'questionings' that Wordsworth raises his 'song of thanks and praise' (l.143). We shall never recapture that primal 'joy'. We cannot even claim to preserve it in some form of memory, but we are given to know that it is there: it is an intimation brought to us by our mind's determination to resist (by 'obstinate questionings') the temptation to despair.

In the penultimate stanza we find a succinct summary of the moral that underpins all the narrative poetry he was to compose for inclusion in *The Excursion*. We can see how appropriate it is for a reading of *The Ruined Cottage*, the poem destined to become Book I of *The Excursion*:

> We will grieve not, rather find
> Strength in what remains behind,
> In the primal sympathy
> Which having been must ever be,
> In the soothing thoughts that spring
> Out of human suffering
> In the faith that looks through death
> In years that bring the philosophic mind.
> (ll.182–9)

The 'Elegiac Stanzas, Suggested by a Picture of Peele Castle' that precede the 'Ode', attach the specific bereavement of John's death, and the poet's manner of coping, to the 'Ode's' broader project of coping with the loss of 'joy'. In what is clearly the pivotal stanza of the poem, Wordsworth describes the effect of seeing Beaumont's painting of Peele Castle in a storm, a dramatic contrast to his own memory of the place as a calm and peaceful scene:

> So once it would have been, – 'tis so no more;
> I have submitted to a new controul:
> A power is gone, which nothing can restore;
>
> A deep distress hath humaniz'd my Soul.
> (*Poems 1807*, 267, 33–6)

There is to be no superhuman defiance of the human condition, and the final verse provides a link to the 'Ode' that follows it:

> But welcome fortitude, and patient chear,
> And frequent sights of what is to be borne!
> Such sights, or worse, as are before me here. –
> Not without hope we suffer and we mourn.
> (*Poems 1807*, 268, 57–60)

Moving in this way from the specific location of the 'Elegiac Stanzas' (a brother's death) to the all encompassing agenda of the 'Ode', is to see Wordsworth replacing (in Levinson's words) 'the picture of the place with "the picture of the mind," such as it might be at any time and in any place'.[20] 'History' in its most formal guise is manifestly displaced in the process because Wordsworth has reversed the creative chronology. By placing the 'Elegiac Stanzas' (1805) before the Ode (1804), a revised version of the narrative of his life has become possible.

The 1807 collection reaffirms Wordsworth's democratic instincts. The range of poetry included is immense, and challenges Augustan principles of aesthetic discrimination so valued by a critic like Jeffrey. But it is not only the range of poetry that is significant. It is also the way that a thematic unity begins to pervade the volume as a whole, pointed up by Wordsworth's attention to the ordering of his material. Alice Fell's grief at the loss of her cloak belongs with a country's fear for its survival against a foreign invader; this in turn involves us with private reflections on robins, butterflies, daisies, celandines and daffodils. All must appear, in the end, as part of an interlinked narration of the life Wordsworth describes in his final poem, a life which can still – he claims – appeal to the influence of an ordering power, even though such things are in the end, para-doxically, beyond the power of knowing with words:

> To me the meanest flower that blows can give
> Thoughts that do often lie too deep for tears.
> (*Poems 1807*, 277, 205–6)

5

Three Narrative Poems: *Peter Bell* (1798/1819), *Benjamin the Waggoner* (1806/1819), *The White Doe of Rylstone* (1807/ 1815)

> He serves the Muses erringly and ill,
> Whose aim is pleasure light and fugitive:
> O, that my mind were equal to fulfill
> The comprehensive mandate which they give –
> Vain aspiration of an earnest will!
> ('Prefix' to *The White Doe of Rylstone*; *White Doe*, 80, 57–61)

I

It was not until 1820, when Wordsworth published the sonnet sequences, *The River Duddon*, that he could begin to consider himself as having achieved commercial success as a poet. There were signs, however, that the tide of critical opinion was beginning to turn in his favour five years before this. John Scott, writing in the *Champion* (June 1815), made the following claim: 'He is now before the public in a variety of works, – of unequal merit certainly, – but in their collective testimony proclaiming the greatest poetical genius of the age.'[1] Scott was reviewing *The White Doe of Rylstone*, one of three extended narrative poems written much earlier, but not previously published. Like the still unpublished *Prelude*, all three narratives are concerned in various ways with the problematic relationship between a public and a private life; all three poems are concerned with a central figure who seeks redemption after suffering a fall from grace. *The White Doe* (published in 1815) had been written in 1807; *Benjamin the Waggoner* was written the year before, and published in the same year as the third in this group, *Peter Bell*, 1819. *Peter Bell* had been written back in 1798. All were ridiculed by what had become a well-established pack of Wordsworth detractors among the critics of the day. Most famously, *Peter Bell* had been pre-empted by a 'Peter Bell' parody written in Wordsworth's 'simple' style by J. H. Reynolds; it was then taken more seriously to task by Percy Shelley in his *Peter Bell the Third* (though Shelley's poem remained unpublished until 1839). The audacity of Reynolds's pre-emptive strike worked to Wordsworth's favour; the reading public was sufficiently entertained and therefore sufficiently intrigued to see if the Lake Poet's *Peter Bell* was as crassly amusing as the anonymous parodist's *Peter*. The consequence was that *Peter Bell* became Wordsworth's best-selling poem to date (there was just a week between the appearance of the two poems).

II

The publication dates of all three poems, 1815 and 1819, place them at a turning point in Wordsworth's literary life. The composition dates of *Benjamin the Waggoner* and *The White Doe* (1806–7) coincide with the move from Dove Cottage and developing links with two wealthy patrons, Sir George Beaumont and Sir William Lowther (see Chapter 4). In this respect *Peter Bell* belongs to a different era. Compared to the other two, it reads as a reminder of the serio-comic mood that marks out other 1798 *Lyrical Ballad* narratives (with the exception of the unremittingly grim 'Female Vagrant'). Viewed as something of an anomaly when it came out, a reminder of Wordsworth at his most perversely 'simple', *Peter Bell* failed to become responsible for a body of critical literature of the kind we can turn to when studying *Lyrical Ballads*, *The Prelude*, or the 1807 *Poems in Two Volumes*. The same is true for *Benjamin* and *The White Doe*, though compared to them, *Peter Bell* at least earns a passing mention in most critical accounts. In Chapter 9 of *Wordsworth: Play and Politics* (1986) John Turner calls the poem 'the culmination of the lyrical ballad poetry', while J. H. Alexander goes so far as to claim that it is one of 'Wordsworth's three supreme achievements' alongside *Lyrical Ballads* and *The Ruined Cottage*. That is on page 1 of *Reading Wordsworth*; he quotes three stanzas from it on page 13 and never mentions it again.[2]

There has been, however, one major critical essay on *Peter Bell* published in recent times. In *Wordsworth and the Enlightenment* (1989), Alan Bewell argues that Wordsworth's poem parodies eighteenth-century anthropological theories, in particular Giambattista Vico's *Principles of a New Science of Nations* (first published in 1725). Vico argued that societies evolved through a cyclic progression that took them from barbarism, through heroism to enlightened reason. Bewell reads *Peter Bell* as a comic recycling of Vico's mechanistic historicism. What Wordsworth found objectionable here was what he also found objectionable in the rationalist theories of Hartley and Godwin. Without a knowledge of Vico and 'hypothetical history', Bewell claims, critics may perceive *Peter Bell* to be an important poem, but remain ignorant of its full range:

> Like 'The Idiot Boy', *Peter Bell* does not provide us with a simple 'hypothetical history', but instead achieves its goals with destructive and parodic merriment. As a comic compendium of eighteenth-century anthropological method, the poem has its own fascinations and pleasures. Equally importantly, the poem merits our attention because it offers us the easiest access to the anthropological paradigms that Wordsworth began with and ultimately displaced in his mature work.[3]

Other critics have described *Peter Bell* as a foil to Coleridge's *Ancient Mariner*. Bernard Groom, writing in 1966, discusses this aspect of the poem with an obvious enthusiasm for what he sees as Wordsworth's affirmation that conversion to Christianity may be achieved without recourse to a 'supernatural world' or a 'mythical heaven': 'Seldom has the transformation of a sub-human brute into a living soul been traced with such subtle originality.' Unlike Coleridge, Groom suggests, in *Peter Bell* Wordsworth portrays a gradual conversion rooted in the poet's own slow journey towards a Christian faith that took place 'step by step, within the bounds of common occurrences'.[4]

Both Wordsworth and Coleridge set out to reveal the power of religion as something that goes far beyond what Vico would have argued for in anthropological terms. As others have suggested, there is probably an alliterative link between Wordsworth's 'Peter Bell' and Pierre Bayle, whose rationalist critique of the Bible in the late seventeenth century became a seminal document for subsequent eighteenth-century religious sceptics. Like Coleridge's Ancient Mariner, Peter travels towards atonement, and in the process both reveal that religion is a far more mysterious, potent force than any rationalist interpretation of historical evolution is prepared to allow. As Peter moves on from a primitive, brutal state of belief in superstition and magic to discover the transforming power of Christianity, Wordsworth implicitly provides an ironically tinged narrative of his own journey from France to London, from London to Racedown, and finally from Racedown to Alfoxden. It is a journey in which the political preoccupations of previous years are being progressively supplanted by humanitarian ('humanising') priorities. In the process, eighteenth-century anthropology is parodied, but so also is the image of what we have come to think of as the 'Romantic poet'. In the Alfoxden coterie atmosphere of 1798 Wordsworth's specific intention was almost certainly to have some gentle fun with the poet of *The Ancient Mariner* and 'Kubla Khan'. In the Prologue to *Peter Bell* he describes being taken on a whirlwind tour of space in a magical boat. The boat derides him for wanting to come home, offering material for his poetic gifts that might well be suggestive both of the *Mariner* and 'Kubla Khan':

> Come, and above the land of snow
> We'll sport amid the boreal morning
> Where thousand forms of light are riding,
> Among the stars, the stars now hiding
> And now the stars adorning.
>
> I know a deep romantic land,
> A land that's deep and far away;
> And fair it is as evening skies
> And in the farthest heart it lies
> Of deepest Àfrica.
> (*Peter Bell*, 50–2, 86–95)

But Wordsworth insists that his place is at home, telling his tale of Peter Bell to a few patient friends, a tale that is essentially a story for the children in the group.

As I have argued elsewhere, much closer to Wordsworth's heart than Pierre Bayle as a model for Peter Bell, is William Wordsworth himself.[5] The poet was doing in a more extended and elaborate form what he had done in 'Simon Lee', 'Anecdote for Fathers' and 'We Are Seven' – he was sending himself up. Peter Bell is a Satanic, unredeemed version of the Pedlar. Both men have spent their lives in close proximity to the natural world. The Pedlar

> wandered far, much did he see of man
> Their manners, their enjoyments and pursuits
> Their passions and their feelings, chiefly those
> Essential and eternal in the heart...
> (*Ruined Cottage*, 359, 190–3)

Of Peter we learn that 'Sure never man like him did roam', but by contrast to the Pedlar:

> As well might Peter in the fleet
> Have been fast bound, a begging debtor;
> He travelled here, he travelled there,
> But Peter never was a hair
> In heart or head the better.
> (*Peter Bell*, 64, 206–10)

It is made very clear that Nature requires the application of a philosophic, discriminating mind if it is to deliver 'that blessed mood' of which 'Tintern Abbey' speaks:

> Though Nature ne'er could touch his heart
> By lovely forms and silent weather
> And tender sounds, yet you could see
> At once that Peter Bell and she
> Had often been together.
>
> A savage wildness round him hung
> As of a dweller out of doors;
> In his whole figure and his mien
> A savage character was seen
> Of mountains and of dreary moors.
> (ll.261–70)

A case might indeed be made for Peter displaying – in a comically distorted form – the symptoms displayed by Wordsworth himself when he first made his way up the Wye Valley, 'more like a man / Flying from something that he dreads, than one / Who sought the thing he loved' (*LB*, 118, 71–3). Peter is also reminiscent of the young Wordsworth of 'Tintern Abbey' once he has tried to take a short cut; this results in him encountering an increasingly difficult terrain. In 'Tintern Abbey' we learn of the poet's anxiety as he makes his way through the rugged landscape: 'deep rivers...lonely streams...the tall rock...the deep and gloomy wood' (ll.66–84). In Peter's case the response is unbridled anger:

> For while he drives among the boughs
> With head and hands and cheeks that burn
> With downright fury and with wrath,
> There's little sign that Peter's path
> Will to the road return.
> (*Peter Bell*, 72, 331–5)

His way leads him into a disused quarry that approximates very closely to the rugged landscape associated with the poet's youth in 'Tintern Abbey'. Once through it, he arrives at a beautiful glade on the far side:

> Now you'll suppose that Peter Bell
> Had some temptation here to tarry,
> And so it was, but I must add
> His heart was not a little glad
> That he was out of the old quarry.
> (ll.366–70)

An autobiographical reading of the poem (sustained in part by a carefully qualified alignment with 'Tintern Abbey') would suggest that by 1798 Wordsworth was looking back to his enthusiasm for Godwinian political philosophy as a short cut he had attempted to make in his own life, leaving the public way to become, like Peter, isolated and increasingly bitter. This recognition of the poem's intimate relationship with Wordsworth's personal history complements Bewell's reading of *Peter Bell* as a parodic attack on rationalist intellectualism.

The clearing Peter has come to is on the banks of the River Swale. The mature poet of 'Tintern Abbey' will have valuable things to say of such a place; in particular, we would expect to learn that its seeming lack of human habitation serves to prompt the poetic imagination to reflect upon the human condition in a way that helps to ease 'the weary weight / Of all this unintelligible world' (ll.40–1):

> wreathes of smoke
> Sent up, in silence, from among the trees,
> With some uncertain notice, as might seem,

> Of vagrant dwellers in the houseless woods,
> Or of some hermit's cave, where by his fire
> The hermit sits alone.
> (*LB*, 116–17, 18–23)

Wordsworth seems to have anticipated these lines in his description of Peter Bell's glade:

> And is there no one dwelling here,
> No hermit with his beads and glass?
> And does no little cottage look
> Upon this green and silent nook?
> Does no one live near this green grass?
> (*Peter Bell*, 74, 371–5)

The answer is no; but there is an ass, and a dead man in the River Swale nearby.

Though there are still a great many stanzas to come, the turning point for Peter Bell is now in sight. He decides to take the ass, but it will not move. It remains faithful to its dead master. Part I of the poem (585 lines in the early 1799 draft being used here) ends with Peter fainting because, having discovered the man's body, he believes 'That 'tis a fiend with visage wan, / A live man fiend, a living man, / That's lying in the river bed' (ll.578–80).

Peter is now set to overcome a series of irrational and fanciful fears. He realises who the drowned man is, and hauls him out of the river. The ass is then happy to depart, but only takes him where he, and not Peter, wishes to go; that is home to break the news to the dead man's wife and child. Even as the Ancient Mariner found himself with the Albatross hung around his neck, Peter now finds himself on the back of the ass, his destiny controlled by its will. In the course of the journey there are various incidents which Peter assumes to have supernatural causes. In each case Wordsworth supplies the reader with a natural cause, though these 'natural' causes point to a spiritual dimension for the story. As the journey continues, Peter begins to review his past life. He is taken past a chapel, and this reminds him that he is a bigamist; he is taken past an inn and discovers that he can no longer find pleasure in the sounds of carousel that he hears. Most disturbingly, he remembers a 'Highland Girl' he seduced, who bore his child, and who 'Died of a broken heart' (*Peter Bell*, 130–2, 1136–65). Though Wordsworth later suggested that he had been thinking of a similar case that dated back to his childhood, it is difficult not to assume that Annette Vallon and Caroline were also on his mind:

> Close by a brake of flowering furze
> He sees himself as plain as day;
> He sees himself, a man in figure
> Just like himself, nor less nor bigger,
> Not five yards from the broad high-way.
>
> And stretch'd beneath the furze he sees
> The highland girl – it is no other –
> And hears her crying as she cried
> The very moment that she died,
> 'My mother! Oh! my mother!'
>   (ll.1171–80)

Redemption is finally won when Peter recognises and responds to the widow's need for comfort. A decisive moment in his transformation comes when he hears the promise of Christian salvation uttered by a Methodist preacher as he rides by the second chapel in his journey (this was, above all else, the moment of piety that angered Shelley beyond endurance). The call to repentance comes at the right psychological moment and Peter is returned, like the Ancient Mariner, to the human race; he is bruised and shaken, but essentially a whole man once more. The bird falls from the Mariner's neck, and Peter will now (before very long) feel free to dismount the ass. But Wordsworth was carefully delineating the differences between his tale and that of Coleridge. One such distinction relates to the fact that it is the sight of the water snakes that moves the Mariner towards atonement, while in Peter's case it is hearing the closing words of a sermon. Where the Mariner is surrounded by portentous symbols, not least the Albatross, Peter has acquired a half-starved ass, along with whatever else his untutored, superstitious mind can conjure out of the shadows; and while the Mariner remains an isolated, haunted figure at the end of Coleridge's poem, Peter seems well on the way to full social reintegration.

III

Peter Bell is an intertextual *tour de force*, and not least among the texts employed within it was the poet's own life. The rational explanations for supposedly supernatural phenomena that Peter experiences reside in a natural world properly perceived, which is to say they remain mysterious in their own terms, as mysterious as the way in which the grief of the widow, once she knows of her husband's death and can begin to grieve, can be seen to comfort her:

> 'Oh God be prais'd! my heart's at ease,
> For he is dead. I know it well!'
> Of tears she poured a bitter flood
> And in the best way that he could
> His tale did Peter tell.
> (*Peter Bell*, 142, 1266–70)

It is a serious poem, and we have Hazlitt's testimony to remind us that this was so: 'Whatever might be thought of the poem, "his face was as a book where men might read strange matters," and he announced the fate of his hero in prophetic tones.'[6] Hazlitt's words should certainly confirm the appropriateness of reading *Peter Bell* alongside *The Ancient Mariner* and alongside the 'strange matters' of the poet's own life, some of which had already been written into the still gestating *Ruined Cottage*, and were shortly to inform the writing of 'Tintern Abbey' (Hazlitt must surely have observed that parts of this poem held meanings for the inner circle to which he was not privy). His insistence on Wordsworth's sense of the seriousness of it prompts a further suggestion that in the context of critical orthodoxy must be considered a profound heresy: 'Tintern Abbey' may now be read as a spin-off from what, at the time of its composition, was the major work, *Peter Bell, A Tale in Verse*.

In a recent reading of *Peter Bell* (1999), John Wyatt has relocated the discussion of the poem by drawing attention to the contents of the volume in which *Peter Bell* first appeared in 1819. The poem was accompanied by four sonnets; three of these sonnets refer to three prints of Yorkshire scenes by William Westall. One print is unnamed; the other two are 'Gordale' and 'Malham Cove'. The fourth sonnet is entitled 'Composed during one of the most awful of the late storms, Feb. 1819'. This circumstance prompts Wyatt to investigate the extent to which the publication of *Peter Bell* may be considered as marking a significant moment in the transition from an early to a late style in Wordsworth's poetry. The decision to include the prints is not difficult to understand: the Westall landscapes feature the part of Yorkshire near where the action of *Peter Bell* takes place, and the fourth sonnet describing the storm includes a moment of religious conversion. Wyatt's book is called

Wordsworth's Poems of Travel, 1819–42, and, as the title suggests, his interest in this material is linked to his study of Wordsworth's journey into his later years as a poet. The first three sonnets are read as reflecting Wordsworth's increasing reliance upon art for inspiration, a tendency that qualified his idea of the Imagination as a formative power. If it was not the case in 1798, by the time of publication in 1819, it had become so. Wyatt's work encourages us, therefore, to reassess *Peter Bell* as a transitional poem, written well before the period normally associated with the appearance of significant changes in Wordsworth's poetry associated with his shifting political and aesthetic opinions. Read in this way, the poem puts us in mind of the 'humanising' process that the poet confronted in the 'Elegiac Stanzas' of 1807, a poem also predicated upon a specific work of art, and lamenting his failing visionary powers. This in turn serves to emphasise the theatricality of the setting of *Peter Bell*. It may be read as a series of tableaux, a gallery where we view a collection of highly contrived scenes.

Wyatt suggests that the fanciful 'Prologue' – which describes the poet's journey in the magic boat – indicates that Wordsworth's commitment to the imagination was already beginning to be less than secure at the time of the initial composition of the poem. The voyage in the boat reveals a mind responding to stimuli that are essentially visual and also associated with the discipline of scientific, rational enquiry. As he sails through the sky what Wordsworth describes is effectively a map. Wyatt concludes:

> Simultaneously with technological advances in mining and transportation, and with military developments, a new technology of map-making was emerging in Europe, a technology demanding a view from above. The first English geological maps were produced in the period 1816 to 1822. In aspiring to a country-wide vision, Wordsworth was a man of his time.[7]

William Westall had worked as a scientific assistant on various expeditions, and when he became a regular visitor to the Wordsworths at Rydal Mount, he would certainly have discussed landscape as a site for scientific activity and discovery as well as a thing of beauty. Indeed, the Yorkshire landscape was being closely studied at this time as a source of geological evidence by William Buckland and others, and Wordsworth would have been aware of the theories that were being formulated as a result.

What Westall's art – with all its implications for the involvement of scientific enquiry alongside imaginative exploration – appears to have done for Wordsworth, is to encourage him to delve beneath the surface of a landscape for essential truths. We should remember how in *Peter Bell* the true explanation for an earth tremor lies below the surface where miners are at work, not in Peter's fanciful, fevered imagination. The sonnets, Wyatt suggests, are 'cool and classical', and are set alongside a poem that aspires to their condition, poetry written 'within the context of art'. Wyatt concludes:

> The scenery on the stage of the 1819 volume is pictorial in *Peter Bell* and in the sonnets. The landscape of Yorkshire with its strange geology is a stage with natural features, a symbolic context for the play of tensions and the resolutions of inner lives. Peter Bell and the nameless traveller of the last sonnet both shift internally into renewal and resurrection. The poet's voice in the Westall sonnets appeals to an underworld of inner certainties, and deep reconciliations. The poet and his readers are presented in 1819 with a travel account in one locality, a world of a didactic and moral narrative conveyed by accounts of people in a foreign setting and by scenes which might well be the subject of a painter's canvas. Such is the poetic material for the travel accounts of the next twenty years of the travelling poet.[8]

The critical issue here is to consider how convincingly we might be able to attach the poet of 1798 to the poet of the later years, in a way which preserves the integrity of both.

IV

In *Benjamin the Waggoner* of 1806 Wordsworth returned to what might almost be described as the next chapter in the same story. Benjamin has a past history similar to that of Peter; he, too, has lived the life of a drunken ne'er-do-well. Now he is a reformed character with a steady job. Will he be able to withstand temptation when – as is inevitably the case – it once more rears its head?

Unlike *Peter Bell*, *Benjamin the Waggoner* has had very little critical attention paid to it since the first dismissive reviews that followed publication in 1819. Mention should be made of Paul F. Betz's Introduction to his Cornell Edition (1981), and Chapter 10 of my *Wordsworth: Romantic Poetry and Revolution Politics* (1989), but there, it seems, the story more or less ends. To even sympathetic contemporary readers, *Benjamin*, like *Peter Bell*, failed to satisfy the formal literary criteria that would qualify it to be considered a major contribution to the canon. Henry Crabb Robinson (reading it in 1811) judged it 'a tale of more naïveté than Wordsworth often displays'. Compared to *Peter Bell* he noted that it 'has far less meaning' and repeated Wordsworth's own description of it as 'purely fanciful': It is a tale 'told with grace and has delightful [passages] of description and elegant playfulness'. Reading it in the year of its publication, William Pearson wrote to Wordsworth that 'the Waggoner is a good deal different from your other poems – it is more light, and merry, and humourous (*sic*)'. He approved of the 'kindly sympathy with human nature in the lower walks of life' that the poem expressed. Many years later Crabb Robinson rediscovered it and felt likewise: 'I discovered in it a benignity and gentle humour'.[9] Everything, including Wordsworth's own insistence that he wrote it without serious intent, 'con amore, and as the Epilogue states almost in my own despite',[10] has combined to diminish the poem, and that verdict has almost universally become the received critical wisdom: wrongly, as it happens.

A number of these contemporary accounts note in passing the presence of a sailor in the poem; 'a fine description' was Crabb Robinson's verdict. The sailor plays an important role in the narrative, and he ought to have been allowed a good deal more critical attention subsequently. Once the details of Benjamin's story are closely considered, and not least the part the sailor has to play in them, we begin to see in Wordsworth a poet with reasons to hide behind the self-deprecating 'con amore' mask. *Benjamin the Waggoner* provided a therapeutic means of working through the turmoil and frustrations of the poet's political life around 1806, frustrations fed by continuing pangs of bereavement following his brother's death.

Beneath the poem's jocular surface runs a stream of bitterness that emanates from a balked humanitarian conscience, and in this respect the sailor is the key figure. Critical opinion then, as now, has largely been deflected from an appropriately rigorous study of the poem by the poet's own diffidence, and this is quite literally displayed at the start of the poem. As Benjamin drives his wagon through Town End he sees the house that used to be the 'Dove and Olive Branch' Inn, now the Wordsworths' house:

> There where the Dove and Olive-bough
> Once hung, a Poet harbours now –
> A simple water drinking Bard.

> Then why need Ben be on his guard?
> He ambles by, secure and bold –
> Yet thinking on the times of old
> It seems that all looks wond'rous cold.
> He shrugs his shoulders, shakes his head,
> And for the honest Folks within
> It is a doubt with Benjamin
> Whether they be alive or dead.
>   (*The Waggoner*, 48, 58–68)

We imagine Wordsworth sheltering in the darkened interior of the cottage, not daring to come too near the window, uncertain of his public reception. Here, as is also the case with *The White Doe of Rylstone*, he is driven to make a political point in very personal terms; in both instances he sought to do so while at the same time using the poetry as a safe haven. *Benjamin the Waggoner* therefore justifiably becomes the subject of analysis that takes count of immediate contextual circumstances, though it is important not to lose sight of its generic literary identity.

The genre is mock-heroic, and Paul F. Betz summarises it accordingly in the Cornell Edition:

> The poem parodies certain patterns in *Paradise Lost* and its sources in Genesis, and in classical tragedy and epic, while yet making a serious point: its story involves a trust given (by his master to Benjamin), a warning that the trust must be fulfilled, temptation, sin, a consequent fall, and suffering by others... as well as by the sinner. (*The Waggoner*, 4)

In slightly more detail, the story is of a wagoner who combines many of the essential qualities of the Wordsworthian hero. He is a solitary traveller of lowly social standing; he lives a reflective life as he steers his wagon through the Lakeland passes. He has put a life of carousing and drunkenness behind him, but not without a struggle, and – as the opening of the poem makes clear – he is still subject to temptation. The situation for Benjamin is shot through with uncertainty, and so it is by implication for the 'water drinking Bard' who watches him and writes about him. Is 'retirement' and 'wise passiveness' in truth equivalent to being 'dead'? Betz comments that 'the poem is suffused with the experimental approach and many of the dramatic and narrative techniques that caused the lyrical ballads to become objects of intense critical interest' (*The Waggoner*, 4). Benjamin makes his lonely way through the Lake District with a heavy, ponderous load, thinking the while of his intoxicatingly exciting youth. Wordsworth sits in a damp cottage in Town End contemplating changing times and friendships, new responsibilities, and his commitment to produce a poem so vast in conception, so ponderous, that he would never complete it. In this respect *Benjamin* may be read as the next chapter of his autobiography; *The Prelude* had been completed in 1805, and to compose this next instalment in mock-heroic terms – creating space for parody and irony – was a defence against depression, perhaps even madness.

Benjamin resists temptation at the next inn he passes, 'The Swan', and begins to toil up 'Dunmal-raise' towards Thirlmere. It is not long before a furious storm blows up, and in the midst of it he comes upon a terrified woman and her child. Whether or not he does it deliberately, the fact that Wordsworth now has Benjamin utter words very similar to those he put in his own mouth in 'Resolution and Independence' should make us look closely at the wagoner's identity. In 'Resolution and Independence' the poet questions the leech gatherer, 'How is it that you live, and what is it you do?' (*Poems 1807*, 128, 126). Benjamin asks the woman:

> 'Now tell,' says he, in 'honest deed
> Who you are and what your need.'
> (*The Waggoner*, 60, 210–11)

However it comes about, it is an intertextual reference that signifies an important subtext for the poem and its narrative. The consequence of Benjamin's generous response is to set in train a series of events that will culminate in a test of his innate goodness in an evil world. The sailor appears:

> Another Voice that was as hoarse
> As Brook with steep and stony course
> Cried out, 'good Brother why so fast?
> I've had a glimpse of you, avast!
> Let go, or since you must be civil,
> Take her at once for good or evil.'

> 'It is my husband,' softly said
> The Woman, as if half afraid.
> By this time she was snug within
> Through help of honest Benjamin.
> (ll.225–34)

Benjamin, the sailor, his wife and daughter, and an ass belonging to the sailor, battle on together through the storm.

At the next village the sailor tempts Benjamin into 'The Cherry Tree', where he begins to drink heavily, and so falls from grace. Not surprisingly, Benjamin is late delivering his load, and his employer finds him considerably the worse for wear. Matters are not helped by the fact that his master's dog, which had been in Benjamin's care, has been injured by a kick from the sailor's ass. Benjamin is sacked, and the loss is twofold, 'both Waggoner and Wain', because no one can manage the wagon with Benjamin's skill (l.751).

To appreciate the political matter embedded in the poem we need to return to the point at which Benjamin is tempted and falls. The part of the Devil in Wordsworth's Lakeland Eden is played by the sailor, who ushers Benjamin through the door of 'The Cherry Tree' before he realises what is happening; 'come in, / Come, come, cries he to Benjamin':

> And Benjamin – ah! Woe is me! –
> Gave the word, the horses heard
> And halted, though reluctantly.
> (ll.315–17)

The woman and her child are forgotten as Benjamin returns with a vengeance to the fleshpots. But Wordsworth had it in mind to do far more than simply deliver a homily on the evils of drink. His target includes nothing less than the conduct of the allies in the war with France. This is the poet who experienced a sickening sense of betrayal as he stood with William Calvert on the Isle of Wight, watching the English fleet prepare to do battle with Revolutionary France in 1793. 'The Cherry Tree' signifies Benjamin's abandonment of duty; it is a place of hedonistic pleasure encapsulating the 'fall' of the would-be honest man. Into this place, to the great delight of its drunken inhabitants, the sailor brings a large model of a man-of-war mounted upon a wheeled frame:

> Surprize to all, but most surprize
> To Benjamin, who rubs his eyes,
> Not knowing that he had befriended
> A Man so gloriously attended.
> (ll.378–81)

The trenchant irony of 'gloriously attended' is immediately apparent (particularly since the man's wife and child are outside cowering in the wagon). This is the devil's toy; it bewitches Benjamin and the rest of the drunken company. It is a model of Nelson's flagship at the Battle of the Nile:

> So said, so done, the masts, sails, yards
> He names them all and interlards
> His speech, with uncouth terms of art,
> Accomplish'd in a Showman's part,
> And then as from a sudden check
> Cries out, ''tis there the Quarter deck
> On which brave Admiral Nelson stood –
> A sight that would have done you good.
> One eye he had which bright as ten
> Burnt like a fire among his men. . . . '
>
> (ll.392–401)

Wordsworth's narrative was, to say the least of it, in bad taste for 1806. No wonder he lingered over publishing the poem, and no wonder the poem finds its way onto paper in a diversionary mock-epic style. We can see him backing away from his Dove Cottage window into the dark interior, though still compelled 'con amore' to write the piece. Less than a year after his death and virtual beatification, Nelson's career is held up by Wordsworth as the focal point for a war he believed to be morally indefensible. It was a war waged by England out of an unhealthy lust for power. While his much loved brother, a paragon of virtue, had died at sea, a tragedy scarcely noted by the world at large, a man of questionable personal morality was being proclaimed martyr to a cause which the poem unambiguously calls into question:

> 'A bowl, a bowl of double measure,'
> Cries Benjamin, 'a draft of length
> To Nelson, England's pride and treasure,
> Her bulwark and her tower of strength!'
> When Benjamin had seiz'd the bowl
> The Mastiff gave a warning growl;
> The Mastiff from beneath the Waggon
> Where he lay watchful as a Dragon
> Rattled his chain – 'twas all in vain;
> For Benjamin, triumphant Soul!
> He heard the monitory growl –

> Heard, and in opposition quaff'd
> A deep, determin'd, desperate draft.
>
> (ll.413–25)

As we have already seen from 'Character of the Happy Warrior', Wordsworth's response to the death of Nelson was, to put it mildly, a muted one. Nelson's ship 'in full apparel' (l.430) is a symbol of the devil's showmanship and seductive skills, against which Benjamin's wagon signifies his worthy, reformed way of life. But the wagon is also slow and ponderous, it moves with some difficulty over the hilly Lakeland roads, and must surely put us in mind of Wordsworth's ungainly poetic project, *The Recluse*, which he is forever being tempted to abandon. Staggering out of the Inn, Benjamin displays just how far he has fallen from grace by suggesting that his wagon might be, after all, not so very different from Nelson's ship:

> 'I like,' said Ben, 'her make and stature
> And this of mine, this bulky Creature
> Of which I have the steering, this,
> Seen fairly, is not much amiss.
> We want your streamers, Friend! You know,
> But altogether as we go
> We make a kind of handsome show...'
>
> (ll.550–6)

Where Wordsworth criticism has taken the poet's political frame of mind on board, the assumption has generally been that by 1806 he had well and truly 'turned'. The truth is that Wordsworth always remained, at heart, a member of the awkward squad, as both *Benjamin the Waggoner* and *The White Doe of Rylstone* make clear. An unquestioning acceptance of the received wisdom with regard to his political beliefs has tended to warp what little analysis there has been of *Benjamin*. Nowhere was this more evident than in Donald Reiman's review of Paul F. Betz's Cornell Edition of the poem in *Studies in Romanticism* (1982).

Reiman looked at the genesis 'of the old sailor who plays so prominent a part in the poem'.[11] Establishing where he comes from is one thing, but the really interesting question is where is he going circa 1806? Reiman declares him to be the 'hero' of the poem. His reason for believing this is his assumption that by 1806 Nelson must have been a hero for Wordsworth. The consequence of this is that the entire logic of the narrative is lost. Wordsworth manifestly identifies with Benjamin, not the sailor who patently acts as his seducer. Reiman's reading totally misses a crucial political facet of the poem's ironic, mock-epic moral. Should there still be any doubt left as to what is really going on in *Benjamin the Waggoner*, two years after completing the first draft, Wordsworth undertook the composition of a lengthy prose pamphlet in which he explicitly gave vent to his intense dissatisfaction with the conduct of the war. The occasion for this was the Convention of Cintra, when – as it seemed to Wordsworth – the British government was prepared to abandon the Spanish and Portuguese nations in their struggle for liberty, and to make a shameful treaty with France. England, he declared, claimed to be the defender of liberty, 'healthy, matured, time-honoured liberty – this is the growth and peculiar boast of Britain'. The Convention had exposed that claim as no longer valid (*Prose Works* I, 280).

Peter Bell is far more than a call to Methodistical virtue, and *Benjamin the Waggoner* is far more than a pious warning against the demon drink (and it was never a panegyric to Nelson or an endorsement of the war with France); both are complex, evasive poems in which Wordsworth approaches his most serious concerns with regard to cultural, historical, political and personal choices in a disconcertingly tangential way; it was what he had been doing ever since poems written for *Lyrical Ballads* began to function as an ironic counter-point to *The Ruined Cottage*. It is the same counter-point that sounds in the closing lines of *Benjamin the Waggoner*, where the poet characteristically insists on the importance of the story even as he seems to be offering to withdraw it from view:

> A sad Catastrophe, say you –
> Adventure never worth a song?
> Be free to think so, for I too
> Have thought so many times and long.
> But what I have and what I miss
> I sing of these, it makes my bliss.
> Nor is it I who play the part,
> But a shy spirit in my heart
> That comes and goes, will sometimes leap
> From hiding-places ten years deep.
> Sometimes, as in the present case,
> Will shew a more familiar face,
> Returning like a Ghost unlaid
> Until the debt I owe be paid.
>
> (ll. 752–65)

V

The third narrative poem, *The White Doe of Rylstone*, begun the year after *Benjamin* had been drafted, differs from its predecessors in that its subject, and its mode of presenting that subject, is unambiguously serious. It may well be primarily for this reason that critics seem to have been more willing to write about it than the other two. Having said that, a majority of commentators have done little more than mention the poem in passing, while what lengthier readings there are reveal interpretative issues no less intriguingly contentious than those that exist for *Peter Bell* and *Benjamin*. In 1940 Alice Pattee Comparetti edited a critical edition of the poem for the Cornell University Press. She began her Preface by reminding the reader that Wordsworth described the poem as 'in conception, the highest work he had ever produced', and that James Russell Lowell had described it in the 1870s as among the most 'Wordsworthian' of Wordsworth's poems.[12] In the event, the ridicule heaped on it when it first appeared in print (from Francis Jeffrey in particular) resulted in its removal from sustained critical scrutiny until Comparetti herself set to work.

The story of *The White Doe* is based on events that took place during the Rising of the North in 1569, an ill-fated insurrection against the rule of Elizabeth I. The Norton family are misguided reactionaries, and their determination to reinstate the Roman Catholic faith lies at the heart of their opposition to Elizabethan 'modernity'. Wordsworth made up his own story about their fate in the wake of the failure of the rising. Though seen by others around him as an attempt to take advantage of the lucrative market for historical narrative poetry that had served Sir Walter Scott so well, Wordsworth had from the first a very different kind of poem in mind.

Wordsworth's Nortons consist of the father, six sons and a daughter. One of the sons, Francis, begs his father and brothers not to take part in the rebellion. His sister Emily is a dutiful daughter and makes a banner for the rebels to take with them, but she shares Francis's abhorrence of their anachronistic ideals. The rebellion was crushed, and the Queen exacted savage reprisals on the guilty. Though in fact all the Nortons bar one escaped to Flanders, Wordsworth has all the rebel members of the family captured and executed. Francis is not implicated, but filial devotion leads him to promise his father that he will take the rebel banner and place it on St Mary's shrine at Bolton Abbey. We are shown the man who has opposed everything the 'unhallowed Banner' (*White Doe*, 97, 505) represents becoming – through this relatively blameless act – an agent of the reactionary cause, an apostate:

> Can he go
> Carrying this instrument of woe,
> And find, find anywhere, a right
> To excuse him in his Country's sight?
> No, will not all men deem the change
> A downward course, perverse and strange?
> (*White Doe*, 129, 1417–22)

There is clearly a strong case for linking Francis with Wordsworth himself.[13] Where *Peter Bell* and *Benjamin the Waggoner* explore an autobiographical strand within their plots using humour and irony, *The White Doe* employs history (substantially rewritten to accommodate the poet's needs) to suit the same end. Wordsworth composed the poem as he returned from Coleorton; his commitment to the radical ideals he had espoused some fifteen years before remained, yet he had every reason to think of himself as having fallen from grace; with Francis Norton, however, he might equally blame his compromised position on the pressure of circumstances beyond his control. By 1806 (as we have seen) he had become substantially indebted to Sir George Beaumont and to Sir William Lowther; beyond them he can hear his accusers speaking the words of the accusers of Francis Norton. They have discovered him with the rebel banner, and they jump to the obvious – but erroneous – conclusion that he does, after all, subscribe to the politics of his father:

> 'Behold the proof,
> Behold the Ensign in his hand!
> *He* did not arm, he walked aloof!
> For why? – to save his Father's Land; –
> Worst Traitor of them all is he,
> A Traitor dark and cowardly!'
> (ll.1480–5)

His fate is sealed – he too must die, a helpless victim of the crossfire. Whatever else he is doing, Wordsworth is most certainly here recreating yet again his own circumstances in the course of his story-telling.

A very different interpretation of the poem has been suggested by Peter J. Manning in Chapters 8 and 9 of *Reading Romantics: Text and Context* (1990).[14] Manning sees the Rising of the North as a radical, not a reactionary, movement. He argues that Wordsworth hesitated over publication because his poem favours the Rising, and could therefore identify him with radical political commitment. It is an unconvincing reading, not least because it sits uncomfortably with the fact that the leaders of the Rising were seeking to put the historical clock back, and also because Wordsworth is clearly expressing sympathy for both Francis, who refuses involvement, and with Francis's sister Emily, who rises above political entanglements. I believe that Manning, like Reiman, has made assumptions about the nature of Wordsworth's conservatism at this time, and read them back into a poem which in fact problematises what undoubtedly were conservative tendencies in the poet's thinking.

All three poems considered in this chapter invite further comment on a critical issue that can now be seen as uniting them. Literary criticism has always had a problem with the *roman à clef*. Regardless of how it is packaged it tends to be regarded as something provided for the 'common reader', a literary game of hide-and-seek, not a serious vehicle for scholarly analysis. This may be the reason why, in all the critical literature there is on *The White Doe*, Francis Norton's role in the story invariably receives short shrift. Almost without exception, commentators have focused their attention on Francis's sister, Emily, the person who is befriended by the mysterious White Doe. Comparetti considered the poem autobiographical to the extent that it bore the unmistakable marks of Wordsworth's continuing grief over the death of John. With other critics, she therefore subscribes to the idea that if Wordsworth himself is represented by a character in the poem, it is Emily, as we observe her coming to terms with the death of Francis in the course of the final Canto. The suggestion that Francis might resemble the poet in some significant way has, she notes, already been mooted by G. M. Harper and H. Fausset. Her response is derisive: 'Both Fausset's and Harper's remarks seem fantastic, and probably it is more satisfactory to refrain from this looser sort of allegorical interpretation.' Enough was known when Harper and Fausset were writing (in 1916 and 1933 respectively) to make the connection a perfectly credible one.[15] What Comparetti reveals is her refusal to see Wordsworth himself as in any way politically engaged. He is the

Romantic Poet: a solitary, feminised, meditative, suffering soul communing with nature that we observed at the beginning of the Introduction to this book, 'Oh! leave me to myself; nor let me feel / The officious touch that makes me droop again' (*Poems 1807*, 146, 11–14).

For Bernard Groom, Wordsworth and Francis are also an incompatible match. The thesis of Groom's *The Unity of Wordsworth's Poetry* is designed to show Wordsworth entering into his Christian inheritance; Francis, though admired for his stoicism, is hardly therefore an appropriate likeness. Emily is once again identified as the central figure in a poem that contrasts 'the martial virtues with the higher fortitude of patience'. Groom takes issue with J. Jones, who in *The Egotistical Sublime: A History of Wordsworth's Imagination* (1954) argued that there is a lack of clarity, 'a theological incompleteness', at the end of *The White Doe*. Groom's response to this is to compare *Peter Bell*, *The Ruined Cottage* and *The White Doe* in a way that both epitomises his Christian agenda, and also illustrates the extent to which *The White Doe*, *Peter Bell*, and I would suggest also *Benjamin the Waggoner*, have been allowed to drift into a critical backwater:

> Instead of deploring Wordsworth's indecision, is it not more noteworthy that, while still working within his own imaginative sphere, he inevitably approached the Christian view of man's moral life – its depths, its needs, its incompleteness without a higher revelation?[16]

An identification of Wordsworth with Francis Norton should not be seen as a denial of the fact that he clearly does also identify very closely with Emily in her bereavement. He identifies with Emily in a way not dissimilar to that in which he identifies with Dorothy in 'Tintern Abbey'; brother and sister are kindred and complementary spirits. This makes it clear that *The White Doe*, while it is a poem about bereavement specifically informed by John's death, engages with a recurring Wordsworthian motif, the imminent death of the poet. 'Tintern Abbey', 'Peele Castle', 'Resolution and Independence' and 'Ode: Intimations of Immortality' are all therefore companion pieces. When Geoffrey Hartman discussed *The White Doe* in *Wordsworth's Poetry* (1964), he described it as the poem that marks the end of the poet's 'great decade'; it introduces 'the leaner years' when Wordsworth was becoming increasingly anxious that his creative powers were failing.[17] In this context, 'Tintern Abbey' and *The*

White Doe illustrate the significance of the poet's relationship with Dorothy, the person who above all others is able to sustain his poetic life after a part of his creative being has 'died' with the passing of time.

Conforming to the genre of popular historical Romance was certainly the last thing on Wordsworth's mind as he wrote. Emily is described as having steadfastly pursued a passive role throughout the story. In the process she gains an inner strength that renders any historical or religious allegiances unnecessary for her attainment of peace of mind. The White Doe symbolises freedom from what the world considers binding upon us. It is this evidence of nonconformity (specifically in the religious sense) that rendered the poem problematic for critics of Comparetti's generation, who understood Wordsworth as primarily a Christian poet. Though by no means anti-Christian, it is never the less a spirit of nonconformist individuality that brings Emily through her crisis – in the same way that we see it 'humanising' the poet in his own grief as he describes it in 'Peele Castle' – and it was this nonconformist individualism that then went on to inform the piety of *The Excursion*.

The Doe is an emanation of the emphatically real world. Wordsworth begins the poem (indeed he uses the whole of the first Canto) to establish this point. Survival in this life is the product of that 'humanising' process, and Emily is reunited with the Doe as she sits beneath 'a mouldered tree, / A self-surviving leafless Oak' (*White Doe*, 137, 1648–9). Mouldering, without leaves, stripped of its external attire, the oak is all-importantly *self*-surviving. It may well seem that for Emily, as for the Wanderer in *The Excursion*, God has been superseded by nature. The message of the poem belongs not with a magical, visionary Doe, but with a real animal. The patient ass of *Peter Bell* and the lowly wagoner's horse (present also in 'The Baker's Cart'), are now fully realised in the Doe as the epitome of nature's gift to the human spirit. The journey from Peter Bell's religious promptings has brought us, via the wagoner's fall from grace and Francis Norton's death, to a point where equilibrium is reached:

> From fair to fairer; day by day
> A more divine and loftier way!
> Even such this blessed Pilgrim trod,
> By sorrow lifted tow'rds her God;
> Uplifted to the purest sky

Of undisturbed mortality.
(*White Doe*, 145, 1867–72)

As Hartman's brief essay in *Wordsworth's Poetry* reminds us, the resolution of the poem is indeed perceived in spiritual terms, but for all that it is a spirituality that Jeffrey – as he read *The Excursion* – became increasingly convinced was tantamount to an earthbound Paganism. Wordsworth, Hartman argues, 'is distracted by his conception (basically Miltonic) of the difference between the Protestant and the Catholic imaginations'. This debate is represented in the narrative by the need to choose between the Norton banner and the Doe. In the process, 'the "Protestant" relationship between Emily and the doe' is judged 'intrinsically purer than the "Catholic" one between the Nortons and the banner'.[18]

The White Doe of Rylstone completes the narrative trilogy discussed in this chapter with a reading of history that focuses upon the part which Christianity has played upon the evolution of British society, a theme that provided Wordsworth with a major preoccupation as he completed *The Prelude* and turned once more to *The Excursion*. *The White Doe* also returns us to the Introduction to this book where we considered the image of the poet communing with nature, a lone voice that seems to stray perilously close to extinction. In the course of the poem he rekindles the trope used by Gray in the *Elegy in a Country Churchyard*: the poet is killed off, the consequence not of Wordsworth's historical researches into the fate of Francis Norton, but the outcome of his pessimistic survey of the prospects for his own survival as the poet and the person he would be. He leaves us with Emily, a feminine trace of the true poet lamenting the fate of her lost brother. This is why – despite the way in which it now demands a very different interpretation from that given it in the early twentieth century – *The White Doe of Rylstone* remains what it was always felt to be, an intrinsically 'Wordsworthian' poem.

6

The Poem and the Poet in Exile: Issues of Textual Identity: *The Prelude (1)*

> What can be toilsome in these pleasant walks?
> Here let us live, though in fallen state, content.
> (John Milton, *Paradise Lost* Book XI, ll.179–80)

I

If there is one critical issue that dominated academic discussion of *The Prelude* in the twentieth century, it was whether or not any such poem properly exists. Since its publication in 1850 *The Prelude* has been the subject of inexhaustible textual scholarship. A summary of this work is to be found in the Norton Critical Edition of the poem edited by Jonathan Wordsworth, M. H. Abrams, and Stephen Gill. First published in 1979, the Norton Edition includes an essay, 'The Texts: History and Presentation', and there we find described the composition of a two-Part *Prelude* of 1799, the subsequent evolution of a five-Book *Prelude* of 1804, a thirteen-Book *Prelude* of 1805, and a fourteen-Book *Prelude* published in 1850. A more detailed account of the procedures involved in textual scholarship of this magnitude, and of the detective work involved, is available in Mark L. Reed's edition of the thirteen-Book 1805 *Prelude*, published in 1991 in the Cornell series. This is a two-volume giant of almost 2500 pages, of which just 435 are given over to a reading text of the poem. Prior to this Stephen Parrish published a Cornell edition of the 1798–99 *Prelude* in 1977, and in 1985 W. J. B. Owen edited the fourteen-Book *Prelude* in one volume of 1222 pages, also for Cornell.

The thirteen-Book *Prelude*, completed by May 1805, had been composed in phases: the 1799 two-Part poem, a series of revisions to that poem made in 1801–3, the further development of that manuscript in 1804 to a five-Book poem, and a spate of composition and revision between March 1804 and May 1805 to produce the thirteen-Book *Prelude*. A brief summary, however, fails to illustrate the full extent to which this 'poem' (or, more properly, this series of poems) evolved as a compilation of fragments subject to periodic reworking, a process that included exclusions as well as inclusions, and also the subsequent publication of further revised segments independently. Eventually, the poem, revised to fill fourteen Books, was published after Wordsworth's death, but not until there had been yet one more round of adjustments to the manuscript by the poet's executors.

In addition to the issue of textual identity that follows from the history of the poem's composition, *The Prelude* has been subject to critical discussion on another, distinct issue: it is a 'long poem', and as such qualifies for inclusion in an on-going debate about how and why long poems evolved in the course of the eighteenth century. This issue has been addressed by (among others) John Sitter in *Literary Loneliness in Mid-Eighteenth Century England* (1982), Susan J. Wolfson in *The Questioning Presence* (1986), and by John Barrell and Harriet Guest in 'The uses of contradiction: Pope's "Epistle to Bathurst"' (1988). Sitter suggests that 'long poems naturally imply a whole picture of the world which they figure', and that they will consequently 'present most of the intellectual uncertainties of a period'. Commenting specifically on James Thomson's *Liberty* (1735–6), Sitter anticipates what has become a point of interest for many recent readers of Wordsworth's *Prelude*. Thomson struggles to resolve 'the relation of the individual to history', and to reconcile 'the values of personal freedom and collective destiny'. The poems discussed by Sitter were, of course, read with equal interest by Wordsworth: Thomson's *Liberty* and *The Seasons* (1726–30), Mark Akenside's *Pleasures of Imagination* (1744, revised 1757) and Edward Young's *Night Thoughts* (1742–5).

In *The Questioning Presence* Susan J. Wolfson argues that, in *The Prelude*, 'the poet's ability to transform despair into hope is often figured as a movement from questioning to resolution, or, at least, to a perspective from which irresolution may be managed'.[1] This is precisely what Sitter describes as the agenda for the eighteenth-century long poem, but it was by no means the way *The*

Prelude was going to be read at the outset. Wolfson's discussion represents a late-twentieth-century critical perspective. Sitter discusses the means by which poets from Thomson through to Wordsworth sought to 'manage' their irresolution. Poets in the mid-century adopted the role of social and political commentator, tending to rely (as Sitter puts it) 'more on solitary than on conversational voices'; 'the self, and not the generalised "Man"' is used as 'the measure of things'. What consequently becomes the 'egocentric perspective' of these earlier poems anticipates critical issues raised by Wordsworth's poetry, and nowhere more so than in the *Prelude* texts.[2]

Though John Barrell and Harriet Guest approach the subject somewhat differently, they come eventually to consider the same issues as Sitter and Wolfson. They begin by identifying a frequent eighteenth-century criticism of the long poem, often summarised as 'want of proper arrangement'. The long poem lacked an Augustan unity of purpose and tone. An overall lack of coherence allowed for the recognition of isolated beauties, but rendered the whole unsatisfactory. For the modern critical sensibility, they suggest, the problem of the long poem has been expressed in different terms; it is that 'such poems regularly contradict themselves'. Barrell and Guest argue that what for the modern reader may constitute a critical issue, may well have been for the eighteenth-century poet and reader an explanation of why the long poem survived as an important genre. At a time when epic and pastoral 'were incapable of representing the modern world', at a time when the modern world was growing in the midst of contradictions – in particular where economic activity and moral values were concerned – the variegated generically mixed format of the long poem allowed (Augustan critics notwithstanding) for a necessary inconsistency. Such poems

> may not have been invented for the *purpose* of giving utterance to contradiction. The power of ideological formations to conceal their function, even and perhaps especially from the class whose hegemony they confirm, is such that we could hardly expect to find evidence of such a purpose; and their power to conceal contradictions, again perhaps especially from those who give them voice, makes it difficult to imagine that new forms could have been invented for a purpose which was not itself open to inspection. But such forms certainly *facilitated* the utterance of contradictions; and we want further to suggest that the institutions of criticism managed to train the readers of poetry in the forms thus invented to read it in such a

way as ensured that they would overlook the contradictory nature of the ideologies those forms were able to express.[3]

As a reader of these long poems, Wordsworth was, therefore, among those being trained by 'the institutions of criticism' to 'admire most the poems which, by their very nature, were most liable to contradict themselves'. He belonged to a generation that would 'make use of those contradictory meanings in the formation of their beliefs and in the conduct of their lives'.[4] Wolfson, Barrell and Guest are reflecting the preoccupations of much recent Wordsworthian discourse, and it is important to consider how the critical issues informing discussion of *The Prelude* have changed since its first appearance as an apparently single text in 1850.

II

In 1850, critics inevitably set *The Prelude* against Wordsworth's other long poem, *The Excursion*, and frequently found the former wanting. The reviewer in *Graham's Magazine* (1850), for example, wrote that

> it cannot be placed by the side of The White Doe, or The Excursion, or the Ode on Childhood, or the Ode on the Power of Sound; and the reason is to be found in its strictly didactic and personal character, necessitating a more constant use of analysis and reflection, and a greater substitution of the metaphysical for the poetic process, than poetry is willing to admit. . . . there is little of that easy yielding of the mind to the inspiration of objects, and that ecstatic utterance of the emotions they excite . . .   (*Prelude*, 554)

In a similarly negative vein, F. D. Maurice described the poem in 1851 as 'the dying utterance of the half century we have passed through' (*Prelude*, 560). The *Examiner* (1850) was – despite misgivings about Wordsworth's standing as a great poet – far more positive in its view: 'The *Prelude* may take a permanent place as one of the most perfect of his compositions' (*Prelude*, 558). A. C. Bradley, writing in 1909, reflects the critical consensus that had emerged: though there are 'dull pages' in both *The Prelude* and *The Excursion*, both are indispensable because both 'contain much of Wordsworth's best and most characteristic poetry' (*Prelude*, 562–4). The chief problem was length. Matthew Arnold made a compelling case in the course of the 1870s that Wordsworth was at his best in

his shorter works. Critics studied the long poems for only moment-
ary evidences of the lyric intensity 'with which Wordsworth feels
the joy offered to us in nature' (*Prelude*, 562).

Though the long poem problem did not go away, the context for
criticism was profoundly altered when the autonomy of the 1850
Prelude text was irretrievably removed by Ernest de Selincourt's
publication of the 1805 text in 1926. De Selincourt's parallel text
format exposed not just a poet whose work was due for reassessment, but also a poet who appeared ripe for psychoanalysis. Fundamental questions began to surface about how to read *The Prelude*
texts, and how to read Wordsworth the poet, because as poet it was
becoming very obvious that the image conjured up in the course of
later-nineteenth-century criticism of a placid, reflective poet whose
life was 'divided by no very profound incidents' would no longer
do.[5]

In 1923, well aware of what was in the offing, H. W. Garrod
characterised a school of criticism that was determined to hold out
for a reading of *The Prelude* as a single opus. His *Wordsworth:
Lectures and Essays* continued to be reprinted and to appear on
university reading lists until the early 1970s. His approach was
reflected in numerous other publications that continued as required
undergraduate reading on through the 1970s. Fairly typical is the
opening paragraph of E. A. Horsman's essay, 'The Design of Wordsworth's *Prelude*' (1966), which was included in *Wordsworth's
Mind and Art* (1969), edited by A. W. Thomson:

> When we are criticising a long poem like Wordsworth's *Prelude*, we
> need to consider not only the quality of its language but also the
> disposition of its materials. I believe that this poem is organised so as
> to compare certain crucial experiences, and that we need to under-
> stand the pointers to this which Wordsworth gives in the argument of
> the poem.[6]

Horsman writes of *The Prelude* as *a* poem 'organised' around *an*
argument. We should also note his recognition of the 'long poem'
status of the work; there will be the customary issue of coherence to
address, therefore, and his rhetoric assumes a unity of purpose and
control by way of response. Bernard Groom, whose book *The Unity
of Wordsworth's Poetry* (1966) has been referred to in previous
chapters, is even more explicit. At the beginning of his chapter on
The Prelude he refers to lines 61–3 from Book IV as 'The key-
passage to the unity of *The Prelude*'.[7]

Textual scholarship has, of course, fundamentally challenged such assertions. Observing the history of the way fractures of this kind have appeared in critical work on *The Prelude* since the 1930s offers valuable insights into the difficulties that Wordsworth himself faced as he wrote the poem. It will be helpful, therefore, to spend some time looking at Garrod's work in the context of more recent scholarship. Ashton Nichols, who published *The Revolutionary 'I': Wordsworth and the Politics of Self-Presentation* in 1998, claims that

> Wordsworth's texts on his own life are also increasingly important to our understanding of literary theory. The prototypical Romantic poet understands, from the earliest stages in his autobiographical project, that his activity is psychologically charged, and linguistically complex. He also reveals – in all of these texts – confusing interactions among speakers and the voices in which they speak, even when the speaking voice belongs to an ostensible 'self'.[8]

By 'texts' Nichols means the many fragmentary passages that come together at different times and in different ways to become different versions of *The Prelude*. This is a vastly different Wordsworth from the one Garrod described: 'Wordsworth himself is our best guide, and in following him we are wise if we emphasise what he emphasises.' Today's critic would have to respond with the question: 'Which Wordsworthian "self" do you have in mind, because *The Prelude* has many?', and would probably be forced to lay Garrod aside at the point at which he states, 'I take the opening of the *Prelude*, then, to be a truthful and exact narrative of fact.'[9]

Whether it be a partner, a doctor, a mechanic, a pension fund or a plumber, most of us tend to spend our lives looking for someone or something we can rely on, and for Garrod, the opening lines of the 1850 *Prelude* sufficed:

> O there is a blessing in this gentle breeze,
> A visitant that while he fans my cheek
> Doth seem half-conscious of the joy he brings
> From the green fields, and from yon azure sky.
> Whate'er his mission, the soft breeze can come
> To none more grateful than to me; escaped
> From the vast city, where I long had pined
> A discontented sojourner: now free,
> Free as a bird to settle where I will.

What, I wonder, were his thoughts on discovering that this 'exact narrative' had previously been written down as:

> Oh there is blessing in this gentle breeze,
> That blows from the green fields and from the clouds
> And from the sky; it beats against my cheek,
> And seems half conscious of the joy it gives.
> O welcome messenger! O welcome friend!
> A captive greets thee, coming from a house
> Of bondage, from yon city's walls set free,
> A prison where he hath been long immured.
> Now I am free, enfranchised and at large,
> May fix my habitation where I will.
>
> > (*Prelude* I, 29, 1–9; 28, 1–10)

He may well have reflected that the sentiment was much the same, and indeed it is; but it would by no means prove to be so with respect to all the alterations that followed. In 1805 Wordsworth began to draw his 'preamble' to Book I to a close with the lines:

> Enough that I am free, for months to come
> May dedicate myself to chosen tasks...
>
> > (ll.33–4)

In the 1850 version he replaced these lines with:

> Dear Liberty! Yet what would it avail
> But for a gift that consecrates the joy?
>
> > (ll.31–2)

In 1805 Wordsworth chooses to remember himself as essentially self-sufficient: he dedicates *himself* to poetic tasks chosen by him. 'In *The Prelude*', Nicholas Roe writes, 'Wordsworth is his own redeemer, and the means of redemption is his imaginative power which must remain inviolate.'[10] The memory preserved by the 1850 lines, however, is of a poet granted a liberty that would go to waste unless it were consecrated by some power outside himself. It may amount to little more than a nuance, but it is enough to establish the gap between the critical culture of Garrod's generation and our own. As Nichols puts it:

> The past three decades of criticism have called into question the stability of all texts, arguing first – deconstructively – that all language uses are potentially equivocal, and more recently – new historically – that no text is less complicated than the cultural circumstances that give rise to its production.[11]

Garrod, as we know, was very aware in 1923 of the textual scholarship going on around him, and he later revised his essay 'The Composition of "The Prelude"' to take account of the de Selincourt parallel text *Prelude*. He responded by reviving the controversies that had accompanied the task of dating when certain sections were written, and his method of arguing is instructive. Thomas Hutchinson, editor of the one-volume Oxford *Poetical Works*, had suggested that although the opening lines of the 1805 *Prelude* recalled Wordsworth's feelings when he left London for Racedown in 1795, they were in all likelihood composed in 1799, and conflated London and Goslar as places of 'bondage' from which the poet had been set free. Garrod insists: 'If the feelings of the "preamble" are those of 1795, then nothing can be more certain than that it was composed in 1795.' On his side in this debate is G. M. Harper, who had noted Wordsworth's reference in the 1850 text to 'the curling cloud / Of city smoke' (*Prelude* I, 33, 88–9), and concluded that the passage might have been written soon after the poet had left London in 1795, resting at a place where he could still see the smoke of the metropolis: Windsor, perhaps. But even this lacked the kind of consistency that Garrod was looking for: 'the journey described by Wordsworth is "A pleasant loitering journey, through *three days*"; and it would tax the powers of Mr. Harper, or anyone else, to accomplish in three days' walking the journey from Windsor...to Racedown.' The answer must be Bristol, 'Bristol is a practicable three-days' saunter.'[12]

My intention here is not to ridicule Garrod, but to illustrate what he felt was expected of him as a scholar. He needs to be clear about the text, its meaning, its intent, its moment of composition; and he needs to be clear about the poet's biography; and then he needs the one to match the other. In this respect his difficulties might be expected to have much in common with those that faced Wordsworth himself, and subsequently continue to dog the genre of biographical criticism. Referring to Stephen Gill's biography of Wordsworth, published in 1989, Nicholas Roe sums up the situation and helps to identify how the priorities have shifted:

> Stephen Gill's wary reading of the poet's history in *The Prelude* differs from Wordsworth's earlier biographers Mary Moorman, Émile Legouis, William Knight and Christopher Wordsworth – all of whom coincided with Wordsworth's own opinion that 'a poet's *Life* is written in his WORKS'. As Gill acknowledges, Wordsworth's selective history in *The Prelude* was achieved by the suppression of

earlier selves (or 'wrong paths') that the poet would not overtly acknowledge as tributary to 'the growth of [his own] mind'.[13]

Whatever the critical approach, the modern reader now works from an edition of *The Prelude* which footnotes the 'preamble' as almost certainly written in the Lake District, while the city referred to 'is partly London, partly Goslar' and partly a reference to Egypt, the 'house of bondage' described in the Book of Exodus Chapter 13 verse 3, and partly a trace from Milton's *Paradise Lost* (1667), a reference that is both destabilising and contradictory. The pervasive influence of John Milton's poetry on Wordsworth, in particular *Paradise Lost*, has always been recognised. But it has been the task of recent criticism to discover in it evidence of imagery that, as David Simpson has claimed, is 'at once appealing and deeply troubling'.[14] In this instance the apostrophe to a new-found freedom is appealing; but when it is aligned with the concluding lines of *Paradise Lost* it is also troubling, for here we see Adam and Eve expelled from Eden and sent into exile for disobeying God's command.

III

In 1993 Nigel Wood charted the critical terrain to be crossed when studying the critical history of *The Prelude* from Garrod's time to ours:

> Where, then, can we find the poem's point of origin?...Even if scholarship were to unearth an unequivocal directive from Words-worth as to what form of the poem best suited him, this...would not prevent some readers identifying this hypothetical pronouncement as 'true' only of the 'Wordsworth' at the date of its utterance.... *The Prelude* is composed by several 'Wordsworths' – and more: Dorothy, who transcribed the verse, and Coleridge, who supplied not just inspiration but also careful advice, to say nothing of Mary and the executors who prepared the 1850 edition.... the roll-call of con-tributors to the 'meaning' derived from *The Prelude* should include Helen Darbishire, Ernest de Selincourt, M. H. Abrams, Jonathan Wordsworth, Stephen Gill, Stephen Parrish, W. J. B. Owen and Mark L. Reed. 'Exit author' means enter reader and most certainly editor.[15]

Appropriately, this extract comes from a section entitled, 'Does *The Prelude* exist?' Wood argues that in *The Prelude* we have an '"object" for interpretation', one that undoubtedly draws on the poet's personal experiences, and that consequently may appear to lay claim to autobiographical veracity; but it is an 'object' that textual scholarship, combined with independent research into the poet's life, has reconstructed as a series of texts that explore a fragmented consciousness.[16] It is a text written from a series of locations (physical and mental) that emphasise the trope of exile. Wordsworth, from a position of exclusion, expresses a longing for wholeness, for belonging, and for reconciliation:

> But peace to vain regrets. We see but darkly
> Even when we look behind us; and best things
> Are not so pure by nature that they needs
> Must keep to all – as fondly all believe –
> Their highest promise. If the mariner,
> When at reluctant distance he hath passed
> Some fair enticing island, did but know
> What fate might have been his, could he have brought
> His bark to land upon the wished-for spot,
> Good cause full often would he have to bless
> The belt of churlish surf that scared him thence,
> Or haste of the inexorable wind.
> For me, I grieve not; happy is the man
> Who only misses what I missed, who falls
> No lower than I fell.
>
> (*Prelude* III, 1805, 116, 492–506)

The immediate context of this passage is Wordsworth's sense of missed opportunities while at Cambridge, and he subsequently chose to emphasise the fact by replacing 'happy is the man' with 'happy is the gownèd youth' (1850 l.494). By contrast, the 1805 text invites us to invest the Cambridge experience with a far broader significance. It is an oddly (but at the same time characteristically) contradictory passage. There are 'vain regrets' that he did not make more of his opportunities at university; perhaps, he goes on to suggest, what he missed was not as desirable as he might be tempted to think. The reference to the sailor suggests a situation akin to Odysseus; in which case it would certainly be wise to avoid going ashore. The best we can say is that no serious harm has been done: 'happy is the man' is a soothing Virgillian antidote with agrarian connotations designed to dispel Odyssean anxieties.[17] But it is precisely the image of a drifting mariner, longing for landfall but unable to secure it, that critics in the late twentieth century have recognised as a preoccupation in the entire poem. Where earlier commentators might point to the way Books I and II of *The Prelude* locate and celebrate a secure sense of place in which the growth of a poet's mind takes place, later generations fastened on the way in which (in both the 1805 and 1850 text) the image of the drifting, dispossessed mariner seems rarely to be far away. It becomes evident within the first dozen lines of both texts: 'in what vale / Shall be my harbour...' (*Prelude* I, 28, 11–12; 29, 10–11).

In *The Politics of Nature* Nicholas Roe searches for what he calls the Wordsworthian selves 'exiled' from *The Prelude*.[18] More mundanely (but no less appropriately), Stephen Gill notes that when Wordsworth had returned from what had effectively been a state of exile in Germany in 1799, bringing with him the two-Part *Prelude* in manuscript, he opted for a literary life that was to retain a persistently marginalised quality. Gill explores the uneasiness of Wordworth's situation, an uncertain stasis between 'positive' and 'negative' that later twentieth-century critics like David Simpson discuss with particular reference to the poet's engagement with Milton, and which critics like Arnold, Pater, Harper, Garrod, Horsman and Groom largely ignore.[19] *The Prelude* began as poetry written in exile. The West Country coterie of 1797–8 had been broken up. If the halcyon days writing *Lyrical Ballads* and *The Ruined Cottage* (not to mention *Peter Bell*) beneath the generous woodlands of Alfoxden were gone, how much more remote must Wordsworth's Lake District childhood have seemed? In the distant and unwelcoming circumstances of Goslar in mid-winter, Wordsworth gave expression to an intense longing for a reinstatement of wholeness and continuity. He then continued to write the poem – as a series of very different kinds of texts – rarely losing sight of that original thematic impulse. In 1799, not yet able to settle to *The Recluse*, separated from what he believed was his true vocation, and from his home, he began the poem in mid-line with a despairing exclamation from exile: 'Was it for this...?'

As his poetic career went uncertainly forward over the next five years, though returned to England and reinstated in the Lake District, the question remained an appropriate one: have the events of my childhood and youth, in England and then in France, been experienced in order to shape me as the poet I now appear to have become?

> Was it for this that I, a four years' child,
> A naked boy, among thy silent pools
> Made one long bathing of a summer's day,

> Basked in the sun, or plunged into thy streams,
> Alternate, all a summer's day...
> > *(Prelude* I, 17–21)

The 'preamble' Wordsworth eventually added to the opening lines of 1799 concludes with his admission that he cannot yet undertake the major work:

> But I have been discouraged: gleams of light
> Flash often from the east, then disappear,
> And mock me with a sky that ripens not
> Into a steady morning.
> > *(Prelude* I, 34–6, 134–7)

He reaches for Milton's *Paradise Lost* to help guide him through a passage justifying his lack of progress. In *Paradise Lost* Book IX Milton sets out what had been on his short list of epic topics; Wordsworth now does likewise:

> Sometimes, mistaking vainly, as I fear,
> Proud spring-tide swellings for a regular sea,
> I settle on some British theme, some old
> Romantic tale by Milton left unsung;
> More often resting at some gentle place
> Within the groves of chivalry I pipe
> Among the shepherds, with reposing knights
> Sit by a fountain-side and hear their tales.
> > *(Prelude* I, 38, 177–84)

In full, the 1805 passage totals 71 lines, and constitutes at best a decoratively self-indulgent detour. Biographical data suggest that Coleridge and Wordsworth were in little doubt as to the form that – in broad terms – the poem in question needed to take. Eventually it is described:

> I yearn towards some philosophic song
> Of truth that cherishes our daily life,
> With meditations passionate from deep
> Recesses in man's heart, immortal verse
> Thoughtfully fitted to the Orphean lyre;
> But from this awful burthen I full soon
> Take refuge, and beguile myself with trust
> That mellower years will bring a riper mind
> And clearer insight.
> > *(Prelude* I, 40, 230–8)

Wordsworth seems here to be attempting little more than to make his inability to write his epic work sound like a matter of being spoilt for choice rather than a matter of laziness and indecision. If we give him the benefit of the doubt, he is labouring his tendency to 'recoil and droop, and seek repose / In indolence from vain perplexity' in order to dramatise the more his original rhetorical question, 'Was it for this...?' (*Prelude* I, 1805, 42, 267–8). The description which then follows of an idyllic first five years of life becomes in consequence as much a reason to doubt its helpful effect on the would-be epic poet, as it is a cause for celebration. This reading is endorsed by the addition a short way into the original passage of the observation that he had grown up 'Fostered alike by beauty and by fear' (*Prelude* I, 1805, 44, 306).

With the Garden of Eden as a persistent point of reference, it is not unreasonable to conclude that Wordsworth suspects that his own presence in the Garden of the Lake District was potentially Satanic, even as John Donne had had cause to suspect his role in 'Twicknam Garden':

> And that this place may thoroughly be thought
> True Paradise, I have the serpent brought.[20]

This tends to be the way that David Simpson reads the poem. Like Nicholas Roe in *The Politics of Nature*, Simpson applies the techniques of new historicism to read the absences, those areas of Wordsworth's life that fail to appear on the surface of the text. He detects their presence by a sensitivity to (among other things) subliminal references in the poem to other texts, and is therefore left to wonder 'what kind of angel, demonic or divine, Wordsworth might be':[21]

> In thought and wish
> That time, my shoulder all with springes hung,
> I was a fell destroyer. On the heights
> Scudding away from snare to snare, I plied
> My anxious visitation, hurrying on,
> Still hurrying, hurrying onward. Moon and stars
> Were shining o'er my head; I was alone,
> And seemed to be a trouble to the peace
> That was among them. Sometimes it befel
> In these night-wanderings, that a strong desire
> O'erpowered my better reason, and the bird
> Which was the captive of another's toils
> Became my prey; and when the deed was done

I heard among the solitary hills
Low breathings coming after me, and sounds
Of undistinguishable motion, steps
Almost as silent as the turf they trod.
                    (*Prelude* I, 44–6, 316–32)

The Garden of Eden secretes a fallen Adam, and God may be heard seeking the sinner to pronounce punishment – 'Low breathings coming after me'. Wordsworth's Eden also contains remembrances of moments of peculiar imaginative significance for him, the so-called 'spots of time' that he refers to in Part One, 1799 (ll.288–96), and Book XI, 1805 (ll.257–9). These were redistributed across the poem and added to as it grew in length. In recent criticism they have come to be read as problematic, contradictory moments of insight rather than unambiguous celebrations of creativity. They are as disturbing as they are illuminating. Simpson's account is representative of a general trend in criticism since the 1980s:

> What *connects* these luminous memories has been less attended to. On close inspection, we find that the kinds of community that the poet tries to return to are all in one way or another ineffective or unstable. To recognise this provides us with a different vocabulary for reading the arguments of the great 'moments' of the poem, which are themselves far from being simply reaffirming.[22]

Simpson would be the first to acknowledge that Geoffrey Hartman was already drawing attention to this kind of 'instability' in *The Prelude* in the mid-1960s: '*The Prelude* leaves many things obscure. Yet its theme is ultimately clear, and its argument no argument but a vacillation between doubt and faith.'[23]

IV

Two of the most celebrated passages of childhood memory that are also 'spots of time', are the account of stealing a boat at night on Ullswater, and of skating on Esthwaite. 'Stealing' may be an overstatement, but we are told that taking the boat 'was an act of stealth / And troubled pleasure' (*Prelude* I, 48, 388–9); it is a crime, and he is conscious of leaving a trail of evidence:

                    Nor without the voice
        Of mountain-echoes did my boat move on,

> Leaving behind her still on either side
> Small circles glittering idly in the moon...

But confidence grows, helped by the child's sense of security within his world:

> I fixed a steady view
> Upon the top of that same craggy ridge,
> The bound of the horizon – for behind
> Was nothing but the stars and the grey sky.

His reassuring knowledge of a known location is then shattered when 'a huge cliff, / As if with voluntary power instinct, / Upreared its head':

> I struck, and struck again,
> And growing still in stature, the huge cliff
> Rose up between me and the stars, and still
> With measured motion, like a living thing
> Strode after me.
>   (ll.389–412)

The child is expelled from his Paradise by this transgression; he has discovered a malevolent world beyond, and he is now denied the delights of the world that previously was his:

> In my thoughts
> There was a darkness – call it solitude
> Or blank desertion – no familiar shapes
> Of hourly objects, images of trees,
> Of sea or sky, no colours of green fields...
>   (ll.420–4)

What is needed – as it was for Coleridge's Ancient Mariner – is a process of atonement. When he describes the experience as a 'purifying' one, therefore, this is far from saying that it was pleasurable; it is a penance 'sanctifying by such discipline / Both pain and fear' (ll.439–40).

The skating appears less traumatic. Initially it is a collective activity, where the children's sport mirrors the hunt, which in turn mirrors the hectic adult world into which they will go:

> All shod with steel
> We hissed along the polished ice in games
> Confederate, imitative of the chace

> And woodland pleasures, the resounding horn,
> The pack loud bellowing, and the hunted hare.

But the disturbing note is soon sounded:

> while the distant hills
> Into the tumult sent an alien sound
> Of melancholy, not unnoticed...

At this point Wordsworth separates himself from 'the uproar'; first he goes into a space occupied only by him; then he abruptly ceases his rapid motion and becomes aware of a very different world, a wordless world of echoes:

> yet still the solitary cliffs
> Wheeled by me, even as if the earth had rolled
> With visible motion her diurnal round.
> Behind me did they stretch in solemn train,
> Feebler and feebler, and I stood and watched
> Till all was tranquil as a dreamless sleep.
> (*Prelude* I, 52–4, 452–89)

For his discussion of the spots of time, Hartman drew heavily on the Christian tradition with which he perceived Wordsworth to be grappling (frequently through Milton) throughout his work. Wordsworth, he suggests, is the 'reader of a prior and sacred text', responding to what he calls 'a silenced ur-fiat', by which he means the initiating, creative word of God that breaks the first great silence with 'a primordial speech-act', the 'Logos': 'In the beginning was the Word, and the Word was with God, and the Word was God.'[24]

Hartman's Wordsworth is striving towards a state of wordlessness within which timeless truth exists. It is an impossible task. What the poet in fact does is to make words, and as he does so he therefore re-enacts the fall: 'The Logos dwells with God and when it comes to men it is not understood. The Light to which it gives Being lights a darkness that is uncomprehending.'[25] With this statement in mind we should note the passage that follows the description of skating:

> Ye presences of Nature, in the sky
> Or on the earth, ye visions of the hills
> And souls of lonely places, can I think
> A vulgar hope was yours when ye employed

> Such ministry – when ye through many a year
> Haunting me thus among my boyish sports,
> On caves and trees, upon the woods and hills,
> Impressed upon all forms the characters
> Of danger or desire, and thus did make
> The surface of the universal earth
> With triumph, and delight, and hope, and fear,
> Work like a sea?
> > (*Prelude* I, 54, 490–501)

The question mark at the end qualifies the notion of a 'ministry', the outcome of which remains unknown despite the words; the 'fiat' has yet to be delivered. The best that can be said is: surely it *will* be, eventually. Eventually this exile will be over and the poet will be allowed to return to Eden.

Critics, many of them taking their lead from Hartman, have been quick to note the use Wordsworth makes of the word 'characters' in *The Prelude* where it signifies written characters, or letters. After the poet exiles himself from his playmates while skating, the experience he has promises to reconstitute the 'presences of Nature' in the form of writing; he will in due course see 'Impressed upon all forms the characters / Of danger or desire' (ll.497–8). Writing is to take place, but as a mysteriously transcendent process which at the same time seems existentially to be locating the numinous within the bounds of the natural world.

An equally important spot of time, the description of crossing the Alps in Book VI, explores the same paradox. Wordsworth, robbed of what he believed would be an inspiring experience (an experience which would owe much to the altitude at which it takes place) is disappointed, only to be overwhelmed by the experience of plunging downwards into the Vale of Gondo:

> > The immeasurable height
> Of woods decaying, never to be decayed,
> The stationary blasts of waterfalls,
> And everywhere along the hollow rent
> Winds thwarting winds, bewildered and forlorn,
> The torrents shooting from the clear blue sky,
> The rocks that muttered close upon our ears –
> Black drizzling crags that spake by the wayside
> As if a voice were in them – the sick sight
> And giddy prospect of the raving stream,
> The unfettered clouds and region of the heavens,
> Tumult and peace, the darkness and the light,

> Were all like workings of one mind, the features
> Of the same face, blossoms upon one tree,
> Characters of the great apocalypse,
> The types and symbols of eternity,
> Of first, and last, and midst, and without end.
> *(Prelude* VI, 218, 556–72)

Writing here is indeed perceived as an act of the creator: 'Characters ... types ... symbols of eternity' are inscribed by God, leaving the writer (and, for that matter, the listener) in limbo.

Hartman, taking his lead from '*A little onward lend thy guiding hand*', a poem Wordsworth wrote for his daughter Dora in 1816 that opens with two lines quoted from Milton's *Samson Agonistes*, describes this situation as one where Wordsworth repeatedly becomes aware of an 'abyss'. Incorporating phrases from Milton's poem in his prose, Hartman suggests that 'Wordsworth's voice has lost, or is always losing, its lyric momentum; formally it is hesitant, disjunctive, "dark steps" over places in nature or scripture aware of the "abrupt abyss" that may, again, open up.' And this in turn brings him to confront the issue as in part one that requires us to return to a consideration of the evolution of the 'long poem'. In the process we encounter Hartman's own recourse to a 'lyric' style when objective critical discourse seems to fail him: 'The result is lyric poetry precariously extended, even *The Prelude's* stumblingly progressive form: a lengthened night music, the residue of a long day's night.'[26] The long poem betokens a precarious lack of unity; it stumbles forward in a fragmentary way, lamenting the poet's exile as it does so, while at the same time it fragments the criticism that seeks to read it.

7

Two Consciousnesses: *The Prelude (2)*

> A tranquillizing spirit presses now
> On my corporeal frame, so wide appears
> The vacancy between me and those days,
> Which yet have such self-presence in my mind
> That sometimes when I think of them I seem
> Two consciousnesses – conscious of myself,
> And of some other being.
>
> > (*Prelude* II, 66, 27–33)

I

The previous chapter has been concerned primarily with exploring how *The Prelude* came to be written, and what the consequences for criticism of that process were. This included taking account of the fact that the poem appeared as a series of proliferating published texts only after the poet's death. Although this chapter will continue to bring forward additional examples from *The Prelude* for discussion, its main purpose is to develop further a consideration of the diversity of critical discourses that confront a reader of *Prelude* texts in our own time. As with the previous chapter, a case continues to be made for suggesting that when Wordsworth described himself in *The Prelude* as a divided being, 'conscious of myself, / And of some other being', he describes a pervasive condition of fragmentation that applies to his readers and critics, and the world in which they live, every bit as much as it applies to his own circumstances.

In an essay of 1988, Ross Woodman applied Geoffrey Hartman's phenomenologist approach to a rigorous deconstructive reading of the so-called 'Arab dream' passage in Book V of *The Prelude*. Lines 49–139 of Book V (1805) tell of a dream described to Wordsworth by a 'friend', in which he meets a Bedouin Arab in the desert. The Arab carries with him a stone and a shell, and proceeds to explain what they signify to his listener. Woodman's technique is to withhold his detailed exposition of the passage until well into the essay, and I will do the same here. Reference to the Book V 'Arab Dream' passage prompts him first to deliver a preliminary discussion on the importance of the 'two consciousnesses' referred to in Book II. The 'two consciousnesses' are best understood, Woodman suggests, as a conflict within the poet's mind between an allegorical and a metaphorical mode of procedure – in other words, the striving to make words connect with phenomena, to 'ground or bury' language 'in time':

> Metaphor operates in a world of Heraclitean flux where the law of perpetual change is the law of life, a world of radical instability, of continuous metamorphosis...Allegory, on the other hand, struggles to arrest and stabilise metaphor by taking it out of the timeless, undifferentiated world.[1]

Woodman (like Hartman and Simpson) is searching for the poet in locations scarcely dreamt of by earlier critics, locations that may still seem to contemporary readers to tend towards the bizarre. Wordsworth's historically located narrative voice only remains as an intensely problematic starting point for this kind of critical analysis, where once it had been a reliable 'given'. Still postponing his discussion of the Arab dream, Woodman turns to a later passage in Book V to explore the fractured persona of the poet. This is Wordsworth's description of the 'Boy of Winander', who stands by the lake as night falls and imitates the hooting of the owls 'That they might answer him':

> And when it chanced
> That pauses of deep silence mocked his skill,
> Then sometimes in that silence, while he hung
> Listening, a gentle shock of mild surprise
> Has carried far into his heart the voice
> Of mountain torrents; or the visible scene
> Would enter unawares into his mind
> With all its solemn imagery, its rocks,
> Its woods, and that uncertain heaven, received
> Into the bosom of the steady lake.

> This boy was taken from his mates, and died
> In childhood ere he was full ten years old.
> (Prelude V, 172–4, 404–15)

Wordsworth describes himself transfixed by the child's grave: 'I believe that oftentimes / A full half-hour together I have stood / Mute, looking at the grave in which he lies' (ll.420–2). For the child the silence would induce 'a gentle shock of mild surprise' in which he heard with his heart 'the voice / Of mountain torrents . . .'; he was reading the characters of nature in the mysterious manner alluded to in the previous chapter. Wordsworth is that same child, rendered dead to the world ('mute') while he communes in spirit with 'the visible scene'. Woodman adopts Hartman's trope of the abyss, along with a good deal of Paul de Man's terminology, to conclude that the poet's creative powers introduce us to 'a metaphysical world of perpetual metamorphosis'; this will continually therefore threaten him with 'annihilation, the presence of nothingness'.[2] The child's 'death' epitomises the struggle between metaphor and allegory which takes place on the edge of 'nothingness'.

Woodman's Wordsworth is an insecure poet with a fragmented consciousness, and the 'Arab dream' of Book V dramatically reveals the consequences of this. The passage uses an account by Descartes of a dream he claimed to have had. A man encounters a Bedouin Arab carrying a stone and a shell, which the Arab describes as two books. One is *Euclid's Elements*, the other is a work of poetry prophesying the end of the world: two consciousnesses indeed! Given the references already noted to the ways in which Wordsworth variously represents writing in *The Prelude* (in particular the 'Characters of the great apocalypse' in Book VI, l.570), it is not surprising to find that *Euclid's Elements* appears as the stone, while the book of poetry is the shell. From the shell comes

> A loud prophetic blast of harmony,
> An ode in passion uttered, which foretold
> Destruction to the children of the earth
> By deluge now at hand.
> (Prelude V, 156, 96–9)

Here we have two consciousnesses leading us to the ultimate abyss, as the Arab flees before 'the waters of the deep / Gathering upon us' (*Prelude* 158, 130–1). For Woodman and Hartman the issues raised here – as elsewhere in Wordsworth's poetry – are essentially linguistic rather than historical. Indeed, in his essay 'Wordsworth Revisited' Hartman is at pains to privilege the significance of 'Nature' over against that of history ('chronology') in the poem.[3]

Other critics have been drawn, frequently from an admiration of Hartman's work, to look further into the relationship between the evolution of Wordsworth's poetry and specific historical events. In 1989 William H. Galperin moved in that direction with a discussion of the revisionary processes that accompanied Wordsworth's method of composition. *The Prelude* of 1799–1800, he suggests, 'immediately deconstructed the very self it promoted'. Later versions of the poem were written to avoid the 'gulf' that threatened to 'negotiate passage *to* self-enclosure'.[4] This discussion edges us towards a more historically located account of Wordsworth's sense of exclusion, and how he attempts to reinstate himself imaginatively in a language of nature that can sublimate the trauma of his involvement with revolutionary politics (what Galperin describes as achieving 'self-enclosure').

Alan Liu's *Wordsworth: The Sense of History* was published in the same year as Galperin's book. He, too, employs the notion of Wordsworth as a poet poised at the edge of an abyss, threatened by a madness comparable to that of the Arab in the dream. Liu historicises the text by suggesting that the Arab dream parallels the passage in Book X where the poet, walking on Leven Sands, hears of the death of Robespierre (*Prelude* V, 156, 71–7; X, 384, 474–80). Liu's Wordsworth is suppressing an uncomfortable historical and political narrative, blocking it out with his own presence. In the process, history is converted into myth: 'The myth is a story of deluge followed by lyric peace . . . Wordsworth's shapeless eagerness is the very genius of transform allowing him at last to deny the deluge of revolution – to recover the antediluvian Loire he knew firsthand in 1792 and to prophecy the postdiluvian zone at Leven Sands.'[5] 'Shapeless eagerness' (a phrase to be found at the beginning of Book IX, line 11) is how Liu characterises the structure of the French Revolution Books of *The Prelude* (IX and X, 1805). It encapsulates for him the way the poet (in eighteenth-century long poem mode) sets about refiguring 'the whole story of history' as 'passages of utterly lyric peace'. The process involves the process of transforming the apocalyptic theme of the Arab dream into the joyful revelation of Leven Sands. Narration and description, Liu argues, are reformulated 'into inward-looking mythos and rhetoric respectively'.[6] The climax of this process, he believes, is to be found in the account of the crossing of the Alps in Book VI. The matter of Book V is completed by the Book VI sequence, which then also instructs us how to read the French Revolution Books which eventually follow.

More recently, Keith Hanley has endorsed the view that Wordsworth was unable to embark on the subject of the French Revolution until he had established a strategy by which he could reinscribe what in political terms was a singularly inglorious phase of his life. In Book VI, Hanley writes:

> The pursuit of the imagination was at last bringing Wordsworth face to face with his revolutionary trauma, revealing both the origin of his discursive alienation and his power of relegitimizing it. The result is a containment and shaping of his Revolutionary history that will enable him to imagine it . . . as the correction of rival British and French usurpations in his historical society by the legitimate power of the imaginary subject.

He goes on to remind us that Wordsworth went on to write Books IX and X after completing Book VI. It was in Book VI that 'the ascendancy of imaginary subjectivity' is established; history is now recast as part of that personal drama.[7]

II

Wordsworth's description of the experience he had when crossing the Alps in 1790 while he was still a student, remains one of the most visited passages of *The Prelude*. He was on a walking tour with a fellow student, Robert Jones, and the two men had become separated from their travelling companions as they approached the Simplon Pass. They arrived at a point where the track they thought they wanted made its way up the mountainside opposite them. Before long they discover that they had already crossed the Alps, and must retrace their steps, and travel downwards. The last thing well-prepared travellers of this era would expect would be to discover that the high point of their crossing had passed unnoticed; both men would confidently have expected an uplifting, sublime *frisson*. The anticlimax results in a 'dull and heavy slackening'; the mind is swept clean of any anticipated excitement (*Prelude* VI, 218, 549). Wordsworth and Jones then headed downward from the Simplon through the Vale of Gondo into the unknown. In the course of this downward path – a path that contradicts the direction they had gone with high hopes of a revelatory experience – Wordsworth describes a visionary experience that defies Guide Book etiquette, and even, it seems, the laws of nature:

> The immeasurable height
> Of woods decaying, never to be decayed,
> The stationary blasts of waterfalls,
> And everywhere along the hollow rent
> Winds thwarting winds...
> (ll.556–60)

Liu suggests that the passage has become 'one of a handful of paradigms capable by itself of representing the poet's work'.[8] This is because we are concerned with a moment when Wordsworth has relegated 'history' to insignificance. Book VI had begun with history in the foreground: Wordsworth arrived in France on July 13th 'on the very eve / Of that great federal day' (ll.356–7). Following the fall of the Bastille and the King's agreement to a revised constitution, a grand Fête de la Fédération was celebrated across the country on July 15th. Initially the poet is governed by a sentimental commitment to the idea of Revolution. This has been acquired from influences outside him; political and cultural forces dominate his individual imaginative capacity and both men are depicted as engaging with the Revolution as voyeuristic tourists:

> In this blithe company
> We landed, took with them our evening meal,
> Guests welcome almost as the angels were
> To Abraham of old.
> (ll.401–4)

As the narrative of Book VI proceeds, however, the poet gradually asserts his authority over events until his imaginative powers seem completely to overwhelm the course of history, banishing not only the mundane historical narrative of the Revolution, but also the identity of the poet himself as an eager, acquisitive tourist. With France put literally behind him, and the descent of the Vale of Gondo before him, the imagination enters as a force from an unknown, unwritten world. It robs Wordsworth (and Book VI) of the structures of an historically ordered narrative. This is the Wordsworth who is now therefore described as 'thwarted', 'lost' and 'halted'; there has been a 'usurpation' by an 'invisible world' culminating in the revelation that

> Our destiny, our nature, and our home,
> Is with infinitude – and only there;
> With hope it is, hope that can never die,
> Effort, and expectation, and desire,
> And something evermore about to be.
> (ll.538–42)

That 'something evermore about to be' explains why Liu can claim that 'History is denied, and "I" engenders itself autogenetically as the very crown of what I have called objectified subjectivity: a mind knowing itself only in the impersonal – "strong in *it*self".'[9] The phrase quoted at the end of Liu's statement comes a few lines on from the passage quoted above, where the emphasis is on imaginative self-sufficiency.

Liu's reading enacts a psychoanalysis of the text, and he concludes that history is being 'screened' from view because it is too painful for the poet to deal with. The 'narrative' of such a poem for Liu constitutes Wordsworth's engagement with history. The Arab dream of Book V with its apocalyptic references is thus read alongside crossing the Alps in Book VI; Books IX and X are written to reconstruct (or 'screen') the realities of Wordsworth's experience and conduct during the Revolution. The link is therefore made (as we have already seen) between the Arab dream and the description of the moment on Leven Sands where Wordsworth hears of the death of Robespierre. Liu argues that in such passages we are able to see how the poet absorbs the historical process into himself; he 'captures it within his own orbit', thereby subjecting it to his imaginative will. The end result is 'that the whole story of history has been folded into passages of utterly lyric peace'.[10]

The final Books of the 1805 text (XI to XIII) then proceed to establish an 'ideology of self' from the preceding matter; this will be a fundamentally conservative ideology, and although (in keeping with its conservatism) it will turn from history to religion, that religion will be of a deeply earth-bound kind. Liu writes of the three final books:

> As such mounting religiosity prophesies, Wordsworth's culminating ideology of self – his great denial of history – will indeed be apocalyptic in the old, high sense. But what sense in particular?

What final doctrine or formalized ideology of transcendence will the Imaginative self choose to invest? This we may take to be the function of Books 11–13 in *The Prelude*: to impose not only a natural limit on Imagination, as Hartman has argued, but also a supernatural limit aligned with the deepest traditions of religious doctrine. The official spots of time in Book 11 address themselves to the task by indoctrinating the Imagination in a regime of nature identical with God.[11]

III

Liu's work is representative of a considerable number of critics (including McGann, Levinson, Simpson and Hanley), all of whom in various ways have been concerned to historicise Hartman. They have analysed Wordsworth's relationship to history, and considered how that relationship constitutes the subject of *The Prelude*. Two relatively recent books, Gary Harrison's *Wordsworth's Vagrant Muse: Poetry, Property and Power* (1994), and Celeste Langan's *Romantic Vagrancy: Wordsworth and the Simulation of Freedom* (1995), do this by setting the politically provocative issue of vagrancy and the socially ubiquitous phenomenon of the wanderer alongside *The Prelude*, and exploring the relationships that emerge between text and historical evidence.

Langan links the repeatedly halted progress of the poem's narrative to her perception of history as similarly 'interrupted' by the poet. In this way she suggests a link between Wordsworth's interrupted journey in Book IV where he encounters the discharged soldier, and the 'interruptive aspect of the apostrophe to imagination in book VI' (crossing the Alps).[12] The consequence is a triumph of imagination over objective perception. Gary Harrison looks at images of poverty and vagrancy in Wordsworth's early poetry, using (among other examples) *The Prelude* to draw attention to the way realistic description began later to be modified in keeping with Wordsworth's perception of his own persona as a poet. Harrison notes, for example, a twitch given to the lines from Book I 1805, 'So, like a peasant, I pursued my road / Beneath the evening sun' (*Prelude* I, 34, 110–11). This was altered to become more respectable by 1850: 'so, like a home-bound labourer...' (*Prelude* I, 35, 101). At some point between 1801 and 1850 the image of the unattached 'peasant' was replaced by that of the domesticated 'home-bound labourer'.[13] This line of criticism has not always been well received because the critic may be seen as colluding with the historical suppression he or she is describing. Annette

Vallon, the landmark in Wordsworth's history he was most anxious to obliterate, the mother of his illegitimate child left behind in France in 1792, is certainly not ignored by Liu; but in describing how the poet's negotiation of a 'private peace' with Annette ran in tandem with his country's negotiation of the Peace of Amiens with France in 1802, Liu does indeed seem to be employed in removing her from the critic's view, even as Wordsworth excises her from his text. By no means all critics have been happy to allow themselves to be appropriated by the poetry to this extent.

In her essay 'Sex and History in *The Prelude* (1805): Books IX to XIII', Gayatri Chakravorty Spivak begins her explanation of what Wordsworth is attempting in the poem by describing what she sees as his need 'to exorcise his illegitimate paternity' and 'to re-establish himself sexually in order to declare his imagination restored'. This is an overtly feminist reading, rigorously attached to a neo-Freudian analysis:

> in these books of *The Prelude*, one may find textual signs of a rejection of paternity, of a reinstatement of the subject as son (rather than father) within Oedipal law, and then, through imagination, a claim to androgyny.

There are also parallels with new historicist interpretation in Spivak's argument that 'Wordsworth...seems more interested at this point in transcending or coping with rather than declaring history...'.[14] But as much as anything, it is Spivak's refusal to indulge in any kind of homage to the 'great poet' that marks her out as different from Liu. She sees an objectionable ego at work rather than a romantic poet, and therefore suggests that reference to the French Revolution in *The Prelude* takes place primarily to display the extent that it can be shown to have moulded the poetic gifts of William Wordsworth. Everything Wordsworth puts into *The Prelude* justifies its inclusion to the extent that it contributes towards the creation of its author as a poetic genius.

Spivak's agenda extends well beyond Wordsworth and *The Prelude*. The poem is seen to epitomise male-dominated critical practice that persists to the present day, a practice most notably enshrined in the concept of a literary 'Great Tradition' associated with the criticism of F. R. Leavis (Leavis's *The Great Tradition* was first published in 1948). Spivak's response to Wordsworth's attitude to the politics of the French Revolution is far less sympathetic than that of any of the critics considered so far. She reflects (like Langan) on the way the historical narrative is repeatedly interrupted, suggesting that this is indicative of his failure properly to understand what was involved. Spivak's Wordsworth is politically uninformed, chauvinist, and intellectually sly. In the end, however, he still resembles the Wordsworth of Liu, Galperin, Simpson and Hanley in so far as he replaces history with myth created around the imaginative autonomy he claims: 'Wordsworth's solution is to disavow historical or genealogical production and attempt to gain control through a private allusive positing of resemblance for which he himself remains the authority and the source'; in short he uses parallel texts ('allusive positing'), specifically Milton, Dion, Plato, Eudemus, and Timonides.[15]

Once we remove the ironic, feminist rhetoric within which Spivak frames her critique, it is possible to identify affinities with Hartman in her discussion of the way the poetry is controlled by 'a private allusive positing of resemblance', and its use of 'parallel texts'. This is Hartman (a passage already alluded to in the previous chapter) on Wordsworth's use of Milton in '*A little onward lend thy guiding hand*':

> Wordsworth's voice has lost, or is always losing, its lyric momentum; formally it is hesitant, disjunctive, 'dark steps' over places in nature or scripture aware of the 'abrupt abyss' that may, again, open up.
>
> It is Wordsworth's own writ, his own poem, that should be disclosed, yet by a fate for which the word Oedipal is appropriate, an oracular 'Discourse of the Other' interposes, one that involves the relation of child and parent, or younger poet and elder. Reacting to these inner 'passions' Wordsworth projects nature as something that speaks 'rememberable things', as something that textualises phantom voice: perhaps 'the ghostly language of the ancient earth', perhaps the language of dream image and phrase. The result is lyric poetry precariously extended, even *The Prelude's* stumblingly progressive form: a lengthened night music, the residue of a long day's night.[16]

Hartman reminds us of the way historicist critics call attention to the hesitancy of Wordsworth's progress, to the 'phantom voice' that the poet seeks to emulate, to the way in which he consequently seems to totter on the edge of an abyss, and to the way he has recourse to allusion, creating an egocentric myth in order to achieve progress (a 'stumblingly progressive form'). While this coincides with Spivak's analysis, it does not share her hawkish determination to expose the poet as an unredeemed reactionary. She strategically counters the philosophical and psychoanalytic rhetoric used to investigate Wordsworth's pursuit of a new language for poetry with a lengthy quote from Marx's 'The Eighteenth Brumaire of Louis Bonaparte'. Wordsworth conducts his own version of class war as he appropriates, revises, and controls the discourse of revolution the better to pursue his own egocentric male agenda. The language of revolution never becomes truly his; he is ' "the beginner who has learned a new language" '; he can therefore only ' "retranslate it into his mother tongue" '. Spivak concludes: 'A new and unknown language has been thrust upon William Wordsworth. Even as its elements are being explained to him, he engages in a bizarre "re-translation" into the old.'[17]

IV

In 'Splitting the Race of Man in Twain': Prostitution, Personification, and *The Prelude*' (1989) Mary Jacobus is, like Spivak, concerned to expose the underlying ideological prejudices of a dominant critical tradition in Wordsworth scholarship. The pivotal name is yet again Geoffrey Hartman, and it seems he walked right into this one:

> 'Every Jack will have his Jill.' With what he calls 'This utopian and "romantic" proverb', Geoffrey Hartman begins a gnomic essay 'On the Theory of Romanticism'. An authorised gloss might run: 'Every intellectual desire will finally find its scholastic fulfilment.' The role of woman (Jill) is to put man (Jack) in possession of his desire. High Romantic critical quests might be said to have been waylaid by this enchanting and discriminatory plot . . . the metaphoric consummation or spousal union of masculine mind and feminine nature haunts A. O. Lovejoy's Romantic heirs, giving M. H. Abrams's shaping narrative its underlying form (that of the History of Ideas) and lingering on in Hartman's 'romantic' proverb.[18]

Earlier in the previous chapter *The Prelude* was described as a poem written from exile. Jacobus is also concerned with exile, but her interest in this respect is with *The Prelude* as an environment where the poet is very much at home and in evidence, while it is 'Romantic Woman' who is rendered 'outcast'. The traditional theme of exile is given a radical Marxist Feminist twist of the kind to be found, for example, in John Barrell's essay on the function of Dorothy Wordsworth in 'Tintern Abbey' and in L. Kramer's 'Gender and Sexuality in *The Prelude*', as well as in Spivak's work.[19] Jacobus concentrates on Book VII (1805), and in particular on Wordsworth's account of Mary Robinson, the 'Maid of Buttermere', in order to argue that Wordsworth's response to sexual difference is a pervasive influence on *The Prelude* as a whole.

In Book VII Wordsworth recalls his impressions of London during the period after he completed his BA in January 1791. Among the plays he saw was *Edward and Susan, or The Beauty of Buttermere*:

> a story drawn
> From our own ground, the Maid of Buttermere,
> And how the spoiler came, 'a bold man'
> To God unfaithful, children, wife, and home,
> And wooed the artless daughter of the hills,
> And wedded her, in cruel mockery
> Of love and marriage bonds. O friend, I speak
> With tender recollection of that time
> When first we saw the maiden, then a name
> By us unheard of – in her cottage-inn
> Were welcomed, and attended on by her,
> Both stricken with one feeling of delight,
> An admiration of her modest mien
> And carriage, marked by unexampled grace.
> (*Prelude* VII, 242–4, 321–34)

The narrative now receives one of its characteristic interruptions as Wordsworth goes on to reflect on the fact that he and Robinson shared a childhood in the same landscape, 'we were nursed... / On the same mountains' (ll.342–3). He then continues:

> She lives in peace
> Upon the spot where she was born and reared;
> Without contamination does she live
> In quietness, without anxiety.
> Beside the mountain chapel sleeps in earth
> Her new-born infant, fearless as a lamb
> That thither comes from some unsheltered place
> To rest beneath the little rock-like pile
> When storms are blowing. Happy are they both,
> Mother and child!
> (ll.351–60)

Here Jacobus recalls the 'Boy of Winander' passage of Book V, another case of infant mortality. The child's death there arguably fixes his identity (and the poet's) in an innocent, pre-sexual past. The death of Mary Robinson's child, Jacobus argues, 'tranquillises her unquiet life':

> allowing her to stand in for the purified, pre-sexual, Lake District poet (himself, one might note, the parent of an 'unfathered' child). This hushing up of the sexual drama is effected by making Mary no longer – or again not yet – a mother, still emphatically the *Maid of Buttermere*.[20]

There is an abundance of material here for a Freudian critic like Jacobus to deconstruct, and she pursues her analysis into the next section of the Book, where our attention is drawn to 'two figures':

> one
> A rosy babe, who for a twelvemonth's space
> Perhaps had been of age to deal about
> Articulate prattle, child as beautiful
> As ever sate upon a mother's knee;
> The other was the parent of that babe –
> But on the mother's cheek the tints were false,
> A painted bloom.
> (*Prelude* VII, 244–6, 367–74)

What strikes the poet is the aura of innocence the child brings to the company of 'dissolute men / And shameless women' (ll.387–8). Though he does not kill this infant off, in the interests of preserving his purity ('Like one of those who walked with hair unsinged / Amid the fiery furnace', ll.398–9), Wordsworth arrests his development in time, the vocabulary suggesting a life-in-death existence:

> He hath since
> Appeared to me ofttimes as if embalmed
> By Nature – through some special privilege
> Stopped at the growth he had – destined to live,
> To be, to have been, come, and go, a child
> And nothing more . . .
> (ll.399–404)

Entry into adult life is denied, a process achieved by destroying the child and banishing the adult, identified here as the fallen woman. Wordsworth claims he can scarcely remember the mother of the beautiful child seen at the theatre. Jacobus explains: 'The reason why the mother is scarcely remembered...is that she has been cast out...so that Wordsworth can throw in his lot with the "embalmed" and separate self figured by the beautiful boy. In order to save the boy, Wordsworth has to get rid of the mother.'[21] Jacobus concludes that Wordsworth's overwhelming desire is for 'single-ness', and she points to the influence in this respect of Milton's *Samson Agonistes* on the composition of Book VII. It is a case of what Spivak described as the 'private allusive positing of resemblance':

> The *locus classicus* for the depiction of a fall from and recovery of this singling, God-given, and above all masculine strength-in-silence is *Samson Agonistes*, which Romantic poets, including Wordsworth, tended to read as Milton's spiritual autobiography.[22]

Drawing on the work of Jim Swan, Jacobus suggests a parallel between Samson, whose strength lies not in his hair, but in his silence, and Wordsworth. Once betrayed into speech by Dalila, Samson falls, and is portrayed by Milton as feminised. This anxiety about a 'fall into language' has been met with repeatedly before. What Jacobus claims is that Wordsworth genders the divide. The woman is cast out as prostitute; the voice of the fallen is feminine, the voice of the chosen is male. The Romantic (male) poet is separated out as destined to inhabit 'the archaic space of the paternal Logos'. So this brings us back to that first creative word of God described in the fourth Gospel, only in Jacobus's reading, while the poet is pointing us in that direction, he himself is dishonestly seeking 'an illicit intercourse with the painted bloom of sin'.[23] Which is to say that across the channel Annette Vallon and her daughter Caroline are still embarrassingly alive and well and abandoned by Wordsworth along with Revolutionary France.

V

Despite the power of psychoanalysis in penetrating the inner workings of the text, a process which reveals a poet engaged in exiling and excising others in order that he might survive, the end result – with Samson still in mind – is to observe an isolated, if not literally exiled, poet, even if he is, as Jacobus memorably describes him, 'the

spoiled brat of *The Prelude*.'[24] Both Spivak and Jacobus historicise
the situation in Marxist terms, echoing what Marxist Romanticists
have said from E. P. Thompson, through to Raymond Williams,
John Barrell, John Lucas and others, about a fundamental fudging
that occurs when Wordsworth contemplates the outcast and his or
her failure to be involved in 'productive labour', and what he says
about the means by which their lot might be judged. Spivak writes:

> Within the historical situation of the late eighteenth century, to offer
> only poetry as the means of changing this definition of 'productive' is
> class-bound and narrow. Since it denies the reality of exploitation, it
> need conceive of no struggle.... Wordsworth's choice of the rural
> solitary as theme, then, is an ideologically symptomatic move in
> answer to a critical question about political economy.[25]

However you come at it, it seems, Wordsworth remains exiled
from the realities of political revolution. In the final Book of *The
Prelude* we are taken into Wales, and then on a trek to the summit
of Mount Snowdon for the poem's final moment of truth. Yet again
the poet stands alone before returning to his small circle of friends
to summarise at length how it is he must remain (as Jacobus would
have it) in a state of 'singleness':

> Here must thou be, O man,
> Strength to thyself – no helper hast thou here –
> Here keepest thou thy individual state:
> No other can divide with thee this work,
> No secondary hand can intervene
> To fashion this ability.
>
> (*Prelude* XIII, 468, 188–93)

In the summer of 1791 Wordsworth and Robert Jones arranged to
be taken by a guide to the summit of Snowdon in the early hours of
the morning to witness the sunrise. The description of the climb emphasises the move upward, away from what is perceived as earth-
bound towards what should surely be a spiritually uplifting
experience: 'With forehead bent / Earthward, as if in opposition
set / Against an enemy, I panted up...' (*Prelude* XIII, 458, 29–31).
The expedition matches that of crossing the Alps. Here, however,
there is no space allowed for the moment of anti-climax that was
such an important ingredient of Book VI. Before he realises what is
happening, Wordsworth steps from the cloud into a moonlit scene

on the summit. His intention has been to rise as far above the earth as
he can, but without warning, he finds himself standing at what would
seem to be the lowest point possible: 'on the shore / I found myself of a
huge sea of mist'; and he is then drawn deeper still than that:

> and from the shore
> At distance not the third part of a mile
> Was a blue chasm, a fracture in the vapour,
> A deep and gloomy breathing-place, through which
> Mounted the roar of waters, torrents, steams
> Innumerable, roaring with one voice.
> (*Prelude* XIII, 460, 54–9)

The profundity of the experience is in direct proportion to the
degree to which it represents a reversal, a thwarting, a contradiction of everything that Wordsworth had been expecting.

Most critics have read this episode as intending to provide a final,
triumphant statement of the way in which the sovereignty of the
Imagination has been dramatically restored to the mind of the poet.
What he claims to have seen is 'The perfect image of a mighty
mind': an image of the mind of God. It 'feeds upon infinity' and
is 'exalted by an under-presence' (ll.66–71). We are to understand
that it is the under-presence, the moonlit prospect, that presents
Wordsworth with the image of that 'mighty mind'. So the quest for
the sun (by now entirely forgotten) was an ill-conceived venture; it
is the 'under-presence' that conveys 'The sense of God' (l.72). This
is a 'Resemblance', 'a genuine counterpart', a 'brother' of that which
exceeds all; we should note that these words all speak of equiva-
lents; they might be thought of as parallel texts, not the ur-text
itself. That ur-text remains beyond the realm of language: call it the
Logos, an 'ur-fiat', the first cause, God (ll.87–90). To approach this
mind ('The sense of God') is to approach the abyss; or perhaps it is
just to approach an extraordinarily complicated way of screening
out historical/biographical material it would be too painfully destructive to articulate. It certainly becomes clear that what would
raise us up may also thrust us down, back into this earth. The
Simplon Pass followed by the Vale of Gondo has prepared us for
this, as have all the spots of time and numerous other incidents.
There is a conviction in these lines that the poet has come near to
the presence of God; but what was true of the Lake District as Eden
in Books I and II has remained true of all the spots of time subsequently. The serpent also is there: the drowned man rises from the

depths of Esthwaite, 'mid that beauteous scene / Of trees and hills and water...a spectre shape – / Of terror even' (*Prelude* V, 176, 470–3). On Penrith Beacon a spirit of 'visionary dreariness' materialises that defies description except in its manifestation as the 'ordinary sight' of a woman walking close to the site of a gibbet-mast (*Prelude* XI, 430–2, 278–327).

The ecstatic joy of entry into bliss is inescapably coupled with the stern rhetoric of exclusion. The poet climbs in vain; he is destined to be brought low:

> Oh, who is he that hath his whole life long
> Preserved, enlarged, this freedom in himself? –
> For this alone is genuine liberty.
> Witness, ye solitudes, where I received
> My earliest visitations (careless then
> Of what was given me), and where now I roam,
> A meditative, oft a suffering man,
> And yet I trust with undiminished powers ...
> (*Prelude* XIII, 464, 120–7)

As Hartman writes, very much in keeping with his roots in phenomenology, Wordsworth is made to 'stand in time once more'. Snowdon is 'a vision of mastery, though a peculiar one';[26] it marks the humanising, the grounding, of Wordsworth's imagination. If he is in Paradise, he is being shown the door marked 'Exit'.

The Prelude is about unfinished business, a home-coming yet to be accomplished, poetry as yet unwritten. For Garrod, therefore, Book XII proved unsatisfactory in a way that subsequent commentators have had little difficulty dealing with:

> We have followed, in close detail, the process by which Wordsworth was 'turned away from Nature' by the 'outward accidents' of the Revolution, and the further process of alienation induced by a false philosophy. . . . But neither Wordsworth himself, nor external sources, suffice to enable us to trace in similar detail the process of restoration and reconcilement. Wordsworth's account of it, in the last books of the *Prelude*, is at once diffuse and uninforming. It may be doubted whether in the indications which he furnishes he is always quite consistent with himself, and towards a chronology of the process of restoration he contributes nothing.[27]

For later critics, it is the indeterminacy of Wordsworth's closure that makes *The Prelude* a seminal text (or series of texts) in the

Romantic canon. William H. Galperin illustrates this when he considers the relationship of the Druid Elders, seen by the poet in a vision on Salisbury Plain in Book XII, to the Snowdon passage of Book XIII. In the latter, 'the poet finds himself, like the teachers on Sarum, between heaven and earth'.[28] Despite the apparent certainty of the rhetoric, Wordsworth, like his long poem, remains incomplete, inconclusive, interrupted, 'between heaven and earth' looking to write the poem that never will be written, *The Recluse*.

Impressive as much of the scholarship is that has been lavished on *The Prelude*, the most interesting consequences of such work may well be not so much what we have discovered about *The Prelude* since the 1920s, as what *The Prelude* has discovered about us. We have engaged with the fragmentary nature of the text; with its habit of dismembering biographical certainties; with its ability to conceal as much as it reveals; and with the way in which it has defined its late-twentieth-century readers as 'exiles' every bit as much as its latter day readers have tended to read its author as a poet in exile. It has become a paradigmatic statement of the indeterminacy of textuality, and of the pervasive insistence of intertextuality and performativity. As the shards of text revolve before us in no set order, we see ourselves reflected several times over: Historicists, Freudians, Jungians, post-Berlin-Wall Marxists, post-Modernists of various persuasions, textual scholars, all readers responding to a poem refracted through a continual flow of printed and virtual critical material celebrating the many poems prefaced by the one tentative, preliminary title provided by its author, 'Growth of a Poet's Mind'.

Like Wordsworth himself, our interest in these texts is defined by a sense of their, and our, incompleteness. So we carry on where he left off, endlessly tinkering with it, content now that it never will be 'complete'.

8

A Choice of Texts, a Choice of Wordsworths: Reading *The Excursion* Over Two Centuries

> Those fervent raptures are for ever flown;
> And, since their date, my soul hath undergone
> Change manifold, for better or for worse:
> Yet cease I not to struggle, and aspire
> Heavenward...
> (*The Excursion* Book IV, ll.123–7, in *PW* 5, p. 113)

I

In *The Spirit of the Age* William Hazlitt memorably described *The Excursion* as falling 'stillborn from the press'.[1] Five hundred copies had been printed in 1814; little more than half of them had been sold by the end of the year. By comparison, Byron's *The Corsair*, also published in 1814, sold 10,000 copies on the day it came out. Wordsworth had certainly made a name for himself as a poet; he had maintained and enlarged a coterie following, but as *The Excursion* made very clear, he was not a commercially successful poet. In 1814 some readers may have had a knowledge of *An Evening Walk* and *Descriptive Sketches*, but most will have known of him solely as the author of *Lyrical Ballads* and *Poems in Two Volumes*. *Lyrical Ballads* had established its place on the shelves of most well-stocked libraries in the course of the first decade of the nineteenth century. Its success can be measured by the fact that Longman's were prepared to set up a print run of 1000 copies of *Poems in Two Volumes* in 1807. Such was the critical drubbing handed out to the 1807 collection, however, that 230 copies still remained unsold when *The Excursion*, a poem in nine books, first appeared in August 1814.

The fact was that the reading public remained unclear what kind of a poet Wordsworth was, a point made by Charles Lamb in the review of *The Excursion* he wrote for the *Quarterly Review*. The piece was heavily edited by the *Quarterly's* editor, William Gifford. Wordsworth's poetry, it was conceded, was not widely popular; the reason proffered was 'the boldness and originality' of the poet's 'genius':

> The times are past when a poet could securely follow the direction of his own mind into whatever tracts it might lead. A writer, who would be popular, must timidly coast the shore of prescribed sentiment and sympathy.[2]

Hazlitt, writing in *The Examiner* in 1814, accused Wordsworth of an inability to produce a poem properly fitted to his intentions and skills:

> if the skill with which the poet had chosen his materials had been equal to the power which he has undeniably exerted over them – if the objects (whether persons or things) which he makes use of as the vehicle of his sentiments had been such as to convey them to all their depth and force, then the production before us might indeed 'have proved a monument' as he himself wishes it, worthy of the author and his country.[3]

Most contemporary reviewers tended to agree that it was difficult to be sure how *The Excursion* should be read, and how its poet should be categorised. Josiah Conder, looking to be generally supportive in the *Eclectic Review* of 1815, reflected the general sense of confusion when it came to assessing the undoubted powers of a somewhat perverse and idiosyncratic poet:

> Corresponding with his originality of mind, he has invented a style more intellectual than that of any of his contemporaries, and in contradiction to his own theory (see the Preface to *Lyrical Ballads*, &c.) as different from the most energetic language of ordinary minds in excitement, as the strain of his argument is elevated above vulgar reasoning.[4]

The critical issues raised by *The Excursion* in 1814 were for the most part very different from the ones familiar to a late-twentieth- and early-twenty-first-century readership. Wordsworth was not known as a writer of long poems; most of his published work came in the form of short pieces, interspersed with the occasional bulky ode and extended narrative poem. The 1802 Preface to *Lyrical Ballads* had established him as a poet with a serious, ambitious and controversial agenda, but there was nothing in his published output to prepare the reader for what had now appeared.

II

The Excursion comprised almost 9000 lines of poetry divided into nine Books. It describes a man, the 'Solitary', who has lost all faith in humanity following personal bereavement, and the subsequent failure of political revolution to bring about a better world. The reader is first introduced to the poet and his mentor in Book I, a reworking of *The Ruined Cottage*. The 'Solitary' makes his appearance in Book II, and from then on we observe the attempt of a small group of friends to cure him of his misanthropy.

The Preface to the poem included an extract from the conclusion of the first part of *The Recluse*; this, it is explained, is the even longer – as yet unfinished – poem of which *The Excursion* forms only the central part. The first paragraph of this extract begins:

> On Man, on Nature, and on Human Life,
> Musing in solitude, I oft perceive
> Fair trains of imagery before me rise,
> Accompanied by feelings of delight
> Pure, or with no unpleasing sadness mixed;
> And I am conscious of affecting thoughts
> And dear remembrances, whose presence soothes
> Or elevates the Mind, intent to weigh
> The good and evil of our mortal state....
>   (*Excursion*, p. 3, 1–9)

The paragraph ends with a quotation from Milton's *Paradise Lost*: 'fit audience let me find though few' (l.23).

The reader of 1814 was thus confronted by a man who aspired to the status of Milton, the most revered religious poet of the seventeenth century. He was a poet determined to do more than merely emulate the writers of long poems that had inhabited the previous century: Alexander Pope, James Thomson, Edward Young, Mark Akenside, James Beattie, William Cowper. His purpose was to address a generation committed to enlarging the nation's political liberties, a generation whose hopes for the future had first been raised, and then dashed by a series of political events that had begun with the American War in the late 1770s, only to end in disaster with the mutation of the French Revolution into a European war driven by a lust for imperial aggrandisement; a mutation for which the reactionary British government was seen by many as in no small way responsible. Unlike his eighteenth-century predecessors, Wordsworth was writing in the shadow of traumatic political and military events, and in sight of fundamental social changes in England accompanied by an agrarian and an industrial revolution. In this, the comparison was to be with Milton, writing *Paradise Lost* in the wake of the collapse of Cromwell's Commonwealth (rather than, say, with Young's *Night Thoughts*, Akenside's *Pleasures of Imagination* or William Cowper's *The Task*).

It was this goal that the author of *Lyrical Ballads* had set himself, with Coleridge's encouragement:

> I wish you would write a poem, in blank verse, addressed to those, who, in consequence of the complete failure of the French Revolution, have thrown up all hopes of the amelioration of mankind, and are sinking into an almost epicurean selfishness, disguising the same under the soft titles of domestic attachment and contempt for visionary *philosophes*.[5]

The Preface of 1814 avoids spelling out any such direct links between the poem and recent events. Wordsworth does little more than state that the *Recluse* project aims to deliver 'a philosophical poem, containing views of Man, Nature, and Society... having for its principal subject the sensations of a poet living in retirement' (*Excursion*, p. 2).

In Book I the reader of 1814 would have recognised without too much difficulty – despite the Miltonic diction – the controversially 'simple' Wordsworth of the *Lyrical Ballads* and the 1807 *Poems*. The central narrator, the fount of all wisdom who defers to the natural world as the medium through which the hand of God might be perceived, and from whence the fortitude might be had to withstand the blows of fate, is the Scottish pedlar already known to us from *The Ruined Cottage*. Progressing to Book II, and the introduction of the character of the 'Solitary', Wordsworth's intentions to address the impact of the course of the French Revolution on British society would have become very clear. What neither readers nor critics of 1814–15 were in a position to do, and what none of them felt obliged even to consider (since the text, it seemed, was still being written), was to go in search of the rest of the poem. The identity of the larger poem has since been the subject of exhaustive research and speculation. De Selincourt's 1949 edition of *The Excursion* included a 'Chronology of the Composition of *The Excursion*', beginning with reference to poetry written in 1795. This information has subsequently been elaborated and threaded into an emerging picture of the poet's ambition to complete *The Recluse*. In 1984 Kenneth R. Johnston produced his seminal study, *Wordsworth and the Recluse*. From this we are to understand that a satisfactory reading of *The Excursion* must take account of the fact that it exists as part of a larger work:

> my conclusion is firm that an epic poem intended as the secular successor to Milton's theodicies, and whose extant sections are longer than *Paradise Lost* and *Paradise Regained* combined, including *The Prelude*, *The Excursion*, 'The Ruined Cottage', 'Home at Grasmere', and several other poems, cannot be dismissed in the illusion that it does not exist or by the misjudgement that it is simply a failure, but deserves full critical consideration in its own right.[6]

This statement is of course predicated upon the existence of a late-twentieth-century readership who have ready access to unpublished fragments demonstrably destined for *The Recluse*, and to the textual revisions that Wordsworth made to later editions of the poem. It is also a readership able to draw on the experience of having read and reflected upon other Romantic 'Epics' from the vantage point of a Modernist-turned-Post-Modernist twentieth and twenty-first century (Johnston cites Shelley's *Prometheus Unbound*, Byron's *Don Juan*, Goethe's *Faust* and Whitman's *Leaves of Grass*).[7]

In this respect the situation now could hardly be more different from the one in 1814. Lamb (in the *Quarterly*) comments on the announcement that *The Excursion* was part of a larger work, but reassures us that it is nevertheless 'not a branch...prematurely plucked from the parent tree to gratify an overhasty appetite for applause; but is, in itself, a complete and legitimate production'.[8] Lamb knew of the genesis of Book I (he refers to 'The Ruined Cottage' by name in the review), and he does allow himself a moment's regret that the 'tale of Margaret' is placed at the beginning of the poem, before the reader is fully acquainted with 'the author's theory'. Before making this point, Lamb has already effectively adjusted the narrative structure of the poem. Having described the Pedlar (now the 'Wanderer'), he largely ignores Book I, moving directly to the matter of Books II and III, the Solitary's character and history, and to the nub of the debate that fuels the poem:

> With this man [the Wanderer], then, in a hale old age, released from the burthen of his occupation, yet retaining much of his active habits, the poet meets, and is by him introduced to a second character [the Solitary] – a sceptic – one who had been partially roused from an overwhelming desolation, brought upon him by the loss of wife and children, by the powerful incitement of hope which the French Revolution in its commencement put forth, but who, disgusted with the failure of all its promises, had fallen back into a laxity of faith and conduct which induced at length a total despondence as to the dignity and final destination of his species . . . .
>
>   The conversations with this person, in which the Wanderer asserts the consolatory side of the question against the darker views of human life maintained by his friend, and finally calls to his assistance the experience of a village priest, the third, or rather the fourth interlocutor (for the poet himself is one), form the groundwork of 'The Excursion'.[9]

This 'groundwork' is what Lamb later refers to as 'the author's theory', expressed through the medium of 'conversations' between the Wanderer, the Solitary, the poet and the village priest. The poem, he explains, is therefore 'of a didactic nature, and not a fable or story'. He is anxious to make it clear that 'it is not wanting in stories of the most interesting kind, – such as the lovers of Cowper and Goldsmith will recognise as something familiar and congenial to them'.[10]

By drawing attention to what should be 'congenial' Lamb seeks to sugar what he knows will prove a somewhat indigestible pill. Hazlitt, as we have seen, had nothing good to say about the poem's mixed format: 'he has chosen to encumber himself with a load of narrative and description, which sometimes hinders the progress and effect of the general reasoning'.[11] Hazlitt, who had himself been on the receiving end of Wordsworth's 'general reasoning' when it came to his standards of personal morality in Grasmere, seized the opportunity to criticise the poet's egotism and mock his pietism:

> An intense intellectual egotism swallows up everything. Even the dialogues introduced in the present volume are soliloquies of the same character, taking three different views of one subject. The recluse, the pastor and the pedlar, are three persons in one poet.[12]

Hazlitt also identifies the origin of Wordsworth's didactic model. It is Plato; and Hazlitt is no great lover of Plato: 'The general and the permanent, like the Platonic ideas, are his only realities.... We ourselves disapprove of these interlocutions between Lucius and Caius as impertinent babbling, where there is no dramatic distinction of character.'[13]

As Hazlitt implies, *The Excursion* is built around a series of disputations in the manner of Platonic dialogue, though much is made of the Lakeland setting and the significance of natural objects as the characters move through the landscape. The reference to Plato is important because it signifies that Wordsworth's sense of affinity with Milton incorporated a political commitment to the Commonwealthman political tradition of the seventeenth century. Plato had become a source of inspiration for Commonwealthman writers and sympathisers from the time of the Civil War on into the eighteenth century, and Wordsworth would have started to become aware of this before leaving Hawkshead School. He was subsequently ably tutored in the tradition by Michel Beaupuy while in France in 1792. Henry Neville's *Plato Redivivus* (1680–1) was a key text in the Commonwealthman canon, and a number of writers made use of the dialogue form, including James Harrington, whose *Valerius and Publicola: Or the true Form of a Popular Commonwealth* was first published in 1659. In *The Prelude* Book IX Wordsworth compares Beaupuy and himself to Plato and Dion (the liberator of Sicily) respectively (*Prelude*, 332, 416). Delivering the Warton Lecture on English Poetry in 1940, J. Crofts explored what he saw as a close affinity between Wordsworth and English poetry of the seventeenth century (adding Traherne to Milton and Marvell). Folcroft Library editions republished this lecture in 1974 at a time when considerable interest was being shown in tracing the links between English Romanticism (specifically as represented by Wordsworth) and seventeenth-century literary culture. Notable here was Zera S. Fink's contribution through the 1940s and 50s ('Wordsworth and the English Republican Tradition' was published in 1948, 'Dion and Wordsworth's Political Thought' in 1952), while in 1959 Caroline Robbins published *The Eighteenth Century Commonwealthman*.[14]

Crofts insists that it is not his business to become involved with 'the position of Wordsworth as a thinker', but for all that it is hard not to notice that the seventeenth-century kindred spirits he unearths are a rare mixture of dissenters: the 'seeker' John Salmon, John Rogers, a 'Fifth Monarchy Man', Rhys Evans, a 'young Welsh prophet', John Bunyan and the 'celebrated "Ranter" Coppe'.[15] In 1965 E. P. Thompson published *The Making of the English Working Class*, the book which drew together so many of these strands of seventeenth-century dissent and the literature they produced, locating their successors in the melting pot of late-eighteenth-century political radicalism and Romanticism. This includes *The Excursion*, with its sense of social and political injustice, its analysis of the French Revolution, and its commentary on the harmful effects of the Industrial Revolution on English society.

III

There were, therefore, plenty of reasons why *The Excursion* might be interpreted by its first readers as potentially a subversive text. Critical work on it during the twentieth century used hindsight and scholarly enquiry to illustrate what was already apparent (but rarely openly stated) to many readers in 1814. When Lamb assures us we will recognise something of Cowper and Goldsmith in the work, he is trying to do more than make a potentially tedious read sound attractive. He is doing his best to play down the religious nonconformity that so clearly marks the poet's writing about nature. The moment Lamb turns (as he eventually must) to Wordsworth as a poet of nature, it is hard for him to avoid commenting on what he knows may prove offensive: 'To a mind constituted like that of Mr. Wordsworth, the stream, the torrent, and the stirring leaf – seem not merely to suggest associations of deity, but to be a kind of speaking communication with it.' The implications of pantheism carry with them implications of dissident political views, and this is later admitted when Lamb refers to a discernible spirit of 'liberal Quakerism' and 'Natural Methodism' in the poem.[16]

Lamb and Gifford were uncomfortably aware of what Francis Jeffrey was going to object to in *The Excursion*, though not even they probably guessed at how ferocious the attack would be when it came. Much of Lamb's review is in consequence defensive, even apologetic, attempting to second guess Jeffrey's arguments. When it was time to offer (almost) unconditional praise, however, Lamb anticipated the judgement of many subsequent readers and reviewers in his choice of Book IV, 'Despondency Corrected':

> For moral grandeur; for wide scope of thought and a long train of lofty imagery; for tender personal appeals; and a *versification* which we feel we ought to notice, but feel it also so involved in the poetry, that we can hardly mention it as a distinct excellence; it stands without competition among our didactic and descriptive verse. The general tendency of the argument (which we might almost affirm to be the leading moral of the poem) is to abate the pride of the calculating *understanding*, and to reinstate the *imagination* and the *affections* in those seats from which modern philosophy has laboured but too successfully to expel them.[17]

Writing in the *Eclectic Review* about the same Book, James Montgomery found himself impressed, but with reservations: 'We do not mean to infer, that Mr. Wordsworth excludes from his system the salvation of man, as revealed in the Scriptures, but it is evident that he has not made "Jesus Christ the chief corner-stone" of it.'[18]

The section of Book IV to which Montgomery and Lamb are referring seems to suggest that primitive religion, as an expression of deeply felt spirituality, is far preferable – no matter how barbaric it might appear to the modern observer – to what all too frequently constitutes current religious practice:

> The repetitions wearisome of sense,
> Where soul is dead, and feeling hath no place;
> Where knowledge, ill begun in cold remark
> On outward things, with formal inference ends...
> Meanwhile, the heart within the heart, the seat
> Where peace and happy consciousness should dwell,
> On its own axis restlessly revolving,
> Seeks, yet can nowhere find, the light of truth.
> (*Excursion* IV, 128, 620–30)

Better by far, the Wanderer argues, the idolatry of the ancient Greeks. At least they possessed a sincerity rarely discovered in the present; and, he suggests, their primitive rituals promoted a spirituality equally rare in early-nineteenth-century Christianity:

> The lively Grecian, in a land of hills,
> Rivers and fertile plains, and sounding shores, –

Under a cope of sky more variable,
Could find commodious place for every God,
Promptly received, as prodigally brought,
From the surrounding countries, at the choice
Of all adventurers . . .
                              . . . in despite
Of the gross fictions chanted in the streets
By wandering Rhapsodists; and in contempt
Of doubt and bold denial hourly urged
Amid the wrangling schools – a SPIRIT hung,
Beautiful region! O'er thy towns and farms,
Statues and temples, and memorial tombs,
And emanations were perceived; and acts
Of immortality, in Nature's course,
Exemplified by mysteries, that were felt
As bonds, on grave philosopher imposed
And armèd warrior . . .

                              (ll.718–42)

Lamb's chief anxiety, however, appears to have been that the poem stubbornly refused to compromise on the one aspect of Wordsworth's 'system' that had resulted in the most bruising critical assaults, 'simplicity'. The Solitary responds dismissively to the Wanderer's description of Primitive religious enthusiasm: 'Is it well to trust / Imagination's light when reason's fails?' he asks (*Excursion* IV, 133, 771–2). The Wanderer reminds him that he has, in the past, answered his own question when in conversation with him:

                    Your voice
Hath, in my hearing, often testified
That poor men's children, they, and they alone,
By their condition taught, can understand
The wisdom of the prayer that daily asks
For daily bread . . .
The Shepherd-lad, that in the sunshine carves,
On the green turf, a dial – to divide
The silent hours; and who to that report
Can portion out his pleasures, and adapt,
Throughout a long and lonely summer's day
His round of pastoral duties, is not left
With less intelligence for *moral* things
Of gravest import.

                              (ll.784–807)

This is the appeal to simplicity, and Lamb knew only too well that it was impossible to defend Wordsworth's choice of a pedlar for his chief narrator against the objections Jeffrey would raise. Reference to *Piers Plowman* and Robert Burns as worthy predecessors were unlikely to cut any ice, and it is not difficult to see that the final bizarre sentence of his piece was written in a mood of desperation: 'After all, if there should be found readers willing to admire the poem, who yet feel scandalized at a *name*, we would advise them, wherever it occurs, to substitute silently the word *Palmer* or *Pilgrim*, or any less offensive designation, which shall connect the notion of sobriety in heart and manners with the experience and privileges which a wayfaring life confers.'[19]

One month after Lamb's *Quarterly* review Francis Jeffrey of the *Edinburgh Review* set himself to blow *The Excursion* and its author out of the water. He began by referring to Wordsworth's 'peculiar system' (essentially the 'simplicity' discussed in the Preface to *Lyrical Ballads* which Jeffrey read as a covert reference to a subversive political agenda); he then moved on to the issue of length (the impending *Recluse* prompts him to refer ironically to *The Excursion* – 'four hundred and twenty good quarto pages' – as a 'small specimen'); he considered the poet's tendency to mysticism, and then ridiculed his determination to live in 'seclusion' among 'those paltry idols which he has set up for himself among his lakes and mountains', adding in parenthesis, 'it is remarkable, that all the greater poets lived, or had lived, in the full current of society'. He summarised the poem as 'a tissue of moral and devotional ravings' in which 'the mystical verbiage of the Methodist pulpit is repeated, till the speaker entertains no doubt that he is the elected organ of divine truth and persuasion'. While graciously acknowledging the effectiveness of several passages, Jeffrey's primary concern is to ridicule at every opportunity, because wherever he looks he can point to 'the learned author's propensity to deal out the most familiar truths as the oracles of his own inspired understanding'.[20]

An indicative demolition job is undertaken in relation to Book VII, 'The Churchyard Among the Mountains'. Here the Pastor tells the story of a young man whose grave the travellers are shown:

> through a simple rustic garb's disguise,
> And through the impediment of rural cares,
> In him revealed a scholar's genius shone;
> And so, not wholly hidden from men's sight,

In him the spirit of a hero walked
Our unpretending valley. – How the quoit
Whizzed from the Stripling's arm! If touched by him,
The inglorious football mounted to the pitch
Of the lark's flight, – or shaped a rainbow curve,
Aloft, in prospect of the shouting field!
The indefatigable fox had learned
To dread his perseverance in the chase...
    One day – a summer's day of annual pomp
And solemn chase – from morn to sultry noon
His steps had followed, fleetest of the fleet,
The red-deer driven along its native heights
With cry of hound and horn; and, from that toil
Returned with sinews weakened and relaxed,
This generous Youth, too negligent of self,
Plunged – 'mid a gay and busy throng convened
To wash the fleeces of his Father's flock –
Into the chilling flood. Convulsions dire
Seized him, that self-same night; and through the space
Of twelve ensuing days his frame was wrenched,
Till nature rested from her work in death.
        (*Excursion* VII, 254–5, 735–46; 259, 861–73)

Jeffrey writes:

> This is lofty and energetic; – but Mr. Wordsworth descends, we cannot think very gracefully, when he proceeds to describe how the quoit *whizzed* when his arm launched it – and how the football mounted as high as a lark, at the touch of his toe; – neither is it a suitable catastrophe, for one so nobly endowed, to catch cold by standing too long in the river washing sheep, and die of spasms in consequence.[21]

Jeffrey is no more prepared to state openly the reactionary political position from which his criticism comes, than Lamb is going to state plainly that his reading of the poem reflects his own politically liberal sympathies. Yet the fact remains that Jeffrey is here seeing off a Jacobin poet; his summing up makes this very clear. The Wanderer is another in a long line of potential malcontents from the lower orders; in its time the *Anti-Jacobin* had had no hesitation in making very clear through parody the political import of Wordsworth's old huntsmen, beggars, ruined shepherds, and discharged, mendicant soldiers. Charles Lamb was right to see Wordsworth hanging out his chin when he chose a retired Pedlar for a mouthpiece:

Did Mr. Wordsworth really imagine, that his favourite doctrines were likely to gain anything in point of effect or authority by being put into the mouth of a person accustomed to higgle about tape, or brass sleeve-buttons? Or is it not plain that, independent of the ridicule and disgust which such a personification must give to many of his readers, its adoption exposes his work throughout to the charge of revolting incongruity, and utter disregard of probability or nature?...A man who went about selling flannel and pocket-handkerchiefs in this lofty diction, would soon frighten away all his customers; and would infallibly pass either for a madman, or for some learned and affected gentleman, who, in a frolic, had taken up a character which he was peculiarly ill qualified for supporting.[22]

'Revolting incongruity' indeed.

Jeffrey was by no means alone in his fear that Jacobinism still skulked in the highways and byways of the land. Just two years after *The Excursion* was published a contributor to the *Quarterly* was drawing attention to the fact that counterparts of the leaders of the French Revolution might be found alive and active in England in 1816:

We have those who unite in themselves wealth, fashion and talent, the gifts of fortune and of nature, like Herault Sechelles and St. Just, – but who like them are corrupted by evil principles and evil desires...we have our literatuli and philosophists like the Girondistes; – our lawyers like Barnave, only without his eloquence... our professors of humanity like Robespierre who wrote a treatise against the punishment of death...[23]

For Jeffrey, *The Excursion* represented an attack on a religious orthodoxy that secured the moral and political fabric of a nation immersed in a perilous period of social change. It threatened to undermine the cultural fabric of society, and in doing so negate the means by which a knowledge of decency, beauty and sound judgement was sustained. It smacked of political subversion, of the eccentric championing of the rights of the lower classes, and it carried with it vestiges of an inherent Jacobinism which from the first had marked the poetic system advocated by the Lake poets. Contrast this with the priorities evident in a late-twentieth-century reading of the poem. Kenneth Johnston writes:

Without the ideal of *The Recluse*, there was no need for *The Prelude*, and by studying *The Prelude*, large as it is, in the still larger context of *The Recluse*, we may see that it is less purely self-reflective than is often supposed, and that its self-reflection arises from and occurs within a framework of accommodating Imagination to the 'residences' of Human Life. In similar fashion, it may be possible to revive more of *The Excursion* if we can view its nine thousand lines as but a subsidiary movement in the larger progress of *The Recluse*...[24]

IV

The long journey for *The Excursion* from Lamb, Jeffrey and the first reviewers to Johnston appears to take its first significant turn in the 1830s; it is an important moment for the larger study of Wordsworth's progression from Jacobin Lake poet (in Jeffrey's eyes) to his arrival in Victorian England as a respected elder statesman and man of letters. Stephen Gill has charted the course of these events in *Wordsworth and the Victorians* (1998), and the topic will be returned to in relation to an assessment of Wordsworth's poetry after 1814 in the next chapter. It is helpful here to recall Gill's reference to Sir William Gomm as indicative of the way Wordsworth's reputation underwent a profound change in the years following the publication of *The Excursion*. Where Coleridge (and Wordsworth) saw the poem as offering a healing balm for a generation in shock following the failure of French Revolution, Gomm found in Book IV a very personal lifeline. He had enjoyed a brilliant military career, but his world was rocked by a series of bereavements, culminating in his wife's death in 1827. The Wanderer's attempt in Book IV to dispel the Solitary's despondency was based on an appeal that minimised the need to resort to religious formulae that Gomm had already no doubt tried and found wanting. The appeal to nature seemed both tangible and attractive in its lack of dogma. Gill writes: 'The Wanderer's theology is capacious enough to have pleased even Keats, who loved passages in this book above all the rest of the poem. It views pagans kindly and does not invoke Christ, revelation, or doctrine.... This is why so many, like Gomm, found in *The Excursion* the balm they sought. Nothing in it was incompatible with Christianity, but here was consolation, spiritual counsel, and imaginative succour unattached to doctrine or sect.'[25]

We need to recognise also the part that other, later poems were to have in helping *The Excursion* to become more popular, notably the *River Duddon* sonnets in 1820 and the *Ecclesiastical Sketches* of 1822. Taste was shifting, rendering Jeffrey's perception of the text as subversive increasingly redundant. As the French Revolution and the Napoleonic Wars became the stuff of history, *The Excursion* was no longer read as a text likely to promote political dissent, the reader's response tended more to discover a poem that offered spiritual solace in a time of 'honest doubt'. The intellectual climate of the 1830s was such that it tended increasingly to promote 'spiritually uplifting books', requiring of them a 'seriousness in religious matters'. *The Excursion* was able to fulfil just this need; the reading public were exhorted to look 'for social conscience in political and economic affairs.... And it was these readers who found that Wordsworth was their poet. Denominational magnifying glasses might find flaws in *The Excursion* or *Ecclesiastical Sketches*, but the overall moral tendency of these poems could hardly be doubted, and Wordsworth's recent publications confirmed his place as preeminently the poet for the age.'[26]

It must remain a moot point as to how many people were beginning to read *The Excursion* in its entirety, even if by the mid-century there was no shortage of people ready to advise others to do so. Ruskin, George Eliot, Henry Hudson, Coventry Patmore, J. S. Mill and Elizabeth Gaskell were all to be found echoing James Pycroft's advice: 'Counselling those who wished through private study to become well informed in the central branches of humane learning, James Pycroft insisted on one Wordsworth poem only in his *A Course of Reading* (1844): "Read *The Excursion*".' It was a poem that would provide a source of hope and moral strength for a religiously doubting age. Charles Darwin is reputed to have read it twice before going on to read his way through the remaining collected poems. What is clear in virtually every case is that none of these readers considered themselves to be in possession of an incomplete work. What precisely was it, then, that left them frequently so impressed, so heartened, and even prompted – as in the case of James Russell – to rank Wordsworth's best work with 'the grand simplicities of the Bible'?[27]

V

The Solitary's story begins to unfold in Book II. After a series of bereavements, hope for a better world inspired by the French Revolution is followed by despair brought about by its failure. Wordsworth had created a figure whose plight could readily be associated with the condition of the country. Relief that Napoleon had finally been vanquished in 1815 swiftly gave way to a sustained period of anxiety for the future, an anxiety that continued unabated through to the accession of Queen Victoria and beyond. In the Solitary's narrative, the natural world has no ameliorating effect whatever. The beauties of nature complement his early days of wedded bliss, but have no power to bring solace when his wife and children die. In Book III he goes in search of the spirit of un-trammelled nature when political enthusiasm has failed to regenerate the world:

> I resolved
> To fly, for safeguard, to some foreign shore,
> Remote from Europe; from her blasted hopes;
> Her fields of carnage, and polluted air.
> (*Excursion* III, 104, 831–4)

He is disillusioned with the 'unknit Republic' (l.914) he finds in America, and presses on deeper into the untamed interior, only to find himself no better off:

> But that pure archetype of human greatness,
> I found him not. There, in his stead, appeared
> A creature, squalid, vengeful, and impure;
> Remorseless, and submissive to no law
> But superstitious fear, and abject sloth.
> (ll.951–5)

Framing the narrative, however, are the beauties of a Lakeland setting, evident in the rewritten *Ruined Cottage*, and introduced with renewed enthusiasm into Book II. Although for much of the poem the evocation of landscape takes second place to narrative and argument, the promise of eventual recovery is associated with a process of reconnection to the natural world. A readership that no longer found it easy to trust the institutions of Church and State, but still believed in the ideals those institutions had been created to maintain, might therefore be expected to find considerable comfort in this text. The Solitary, who has been both Parson and political activist, who has recoiled from both occupations in the face of personal and political calamities, is urged in Book IV to seek reassurance in a quite literal sense from the world around him:

> Acknowledge that to Nature's humbler power
> Your cherished sullenness is forced to bend
> Even here, where her amenities are sown
> With sparing hand. Then trust yourself abroad
> To range her blooming bowers, and spacious fields,
> Where on the labours of the happy throng
> She smiles, including in her wide embrace
> City, and town, and tower, – and sea with ships
> Sprinkled . . .
>
> (*Excursion* IV, 147–8, 1190–8)

The worlds of labour and commerce are incorporated, 'City, and town, and tower', but in a tangential fashion. While they are clearly to be included in the discussion, they are not present here as part of the environment experienced by priest or politician in the course of their work. They are to be observed 'In peace and meditative cheerfulness'; there will be no sermon in the church, no political speeches in the city square; quite the opposite, for what speaks here is the 'inarticulate' language of the natural world conveyed to 'social reason's inner sense' (ll.206–7). It is a language communicated by that which lies around the travellers as they set off to find the Pastor at the end of Book IV; it is communicated (as the passage goes on to claim) by feeling. Wordsworth means exactly what he says: the man who 'communes with Forms / Of nature . . . needs must *feel* / The joy of that pure principle of love' (my italics):

> For, the Man –
> Who, in this spirit, communes with the Forms
> Of nature, who with understanding heart
> Both knows and loves such objects as excite
> No morbid passions, no disquietude,
> No vengeance, and no hatred – needs must feel
> The joy of that pure principle of love
> So deeply, that, unsatisfied with aught
> Less pure and exquisite, he cannot choose
> But seek for objects of a kindred love
> In fellow-natures and a kindred joy.
>
> (ll.1207–217)

In Book II the Solitary shows himself still well able to engage in just such an experience of feeling (describable, but ultimately 'inarticulate'), an experience comparable to Wordsworth's crossing of the Alps or climbing of Snowdon. It is a vision of the Heavenly City, but one kept apart from the controlling influence of the religious establishment. It is spontaneous, and it is 'natural'. As the Solitary returns home through the mountains one day he steps out of the mist:

> A single step, that freed me from the skirts
> Of the blind vapour, opened to my view
> Glory beyond all glory ever seen
> By waking sense or by dreaming soul!
> The appearance, instantaneously disclosed,
> Was of a mighty city – boldly say
> A wilderness of building, sinking far
> And self-withdrawn into a boundless depth,
> Far sinking into splendour – without end!
> Fabric it seemed of diamond and of gold,
> With alabaster domes, and silver spires...
> (*Excursion* II, 71–2, 830–40)

There is no intervention here by priest or prayer book: 'By earthly nature had the effect been wrought / Upon the dark materials of the storm / Now pacified', and the Solitary concludes, 'I saw not, but I felt that it was there' (ll.846–8, 872).

The Excursion abounds in fervent Christian rhetoric, but it belongs for the most part in the open air. There is one relatively brief interlude in Book V when the travellers enter a church. They do so to escape the heat of the day, and end up studying the memorials, but within a few lines Wordsworth is exploring the extent to which the building may be perceived as having affinities with the natural world, and it is on this basis that it is judged:

> Not raised in nice proportions was the pile,
> But large and massy; for duration built;
> With pillars crowded, and the roof upheld
> By naked rafters intricately crossed,
> Like leafless underboughs, in some thick wood,
> All withered by the depth of shade above...
>   ...The floor
> Of nave and aisle, in unpretending guise,
> Was occupied by oaken benches ranged
> In seemly rows; the chancel only showed
> Some vain distinctions, marks of earthly state
> By immemorial privilege allowed;
> Though with the Encincture's special sanctity
> But ill according.
> (*Excursion* V, 158, 144–9, 153–60)

This description endorses what is most 'natural' in the building, and what is most natural is what is oldest and most akin to the natural world that surrounds it. Where there are 'marks of earthly state / By immemorial privilege allowed', they are man-made and represent 'vain distinctions'.

Wordsworth's appeal to the power of nature as the ultimate arbiter in all things was made in a way that rendered it consistent with a belief in England as the time-honoured guardian of the principles of political liberty. For the nineteenth-century reader there was no mistaking the view that these principles had been protected, refined and sanctified through the mediation of the Church of England; it was equally admitted that they had come under particular attack of late, but had survived the battering of ten years of European warfare. The past and its political traditions were therefore celebrated as a matter of patriotic pride. But the State was not blameless, and Wordsworth continued to call the government of the 1790s to account for its repressive conservatism. This is the judgement of both the Wanderer and the Solitary:

> But all was quieted by iron bonds
> Of military sway. The shifting aims,
> The moral interests, the creative might,
> The varied functions and high attributes
> Of civil action, yielded to a power
> Formal, and odious, and contemptible.
> (*Excursion* III, 104, 821–6)

But the political and religious convictions of the British patriot are removed from their traditional context: the palace, the cathedral, the parliament building, and the city that surrounds them. Their dwelling place is relocated to the cottage, the rural church, the chapel, and chiefly to a landscape that either remains aloof from the works of man, or reflects (for the most part) a respectful relationship between humanity and the natural world and the rhythms that order it. The temple that matters in *The Excursion* is the Lake District; vexed questions of political and religious division, generally to be found encapsulated by the buildings that represent them, are laid to one side in what was in every respect a profoundly attractive alternative setting.

This conviction is very clearly illustrated in Book VI, where the Pastor describes how 'Two doughty champions; flaming Jacobite / And sullen Hanoverian' retire to live in his parish. At first they are to be found bickering: "'mid the calm / Of that small town encountering thus, they filled, / Daily, its bowling-green with harmless strife ...'. But gradually, though neither will renounce their principles, they learn mutual respect. It is clear that this reconciliation could only be achieved in the open air, and indeed there is a 'boundary' involved that helps to foster their relationship; it also prevents them entering the church:

> A favourite boundary to their lengthened walks
> This Churchyard was. And, whether they had come
> Treading their path in sympathy and linked
> In social converse, or by some short space
> Discreetly parted to preserve the peace,
> One spirit seldom failed to extend its sway
> Over both minds, when they awhile had marked
> The visible quiet of this holy ground,
> And breathed its soothing air; – the spirit of hope
> And saintly magnanimity; that – spurning
> The field of selfish difference and dispute,
> And every care which transitory things,
> Earth and the kingdoms of the earth, create –
> Doth, by a rapture of forgetfulness,
> Preclude forgiveness, from the praise debarred,
> Which else the Christian virtue might have claimed.
> (*Excursion* VI, 201–2, 475–90)

As we have already seen, the interior of the church contains memorials that insist on 'vain distinctions, marks of earthly state'. The churchyard counters that concern for 'transitory things, / Earth and the kingdoms of the earth ...'. We therefore find these 'courtly figures, seated on the stump / Of an old yew'. They decide to be buried in that place, and have a memorial raised there, an ornamental sundial:

> A work of art more sumptuous than might seem
> To suit this place; yet built in no proud scorn
> Of rustic homeliness; they only aimed
> To ensure for it respectful guardianship.
> (ll.506–9)

The sundial, responding only to the dictates of nature, challenges the assumed authority of the Church; it marks out a space where the two men may coexist in a way they could not have done had they been forced into the church building. The inscription on the dial urges its readers to recognise the transience of our differences: to do so is to 'serve the will / Of time's eternal Master'. This is the God revealed to us when we pass through the church building, out into the churchyard and then on out into the open, untrammelled Lakeland countryside beyond. The Solitary is quick to point this up – 'the strain of thought / Accords with nature's language' – and in this he implies that his own despondency is redeemable (*Excursion* VI, 203, 523–35).

These are sentiments that would certainly have found sympathetic readers in the early nineteenth century. A reviewer of *The Works of William Paley* (published in 1825, reviewed in the *Quarterly* in 1828) read Paley's teachings in a very similar light to the advice Wordsworth offers through the Pedlar to the Solitary, as he struggles with honest doubt. The Solitary recognises 'nature's language' speaking through the sundial's inscription; in 1828 Paley was recommended on similar grounds:

> Surely, the book of nature thus read is not lightly to be thrown away, wherein is written, in the plainest characters, the existence of a God, which Revelation, it should be remembered, takes for granted, – of a God how full of contrivance! How fertile in expedients! How benevolent in his ends! At work everywhere, everywhere, too, with equal diligence, leaving nothing incomplete...

Wordsworth and Paley are not entirely comparable, however. The inscription on the sundial is in Latin. Wordsworth's function is to translate 'The appropriate sense' to his readers. For the poet of *The Excursion* there remains that mysterious gap between the sense of what nature has to teach us and our understanding of it. Paley's is a far more simplistic view, though his reviewer endorses Wordsworth's use of the anecdote as a means of dispelling what lingering sense of mystery might remain: 'what is the whole scheme of teaching by parables, but a scheme whereby the natural world is made subservient to the spiritual world, and the wisdom of heaven is taught to find a tongue in the streets, in the fields, and in the sea?'[28]

Book IV of *The Excursion* establishes a firm belief that the Solitary's depression and doubt may be healed, and that the healing would come from God speaking through nature, 'Nature fails not to provide / Impulse and utterance' (*Excursion* IV, 146, 1169–70). If Book IV had also, as the first reviewers noted, seemed to endorse primitive religious beliefs, in Book VI the Wanderer appears to make amends by paying fulsome tribute to the English Church and State:

> Hail to the crown by Freedom shaped – to gird
> An English Sovereign's brow! And to the throne
> Whereon he sits! Whose deep foundations lie
> In veneration and the people's love ...
>   ... And conjoin
> With this a salutation as devout,
> Made to the spiritual fabric of her Church;
> Founded in truth ...
>   (*Excursion* VI, 186, 1–9)

As the passage continues, however, it becomes clear that nothing may be taken for granted; this is a tribute to a tradition of religious and political liberty that is under threat from 'the blinder rage / Of bigot zeal' and 'the destroying hand of war', and from the consequences of rapidly changing patterns of social life, where 'the thronged abodes of busy men' – specifically in wartime – breed materialism, and an attitude 'Depraved, and ever prone to fill the mind / Exclusively with transitory things' (ll.31–41). The image of England as a country destined for decline haunts these lines, and it was a sentiment that remained to touch a raw nerve throughout the century:

> Is't England's parting soul that nerves my tongue,
> As other Kingdoms, nearing their eclipse,
> Have, in their latest bards, uplifted strong
> The voice that was their voice in earlier days?[29]

Coventry Patmore's Proem to 'The Unknown Eros' of 1877 renews the warning note sounded by Wordsworth in 1814. The country – embodied by Wordsworth in the well-meaning but deluded Solitary – had remained unmoved by the Wanderer's arguments. Sixty years on, Patmore was far from alone in suggesting that it now stood on the brink of oblivion, that it was 'A dim, heroic Nation long since dead' (l.67). Though 'The Unknown Eros' received less than enthusiastic notices when it was first published (it did not help that its author was a recent convert to Roman Catholicism), its readers nevertheless had reason enough to take its warning seriously. Before Patmore, Arthur Hugh Clough had also written in a way that suggested the Solitary was indeed far from 'corrected'. In 1849 Clough offered an iconoclastic view of the Nation and the way it had converted Christianity into a matter of pounds, privileges and pence:

> And dignitaries of the Church came by.
> It had been worth to some of them, they said,
> Some £100,000 a year a head.
> If it fetched so much in the market, truly.
> 'Twas not a thing to be given up unduly.[30]

This was territory frequently traversed in nineteenth-century literature, and widely disseminated. 'King, Constitution, and Church forever!' exclaims a character in Bulwer-Lytton's popular novel of 1830, *Paul Clifford*:

> 'which, being interpreted, means, first, King, or Crown influence, judgeships, and gaiters; secondly, Constitution, or fees to the lawyer, places to the statesman, laws for the rich, and *game laws* for the poor: thirdly, Church, or livings for our younger sons, and starvings for their curates!'
>
> 'Ha, ha!' said Brandon laughing, sardonically: '*we* know human nature!'[31]

It is not surprising that readers turned to *The Excursion* for a message of reassurance that did not insist on regular attendance at Sunday worship. Though the second paragraph of Book VI (ll.17–41) urges the importance of maintaining the country's ancient churches and cathedrals, Wordsworth's chief concern is not with boosting the weekly attendance figures. The presence of church buildings as objects viewed from outside rather than from inside, may be guaranteed to help sustain proper Christian virtues in a land in danger of reconstructing the worship of God as the worship of power and money. The appeal is essentially an aesthetic rather than a theological one. We encounter 'the church' in the same way that we encounter it, for example, in the sentimental representation of rural landscapes by Wilson, Gainsborough or Constable. Such a landscape will contain the essential ingredients of social harmony, already being mourned as lost by Goldsmith in 1770 in 'The Deserted Village', the 'decent church' alongside 'The sheltered cot, the cultivated farm, / The never failing brook, the busy mill'.[32]

Christianity here is not defined by liturgical practice of any kind. It represents the means by which a Christian God made manifest in the works of nature may be rendered tangible as a loving creator in the course of daily life. The Christian faith is being returned to its God, and in the process the inadequacies of the established Church (pilloried in Jacobin novels, worried over by so many Victorian novelists, mourned by poets in both centuries) are set to one side in favour of a religion that, rooted in a pre-industrial society, will remain incorruptible. If the Church of England is to survive, it will be because the roots of its spirituality are located 'on rustic wilds'. Its churches

> shall continue to bestow,
> Upon the thronged abodes of busy men
> (Depraved, and ever prone to fill the mind
> Exclusively with transitory things)
> An air and mien of dignified pursuit;
> Of sweet civility, on rustic wilds.
> (*Excursion* VI, 187, 36–41)

Similarly, the church's ministers should emulate the Pastor of *The Excursion*. Wordsworth's Pastor is the guardian of a rural parish, a man who clearly spends far more time wandering through the countryside than he does in his church building; a man who, in Book IX (the final Book) of the poem, conducts its concluding act of worship in the open air.

VI

Matthew Arnold, one of the most influential of Wordsworth's critics in the late nineteenth century, had very clear views on him as a poet of nature, and how that should be understood by those who read him for spiritual guidance. In 1888 he insisted that:

> Wordsworth's poetry is great because of the extraordinary power with which Wordsworth feels the joy offered to us in nature, the joy offered to us in the simple primary affections and duties; and because of the extraordinary power with which, in case after case, he shows us this joy, and renders it so as to make us share it.[33]

Arnold's endorsement of Wordsworth rests on his sympathy with the idea of nature acting as the fountainhead of profound wisdom.

Wordsworth, through the Wanderer, refers to the natural world in a way that Arnold believed he was best able 'to make us share it':

> In flower and tree, in every pebbly stone
> That paves the brooks, the stationary rocks,
> The moving waters, and the invisible air.
> (*Excursion* IX, 286, 7–9)

What Arnold was not prepared to countenance was Wordsworth's attempt to write up this 'sacred energy' as a 'doctrine'; to present it as a 'scientific system of thought', or as 'an ethical system...distinctive and capable of systematic exposition'. Despite his use of the phrase 'sacred energy', Arnold's intention is to differentiate clearly between the exposition of a religious conviction, and what Wordsworth ('at his best') can do when working from 'Nature': 'Wordsworth's poetry, when he is at his best, is inevitable, as inevitable as Nature herself. It might seem that Nature not only gave him the matter for his poem, but wrote his poem for him.' At his least satisfactory (in *The Excursion* and *The Prelude*) we are given 'ponderosity and pomposity...Doctrine such as we hear in church', and no matter how true such doctrine may be 'it has...none of the characters of *poetic* truth, the kind of truth which we require from a poet, and in which Wordsworth is really strong.'

Arnold's argument was partly provoked by his own religious scepticism, and partly by the existence of an enthusiastic band of Wordsworth readers who stood in need of correction. These are people he variously refers to as 'fervent' or 'attached' Wordsworthians. Arnold argues poetry inhabits an altogether different sphere from religion. When Wordsworth is getting it right, therefore, 'Nature herself seems...to take the pen out of his hand, and to write for him with her own bare, sheer, penetrating power.'[34] This was not where Wordsworth himself intended to take us – and leave us – in *The Excursion*, and Arnold was prepared to accept that there were many who, throughout the nineteenth century, found Book IX of the poem a reassuring and stimulating blend of religious fervour and love of nature, and who agreed with Leslie Stephen that Francis Jeffrey had been guilty of a 'dogged insensibility'.[35]

Book IX opens with the Wanderer's reflections on the '*active* Principle' that informs all things:

> 'To every Form of being is assigned,'
> Thus calmly spake the venerable Sage,

'An *active* Principle: – howe'er removed
From sense and observation, it subsists
In all things, in all natures; in the stars
Of azure heaven, the unenduring clods,
In flower and tree, in every pebbly stone
That paves the brooks, the stationary rocks,
The moving waters, the invisible air.
Whate'er exists hath properties that spread
Beyond itself, communicating good,
A simple blessing, or with evil mixed;
Spirit that knows no insulated spot,
No chasm, no solitude; from link to link
It circulates, the Soul of all the worlds.
This is the freedom of the universe;
Unfolded still the more, more visible,
The more we know…'
                    (*Excursion* IX, 286–7, 1–18)

Besides emphasising the unorthodoxy of Wordsworth's ideas about how all nature is imbued with life, this passage also illustrates the way *The Excursion* seeks to resolve the restless, troubled, visionary imagery that haunts the earlier poetry. In his description of his descent of the Vale of Gondo in *The Prelude*, we are shown

            The immeasurable height
Of woods decaying, never to be decayed,
The stationary blasts of waterfalls,
And everywhere along the hollow rent
Winds thwarting winds, bewildered and forlorn,
The torrents shooting from the clear blue sky…
                    (*Prelude* VI, 218, 556–61)

In *The Excursion* we have 'the stationary rocks, / The moving waters, and the invisible air'; we have a 'Spirit that knows no insulated spot, / No chasm, no solitude' because all things are resolved into an integrated whole. *The Excursion* is a work that purports to provide answers. The passage begins with a didactic statement; what follows is not written as though it were a quest or an adventure. It is a resolution, 'calmly spoken'. There is still a mystery, but no longer one that need concern or alarm us because we may be confident that our knowledge is advancing steadily towards the goal, 'Unfolded still the more, more visible, / The more we know' (ll.17–18).

The reader knows, of course, that because the Wanderer has stated confidently and 'calmly' that it is so, has not necessarily made it so. Twentieth-century critics have tended to make much of the way *The Excursion* abounds in contradictory elements which repeatedly challenge the poem's intended resolutions. One reason for the uncertainty of tone is the manner in which *The Excursion's* four protagonists debate the Solitary's 'despondency'. Geoffrey Hartman, Judson Lyon, Frances Furguson, David Simpson, Kenneth Johnston and Peter Manning have all drawn attention to the way the imagery and the use of literary references frequently work to check or modify the poem's overt stance. An important critical issue has therefore become the extent to which the poet seems no longer prepared to allow such ambiguities to appear on the face of the poem. There has always been a sense of space between the poet's poem and the reader's meaning (or response); but in the case of *The Excursion* reading Wordsworth seems to have become a subversive, covert act: we need to wait until the poet's back is turned before we can interpret the text in full. Yet we feel he, too, shares our experience of the text. This is probably nowhere more apparent than in the set piece with which the poem concludes. The major protagonists, to whom are added the Pastor's family, set out on a picnic, and the afternoon's outing terminates upon a hillside from which may be seen the major features of the landscape that has played such an important part in the poem:

> far off,
> And yet conspicuous, stood the old Church-tower,
> In majesty presiding over fields
> And habitations seemingly preserved
> From all intrusion of the restless world
> By rocks impassable and mountains huge.
> (*Excursion* IX, 305, 574–9)

Here are the fields, the lake, the dwellings of the people who have provided narratives throughout the Book; and not least here is the Church, viewed as ever from the outside, symbolising the religious import of the landscape (Wordsworth wants it both ways, 'far off, / And yet conspicuous').

Initially the travellers talk with each other about the beauties of the prospect, but then the sunset imposes an awed silence upon them; nature itself contrives to establish a sense of appropriate humility in the face of God:

> Already had the sun,
> Sinking with less than ordinary state,
> Attained his western bound; but rays of light –
> Now suddenly diverging from the orb
> Retired behind the mountain-tops or veiled
> By the dense air – shot upwards to the crown
> Of the blue firmament – aloft and wide:
> And multitudes of little floating clouds,
> Through their ethereal texture pierced – ere we,
> Who saw, of change were conscious – had become
> Vivid as fire; clouds separately poised, –
> Innumerable multitude of forms
> Scattered through half the circle of the sky;
> And giving back, and shedding each on each,
> With prodigal communion, the bright hues
> Which from the unapparent fount of glory
> They had imbibed, and ceased not to receive.
> That which the heavens displayed, the liquid deep
> Repeated; but with unity sublime!
>
> (ll.590–608)

George Eliot, like many of her generation, was drawn in particular to Book IV of *The Excursion*, but she studied the poem in its entirety over a considerable period of time, and in *Adam Bede* (1859) we find what is probably an echo of this passage in the first paragraph of Chapter 53:

> The low westering sun shone right on the shoulders of the old Binton Hills, turning the unconscious sheep into bright spots of light; shone on the windows of the cottage too, and made them a-flame with a glory beyond that of amber or amethyst. It was enough to make Adam feel that he was in a great temple, and that the distant chant was a sacred song.[36]

The Pastor in *The Recluse* has taken his guests into nature's 'great temple':

> – 'Observe,' the Vicar said, 'yon rocky isle
> With birch-trees fringed; my hand shall guide the helm,
> While thitherward we shape our course; or while
> We seek that other, on the western shore;
> Where the bare columns of those lofty firs,
> Supporting gracefully a massy dome
> Of sombre foliage, seem to imitate
> A Grecian temple rising from the deep.'
>
> (*The Excursion* IX, 303, 495–502)

The moment in *Adam Bede* is brief, and Adam's thoughts at this time far briefer than the oration into which Wordsworth's Pastor now launches; but his reflections are reminiscent of what both the Wanderer and the Pastor have been saying to the Solitary:

> It's like what I feel about Dinah: I should never ha' come to know that her love 'ud be the greatest o' blessings to me, if what I counted a blessing hadn't been wrenched and torn away from me, and left me with a greater need, so as I could crave and hunger for a greater and a better comfort.[37]

Wordsworth's Pastor delivers a lengthy sermon celebrating the power of nature at all times (including the pre-Christian era) to inspire humanity with a sense of its own inferiority before a creator God, and its need for 'a greater and a better comfort'. The onset of Christianity means now that worshippers 'come / To kneel devoutly in yon reverend Pile, / Called to such office by the peaceful sound / Of sabbath bells'; but the coterie within the poem have been privileged to witness a visionary moment that transcends the mundane business of churchgoing (*Excursion* IX, 310, 724–7). Addressing his absent congregation (those gathered in church 'and ye, who sleep in earth' l.77), the Pastor explains:

> For you, in presence of this little band
> Gathered together on the green hill-side,
> Your Pastor is emboldened to prefer
> Vocal thanksgivings to the eternal King;
> Whose love, whose counsel, whose commands, have made
> Your very poorest rich in peace of thought
> And in good works; and him, who is endowed
> With scantiest knowledge, master of all truth
> Which the salvation of his soul requires.
>
> (ll.729–37)

Already he has acknowledged the continued shortcomings of many who call themselves Christian, but prefer 'Bonds and darkness to a state / Of holy freedom' (ll.655–6). We are left in no doubt that the Christian faith stands in need of spiritual renewal, and equally that the place where a reinvigoration of Christianity will take place is in the open air; from thence it may be reintroduced into the church building, a symbol for the Anglican Establishment. It is small wonder that Charles Lamb was put in mind of Methodism, and Francis Jeffrey of something far worse:

These barren rocks, your stern inheritance;
These fertile fields, that recompense your pains;
The shadowy vale, the sunny mountain-top;
Woods waving in the wind their lofty head,
Or hushed; the roaring waters, and the still –
They see the offering of my lifted hands,
They hear my lips present their sacrifice...
(ll.743–9)

A nineteenth-century reader struggling with honest doubt every bit as debilitating as that which continues to haunt the Solitary in this final Book, might find here a measure of reassurance when faced with traditional religious rites which, if not always hypocritical, were invariably tedious – as Clough never tired of pointing out:

Amid these crowded pews must I sit and seem to pray,
All the blessed Sunday-morning while I wish to be away,
While in the fields I long to be or on the hill-tops high,
The air of heaven about me, above, the sacred sky?[38]

Clough, like Arnold, was for maintaining the distinction between religion and nature, and readers of Wordsworth were also reading Clough, and reading Arnold with considerable attention as honest doubt progressively gave way to Modernist cynicism and despair. *The Excursion* was changing with the times.

VII

We have seen how *The Excursion* has become part of a critical debate about *The Recluse*, and how twentieth-century textual scholarship has steadily transformed the critical terrain in that respect. Perhaps the most obvious difference between nineteenth-century critical writing on *The Excursion* and what followed was the disappearance of the idea that it was a text from which society might benefit in any practical sense. *The Excursion* becomes instead a means of gauging what exercised the minds of intellectuals in nineteenth-century Britain. It provides us with an insight into Wordsworth's state of mind as he moved into his 'late' period; it becomes grist to the mill in a complex discussion of textuality, and how any writer is read, not just Wordsworth. The overwhelming impression is that *The Excursion*, now no longer a fixed textual point in the poet's canon, is there to be used as a tool for literary critical purposes.

In 1933 Edith C. Batho published *The Later Wordsworth*, intended as a corrective to the view that the nature of the decline of Wordsworth's poetic powers after 1814, accompanied by political apostasy, was unproblematic. The following extract is characteristic of the way *The Excursion* was now finding its way into the argument:

> [Wordsworth's] support of the Crown, however, was remarkably unsentimental: he had not Oastler's zeal for 'Throne and Altar', even though in Book VI of *The Excursion* the Crown and Throne are symbols of freedom; and at least until long after the accession of Queen Victoria, he had no particular reverence for the wearers of the crown. He did not share Scott's romantic devotion to the monarchy and its representative.[39]

Judson Lyon's *The Excursion: A Study* of 1950 failed to encourage a return to the text in its own right, and in 1971, Gordon Kent Thomas is to be found using the poem to illustrate his point about apostasy in *Wordsworth's Dirge and Promise*: 'It is common among believers in Wordsworth's apostasy to attribute the change in his principles to his changing attitudes about France. In Book III of *The Excursion* . . . the Solitary describes these results from the events in France when revolution turned to terror. . .'.[40] Batho and Thomas illustrate the fact that only very few twentieth-century critics have been prepared to suggest that *The Excursion* (as opposed to *The Ruined Cottage*) possesses any intrinsic value as a poem. Paul Hamilton's verdict of 1986 is characteristic:

> the poem is encrusted with Christian doctrine which grows more explicit in successive revisions. . . . *The Excursion* is his own enormous epitaph, but followed this time by no new beginning. The poem's solutions and destinations prevent it from finally escaping the immobility of the Solitary it sets out to criticise, and make it impossible for Wordworth's poetry any longer to celebrate as its own possession 'the mind's *excursive* power'.[41]

Kenneth R. Johnston's *Wordsworth and The Recluse* had already been in print for two years when this was written. Evidently nothing Johnston had done had been able to convince Hamilton that *The Excursion* was anything other than an anticlimax. Hamilton and Johnston do, however, represent two different critical approaches. The Harvester 'New Readings' series to which Hamilton was contributing had as its rationale the location of its subjects 'in his or her social, political and historical context'. This is a familiar enough aspiration, and of course Johnston shares similar interests. However, Johnston's close readings of *Excursion* passages focus on the internal workings of the text. We may see the consequences of this from his discussion of a passage from towards the end of Book IV:

> Within the soul a faculty abides,
> That with interpositions, which would hide
> And darken, so can deal that they become
> Contingencies of pomp; and serve to exalt
> Her native brightness. As the ample moon,
> In the deep stillness of a summer even
> Rising behind a thick and lofty grove,
> Burns, like an unconsuming fire of light,
> In the green trees; and, kindling on all sides
> Their leafy umbrage, turns the dusky veil
> Into a substance glorious as her own,
> Yea, with her own incorporated, by power
> Capacious and serene. Like power abides
> In man's celestial spirit; virtue thus
> Sets forth and magnifies herself; thus feeds
> A calm, a beautiful, and silent fire,
> From the encumbrances of mortal life,
> From error, disappointment – nay, from guilt;
> And sometimes, so relenting justice wills,
> From palpable oppressions of despair.
> (*Excursion* IV, 142–39, 1058–77)

Johnston writes:

> Lamb singled out this passage as 'high poetry', and despite ornate diction Wordsworth's figure is aptly chosen and provides an emblem for the entire argument of Book IV. He has taken a traditional image of incarnation, immanence, or spiritual indwelling (e.g., The Burning Bush) and adapted it to psychologised landscape description by exploiting the visual ambiguities of the veil image: it conceals, reveals, and reveals-by-concealing. The result illustrates the special mode of human domination over natural contingency which *The Excursion* consistently projects. There is no vision here, no obliteration of common experience. The veil of flesh is not rent, it is incorporated... with a source of spiritual energy. The irradiating source is called Virtue rather than Imagination, but this instance is one among many

in the latter parts of Book IV where the Solitary is urged to inspire his seeing with an impulse from his soul called, alternatively, 'virtue', 'Imagination', 'the imaginative will', or 'the mind's *excursive* power'.[42]

Johnston's emphasis throughout tends to be on the quality of balance the poetry achieves, on a kind of ordering and control in creativity that he finds admirable, and offers to us in that light. What we have here is teaching on goodness that accords with the liberal humanist tradition; it does not over-emphasise its religious bias, it is honest – there is 'no obliteration of common experience' – yet it is literary, aware of cultural and religious roots.

Important as Johnston's book is, it has failed (along with others) to clear the way for a focused critical appraisal of *The Excursion*; indeed, the process of textual criticism has tended to result in a losing of the poem as a readable entity rather than a finding (or rediscovery) of it. There remains, as Peter J. Manning suggested in 1990, little interest in the study of Wordsworth's later poetry in general, 'the notorious conservatism of the later years remains a stumbling block'. Manning nevertheless sets about redefining the critical territory:

> Distaste for Wordsworth's views has thus far largely precluded asking what kinds of poetry he evolved to convey them and what sorts of interest such poems might repay. The late poems deliberately no longer offer the richly represented self of, say, *The Prelude*, but once understood within their historical situation, their contexts steadily widen and their procedures gain meaning.[43]

Very little is said subsequently about *The Excursion*, though Manning's first chapter offers a detailed discussion of the evolution of Book I. Like John Wyatt, writing in 1999, Manning concentrates on a selection of the poetry that came after *The Excursion*.

One important exception to this tendency has been David Simpson. He was able to justify a final chapter on *The Excursion* in *Wordsworth's Historical Imagination* because of its relevance to the new historicist preoccupations of his research. The arguments to be found within the poem, he writes, are evidence of 'some of Wordsworth's most searching and anxious inquiries into the relations between poetry, property and labour, and into the potential in the agrarian life to respond to or modify the challenges of urbanization'.[44]

Simpson is interested in the poem as a source of evidence which shows the extent of Wordsworth's ambivalence in relation to the major issues raised there. Urban life is destructive, but so may be rural life, and not just because it is increasingly infected by the fallout from urban life, but because it can itself be demeaning and diminishing. The regeneration of humanity may be aided by social action, but there is always evidence of endemic depravity that will remain even were the brutalising consequences of poverty to be removed. Education is proposed as a way forward, but here liberal tendencies are offset by reactionary influences, and the religious teaching remains at best heterodox, and thus incapable of offering a firm lead. We are reminded that the Solitary's despondency has not been corrected by the end of the poem, and that the use of the four protagonists problematises the authority with which any of them may deliver moral teachings. Finally, Simpson draws our attention to a comment made by the Pastor's wife to the poet in Book IX:

> I love to hear that eloquent old Man
> Pour forth his meditations . . .
> While he is speaking, I have power to see
> Even as he sees; but when his voice hath ceased,
> Then, with a sigh, sometimes I feel, as now,
> That combinations so serene and bright
> Cannot be lasting in a world like ours . . .
> (ll.459–69)

The fragility of the entire enterprise is thus set starkly before us, and Simpson goes on to reflect on Wordsworth's own uncertain state, a man still capable of radical political impulses while working within the patronage of Lowther and Beaumont. With reference to the concluding act of worship at the end of Book IX he writes:

> We are left . . . in a movement that suggests not only the frailty of the social and spiritual consensus that has just been achieved, but also the larger narrative irony of the projected great work itself, which has still to happen. There *is* an aura of contentment about the end of *The Excursion*, and the view from the 'exalted station' is not marked by the same giddying glimpse *down* into infinity as featured in its prototype (and post-type), the account of the ascent of Snowdon; but it is not unqualified by dissonant allusions.[45]

What has, however, been lacking to any significant degree throughout most of Simpson's discussion, is any commentary on the quality of the poetry. We may detect here, as in most twentieth-century critical work on *The Excursion*, a ghostly tribute to Matthew Arnold who raised, though not in the language of latter-day theory-based criticism, a critical issue that continues to brood over the reading of this text (whichever version of it we use), as indeed it does over most of Wordsworth's later poetry:

> He has no style. He was too conversant with Milton not to catch at times his master's manner, and he has fine Miltonic lines; but he has no assured poetic style of his own, like Milton. When he seeks to have a style he falls into ponderosity and pomposity... and although Jeffrey completely failed to recognise Wordsworth's real greatness, he was yet not wrong in saying of the *Excursion*, as a work of poetic style: 'This will never do.'[46]

9

Making the Best of It: The Later Poetry

> Even so, and unblamed, we rejoice as we may
> In Forms that must perish, frail objects of sense ...
> ('At Vallombrosa', 1842, *PW* 3, 224, 33–4)

I

After 1814 Wordsworth's compulsion to write was increasingly matched by a concern to edit, order and anthologise his steadily growing body of work. The first collected edition of poems appeared in 1815, to be followed by a four-volume edition in 1820. A five-volume edition including *The Excursion* appeared in 1827, then another in 1832; a six-volume edition came out in the course of 1836–7. All the time revisions were being made to existing work, while new poetry was being added. Wordsworth had first begun to group his poems into categories in the *Poems in Two Volumes* of 1807, and the collected editions illustrate the increasing importance this process came to hold for him. In *Wordsworth: Language as Counter-Spirit* (1977), Frances Ferguson suggests that the classification of the poetry becomes an integral part of the poet's creative drive: 'the classification reflects an effort to understand not only the problem of the imagination but also to probe the question of the use of linguistic signs generally'. But she goes on to imply that Wordsworth's engagement with classification is a symptom of decline in the quality of his poetry. In her final chapter she suggests that *The Excursion* 'may not be a fully successful poem' because it is 'an inevitable corollary to the renunciatory drive which we have traced in Wordsworth's classification'.

What began as a celebration of the 'simple' had become, through the increasing recognition of the complexity of so-called 'simplicity', a process of withdrawal from any pretensions to be able to master the subject:

> It is almost as if he were repeatedly saying (especially in the Lucy poems), 'I spoke too soon; I now know that I did not fully comprehend the nature of what I was talking about.'[1]

Ferguson's argument is both subtle and sympathetic, but no matter how circuitous or carefully planned the route, we seem fated – as I suggested at the end of the previous chapter – to return in the end to Arnold's trenchant summary of Wordsworth in his later years:

> Work altogether inferior, work quite uninspired, flat and dull, is produced by him with evident unconsciousness of its defects, and he presents it to us with the same faith and seriousness as his best work.[2]

Wordsworth did indeed bequeath the critical fraternity a vast amount of manifestly mediocre poetry, and the truth is that critics and readers alike have never quite known what to do with it. The one thing we have been congenitally unable to do, of course, is to leave it alone. The principal critical issue here, then, is to find a way of making a case for the study of such poetry. One way critics have approached this has been to reflect on Wordsworth's own acknowledgement that there was a problem of this nature, and at how he then went on to make that problem the subject of much of his later poetry.

Another familiar way in which the later poetry finds a place in critical discourse may be illustrated by reference to Geoffrey Hartman's *Wordsworth's Poetry* (1964). Hartman there discusses *The Excursion* and a selection of the work that came after it primarily as a means of emphasising the greatness of the poetry that preceded it. Writing about *The White Doe of Rylstone* he argues that in his later work the poet has become 'as careful about an idealising impulse as about the apocalyptic intimation':

> The presence of a Sympathetic Nature, which is the one superstition for which he had kept his respect, for it is vital not only to poetry but also to human development, being a necessary illusion in the growth

of the mind, this too is falling away. Yet the story of the white doe is his attempt to save the notion once more in some purer form. He knows that to give it up entirely is to return to a holy, but stern and melancholy, imagination.[3]

We read this, as we do Hartman's preceding chapter on *The Excursion*, with a sense of constant referral back to the superior qualities of the earlier work.

We have seen Ferguson working from essentially the same premise to reinforce her reason for discussing *The Excursion*. In 1990 Peter J. Manning made the point yet again, but this time by way of attempting to move the discussion forward:

> I want to suggest, therefore, that one advantage of giving more serious consideration to the poems Wordsworth wrote after 1807, or 1814, or wherever critical opinion draws the line, will be a more fruitful understanding of the works written before that boundary. I want it both ways, however. I want also to argue that a poet's final period should not be held in thrall to his earlier one, just because that earlier is more appealing.[4]

This comes in his essay 'Wordsworth at St. Bees: Scandals, Sisterhoods, and Wordsworth's Later Poetry' (1985). In the latter part of the essay Manning claims to have shown that 'St. Bees' is characteristic of a 'complexly situated rhetoric' to be found in much of the later poetry.[5] It is an argument which has a good deal in common with David Simpson's thesis on *The Excursion*: Wordsworth moves from being an insecure radical to becoming an equally insecure conservative; his 'resolutions' in the later poetry are found to be every bit as problematic and therefore interesting as they are in the earlier work. The issue here begins to be far more one of reader response than of applying Arnoldian categories of incontrovertibly great, not so great, and inferior art to Wordsworth's poems. If anyone is tempted to think of Wordsworth as a lesser poet in his latter years because the anxieties that had previously fuelled his creative soul have ebbed away, then they are mistaken. The choice we make is between two equally insecure poets, and critical judgement has as much to do with the reader's sympathies in relation to matters more far reaching than the quality of work produced by a single poet; it is a matter of how we find ourselves responding to 'radical' and 'conservative' ideology.

II

The issue is a different one when we make the attempt to see it through Wordsworth's eyes. The issue here is to try and appreciate why he continued to write, edit and revise his work after he appears to have recognised that the 'visionary gleam' referred to in the 'Ode, Intimations of Immortality' was on the wane. By 1814, when *The Excursion* was in the hands of the printers, the 'visionary gleam' characterised in that poem by the passage in Book IX (ll.437–51) which describes the reflection of the ram in still water so easily shattered, is replaced by a narrative that unambiguously displays the absence of 'the glory and the dream', and proceeds to make poetry of it.

Wordsworth, Mary, her sister Sara and the young John Wordsworth embarked on a tour of Scotland in July 1814, and *Memorials of a Tour of Scotland 1814* brought together four poems describing the places that were visited. The third poem is called 'Effusion', and is subtitled, 'In the Pleasure-Ground on the Banks of the Bran, near Dunkeld'. The poem describes the way in which a theatrical device has been deployed to enhance the scenic effect of a waterfall. Any hope of experiencing the landscape in its pristine form is gone, the location has been made into a 'Pleasure-Ground' for trippers. This absence is made all the more disturbingly bizarre by the fact that with unwitting irony the mechanical device intended to enhance the view enacts the destruction of Ossian, the great bardic poet. The poem is headed by Sara Hutchinson's enthusiastic account of their experience:

> The waterfall, by a loud roaring, warned us when we must expect it. We were first, however, conducted into a small apartment, where the Gardener desired us to look at a picture of Ossian, which, while he was telling the history of the young Artist who executed the work, disappeared, parting in the middle – flying asunder as by the touch of magic – and lo! We are at the entrance of a splendid apartment, which was almost dizzy and alive with waterfalls, that tumbled in all directions; the great cascade, opposite the window, which faced us, being reflected in innumerable mirrors upon the ceiling and against the walls.

Wordsworth's poem implicitly chides the prose account with a lament for the fate of Ossian:

What He – who, mid the kindred throng
Of Heroes that inspired his song,
Doth yet frequent the hill of storms,
The stars dim-twinkling through their forms!
What! Ossian here – a painted Thrall,
Mute fixture on a stuccoed wall;
To serve – an unsuspected screen
For show that must not yet be seen;
And, when the moment comes, to part
And vanish by mysterious art;
Head, harp, and body, split asunder,
For ingress to a world of wonder;
A gay saloon, with waters dancing
Upon the sight wherever glancing;
One loud cascade in front, and lo!
A thousand like it, white as snow –
Streams on the walls, and torrent-foam
As active round the hollow dome,
Illusive cataracts! Of their terrors
Not stripped, nor voiceless in the mirrors,
That catch the pageant from the flood
Thundering adown a rocky wood.
What pains to dazzle and confound!
What strife of colour, shape and sound
In this quaint medley, that might seem
Devised out of a sick man's dream!
Strange scene, fantastic and uneasy
As ever made a maniac dizzy,
When disenchanted from the mood
That loves on sullen thoughts to brood.
                    (*PW* 3, 102–5, 1–30)

The poet's opinion is clear; a clumsy attempt has been made, 'Devised out of a sick man's dream', to display the illusive powers of the scene by embellishing them. In his subsequent affirmation that Nature is 'Ever averse to pantomime' we catch a strain that surely originates in a memory of his account of crossing the Alps in *The Prelude* (the 'rock that frowns, and stream that roars'), and this second section concludes by returning to a lament for the fate of Ossian in particular, and poetry in general:

O Nature – in thy changeful visions,
Through all thy most abrupt transitions

> Smooth, graceful, tender, or sublime –
> Ever averse to pantomime,
> Thee neither do they know nor us
> Thy servants, who can trifle thus;
> Else verily the sober powers
> Of rock that frowns, and stream that roars,
> Exalted by congenial sway
> Of Spirits, and the undying Lay,
> And Names that moulder not away,
> Had wakened some redeeming thought
> More worthy of this favoured Spot;
> Recalled some feeling – to set free
> The Bard from such indignity!
>
> (ll.31–45)

At the end of the poem, 'thirsting for redress' Wordsworth describes himself recoiling 'into the wilderness' (l.128).

This makes the point. The poem itself is not about the 'wilderness', but about the harmful effect of its absence on the poet. It is competent, thought-provoking poetry, but it cannot rival 'Tintern Abbey' because its subject is fated to be 'all the perishable gauds / That heaven-deserted man applauds' (ll.109–10). The problem is that already lamented in the 1800 Preface to *Lyrical Ballads*, a problem for poetry in a society increasingly ill-adjusted to what Wordsworth understands to be the priorities of poetry: the exposure of our 'essential passions' and 'our elementary feelings'. To achieve this he had sought out people whose lives were 'incorporated with the beautiful and permanent forms of nature' (*LB*, 743–4). 'Effusion' reports on the desecration of such forms, and therefore on the highest aspirations of the poet as doomed. Wordsworth would have us understand that his personal struggle to sustain the visionary gleam is symptomatic of a widespread cultural malaise, and as a professional poet it is his duty to continue writing poetry about that malaise. However, it should be added that in these latter years we see him campaigning for what he believed in through ever more extended undertakings in prose; the letters he wrote during this later period alone indicate a significant scaling down of the time that might otherwise have been spent on poetry.

The final poem in *Memorials of a Tour of Scotland 1814*, 'Yarrow Visited', is somewhat less despairing than 'Effusion', but the point remains the same. We are shown a picturesque valley, but beautiful as it is, it inspires a sense of loss because until now the place has been embodied solely within Wordsworth's imagination, a presence enhanced by his knowledge of local folklore and balladry. The poem celebrates a postponed visit to Yarrow, but at the same time responds to the experience as evidence of a further dampening of the poet's visionary powers:

> And is this – Yarrow? – *This* the Stream
> Of which my fancy cherished,
> So faithfully, a waking dream?
> An image that hath perished!
> O that some Minstrel's harp were near,
> To utter notes of gladness,
> And chase this silence from the air,
> That fills my heart with sadness!
>
> (*PW* 3, 106, 1–8)

This is poetry made out of the poet's recognition that, through no fault of his own, he is unable to write the poetry he should. Its presence on the page, however, insists that this is not an acceptable reason to cease writing and publishing poetry. One significant reason for Wordsworth's persistence after 1814, despite the strength of continuing negative critical opinion about his work, was that he was also becoming aware of an increasingly sympathetic readership beyond his immediate coterie of admirers. This fact alone differentiates his perception of his later work from those who began to assess his achievement after his death.

III

Suggestions as to when precisely after 1814 Wordsworth began to shed the reputation he had acquired of a perverse and even dangerous poet vary. Stephen Gill has argued that the publication of the *River Duddon* sonnets in 1820 constitutes a turning point.[6] What is beyond doubt is that the period between the establishment of Wordsworth as a 'great poet' in the course of the nineteenth century and our own time witnesses an intriguing degree of critical vacillation. Twentieth-century criticism has endorsed a canonical poet from the writings belonging to the 20 years between 1790 and 1810, setting alongside that a largely burnt-out genius heralded by *The Excursion*. This perception begins early on with Arnold's critical essays and his edition of Wordsworth's poetry published in 1879. Compared to the way Wordsworth's contemporaries attacked the early work, the later poetry has been treated with far less brutality by subsequent critics, though as we have seen from the tenor of Arnold's comments, plain speaking was not infrequently the order of the day. For many Victorians, however, it was *The Excursion, The River Duddon* (1820), and *Ecclesiastical Sketches* (1822) that were primarily responsible for elevating Wordsworth to the role of poet sage, a role that was in due course endorsed when he was offered the laureateship in 1843.

In the early decades of the twentieth century, a number of changes begin to be apparent in the critical response to the later work. Herbert Read was in many respects characteristic of twentieth-century critics in England writing on Wordsworth before the Second World War. Initially he appears not to be in dispute with his predecessors, and in *William Wordsworth* (first published in 1930) he echoes Arnold's verdict:

> From about 1800 he composed, not merely with difficulty, but... with a real sense of pain and physical exhaustion. He was fighting against frustration and inhibition. Remorse was completing its deadly work. He was to live for another fifty years, his powers at first swiftly, and then slowly but completely giving out. The dying embers emit an occasional spark, but nothing that in any degree adds to the total impression of his genius.[7]

It soon becomes apparent, however, that Read felt he did have something new to add, but it was not to do with the quality of the late work, 'to this day we might say that the Wordsworth who survives is Arnold's Wordsworth – a lyrical or pastoral poet, anything but the great philosophical poet of his own and Coleridge's conception'.[8] In 1922 Emile Legouis published *Wordsworth and Annette Vallon*, the first public account of Wordsworth's involvement with Annette while in France in 1792. We need to remind ourselves that the popular perception of Wordsworth up to this point (and indeed it lingers on) was of a largely solitary, contemplative poet whose life, as Walter Pater suggested in his essay on Wordsworth of 1874, was 'divided by no very profound incidents'.

Read, reflecting on the rediscovered emotional turmoil of Wordsworth's youth and early manhood, now declared an interest in biographical criticism, proposing that Wordsworth's poetry as a whole should be read in the light of the 'emotional development' of his personality, a subject that has 'too often and too exclusively been treated as an intellectual development'.[9] For Read, the quality of the late work, of *The Excursion* and *The Prelude*, was not waiting to be rediscovered as better poetry than Arnold had supposed. The later poetry was, however, beginning to look far more interesting because Read was undertaking the kind of reading one might expect from an enthusiastic writer on surrealism and a devotee of Freud and psychoanalysis. Read's book is one of a number of early twentieth-century monographs that prepare the way for the major biographical and critical work that was to appear after the Second World War; in particular, we can find intimations of Hartman's approach (to be described as 'phenomenological' at a later date by others), and of the painstaking biographical research and consequent revisionary readings of the poetry undertaken by Mary Moorman:

> Why didn't Wordsworth marry Annette? Why did he desert her as soon as the child was born? How can we explain his conduct during this year in France; how can we condone his conduct in the years that followed? It is possible that if he had not so completely covered his tracks, the real motives underlying his actions would be more creditable than those we are compelled to assign him. Why pry into the matter at all? it may be asked. I have already answered that question. Wordsworth, as a character and as a poet, is inexplicable without this key to his emotional development. With this key he becomes, not indeed, a rational being, but a man whose thwarted emotions found an external and objective compensation in his poetry.[10]

With reference to Arnold, Read manages to endorse the earlier critic's judgement while at the same time fundamentally remapping the terrain of critical activity:

> For the moment I merely want to glance at whatever direct evidence of the experience survives in Wordsworth's poetry, in spite of his careful attempts to suppress the facts. Such evidence is almost entirely confined to one poem, that known as *Vaudracour and Julia*. Hitherto regarded as one of his dullest poems (Arnold thought it was his very worst) it has suddenly taken on a new interest. It remains a bad poem – one more warning, if that were needed, of the danger of attempting a direct transcript of one's own emotional experience. But it is no longer a dull poem. It is almost a 'human document'.[11]

Read was not only responding to Legouis's biographical work and de Selincourt's textual research; his commitment to surrealism reminds us that the larger context for his criticism includes a concern to register the impact of the First World War on the cultural life of his own time (he had been a combatant), and the emergence of 'Modernism'. Wordsworth was rediscovered as a poet caught up in the drama of rapidly changing times in the 1790s. He was both a poet inclined to radical politics and a man with a guilty secret, and as such he became available as a potential figurehead for those concerned to argue that the cultural life of the nation was ripe for a revolutionary impetus after 1918. As Read gradually developed his picture of Wordsworth in the context of the early nineteenth century, we can detect his enthusiasm for the surrealist manifesto of the early twentieth century, a manifesto produced by a 'period of emotional stress' experienced by Europe after the First World War:

> In that period of emotional stress which followed his experiences in France, Wordsworth evolved not only a new attitude towards the purpose of his art, and the way in which that purpose was to be achieved, but also a general philosophy of life to which his art was subordinate. Actually each theory grew out of the same process of mental adjustment; the theory of art and the theory of life are different aspects of the same growing conviction.[12]

Wordsworth, he suggests, has been misrepresented in the past by readers 'more anxious to discover a new religion than a new poet'; it was against this tendency that Arnold reacted 'almost too violently, going even so far as to make a severe separation between Wordsworth's poetry and his philosophy'. In hastening to dismiss what is 'conventionally pious' and 'moralistic in a common-sense and unemotional fashion', Read argues that Arnold loses what remains of value in Wordsworth's philosophical poetry. At best, he suggests, this is poetry that 'belongs to that rare species of poetry in which *thought is felt*'.[13]

Although he affirms that the later poetry becomes 'conventionally pious', Read finds within it evidence of unorthodox, even atheistic ideas established earlier on in Wordsworth's life which refuse to go away. As his sixth chapter builds towards its conclusion, we see him matching the impasse he perceives within Wordsworth's 'philosophy' to the impasse he diagnoses in contemporary culture, eventually presenting a scenario where the late poetry is doomed to failure, but where it is no less enticing as a body of work justifying critical attention. It carries with it an important message for readers in the 1930s, a message that will not be appreciated unless the full range of Wordsworth's poetry is read in the way he chose to present it, in full, edited and ordered by himself:

> Our attitude towards Wordsworth's philosophy must inevitably be our attitude towards humanism; it is the highest expression of humanism.... The objection to humanism, and it seems to me to be a final one, is that it necessarily assumes this very infinitude of the human mind which inspired Wordsworth. That is an immense assumption. There is nothing in the history of humanity, nothing in our present experience, to justify such a belief. Rather everywhere we have evidence of the mind's finiteness, and mankind's limitation.... What philosophy must we base on that fact? The choice can only lie between stoical scepticism and an uncompromising supernaturalism. Either we are the sport of chance or the children of God. Wordsworth once confessed to Crabb Robinson that the pressing difficulty on his mind had always been to reconcile the prescience of the Almighty with accountability in man. Exactly! The difficulty is not resolvable within the terms of his humanistic philosophy. Either God is prescient and in his will is our peace, or man is accountable to his own Conscience and Intelligence and has no need of a God. There is no compromise between these alternatives. But Wordsworth pretended there was, and his whole philosophy is vitiated by this inherent inconsistency. Wordsworth knew this, and the last phase of his life shows him vainly attempting to hide the heretical significance of his philosophy of nature under a screen of orthodox beliefs.[14]

It is a short step from this to the Wordsworth of 'doubts, revisions and vacillations' discussed by Geoffrey Hartman in 1964. Here the poet is anxiously engaged in exploring the interface between the 'everyday world' and the 'otherworldly power of imagination'. He is increasingly self-conscious about his development (and disintegration) as a poet, and consequently increasingly drawn into editing and categorising, exhibiting a 'tendency to calculation' and an 'increasingly fussy scrutiny of what moved in his mind'. It was this, Hartman, explains, that 'hastened his decline':

> One part of him said, leave nature and cleave to imagination. The other part, fearing that imagination could not be cleaved to, indeed that it would take him beyond human-heartedness even out of this world, answered, cleave to nature and leave vision and romance, those errors of the childhood of poetry.[15]

The dichotomy Read perceived between humanistic stoicism and 'uncompromising supernaturalism' has become a dichotomy between 'nature' and 'vision and romance'. With Wordsworth now established as the epitome of creative tension, as a poet whose work is characterised by what Jonathan Wordsworth has called 'a vulnerable human voice', one who finds himself writing in opposition to 'his personal fear of oblivion', the nineteenth-century Wordsworth, bringer of spiritual resolve in the face of 'honest doubt', is no longer tenable.[16] This transition helped define a way forward for a reappraisal of the later work.

IV

'Laodamia' of 1814 is a poem that displays Wordsworth as a poet grappling not only within the poem, but through a series of revisions of the text, with unresolved tensions between the demands of this world and the next. Herbert Read (the shadow of Arnold notwithstanding) therefore had all he needed to justify his decision to discuss what he described as 'nearly a great poem'.[17] Like Hartman, he was working from the premise that you could, and indeed should, read back into Wordsworth's greatest poetry from work of the calibre of 'Laodamia'.

Laodamia was the wife of Protesilaus. Protesilaus, despite the warnings of Thetis that the first Greek to come ashore in the invasion of Troy would lose his life, led the charge and was finally killed by Hector. When she heard of her husband's death, Laodamia prayed that he might be returned to her. Zeus agreed, but gave Protesilaus only three hours during which he might animate a statue Laodamia had had made. There are at least two versions of what happened next: one is that after the three hours Laodamia stabbed herself to be able to follow Protesilaus; the other is that she was forced by her father to remarry. When her new husband, Acastus, discovered her worshipping the statue of Protesilaus, he ordered it to be burnt. Laodamia then destroyed herself by leaping into the fire.

The poem is a meditation on the consequences of being unable to accept the will of the Gods. When Hermes brings the shade of Protesilaus to her, he explains the terms:

> He comes to tarry with thee three hours' space;
> Accept the gift, behold him face to face!
> (PW 2, 267, 22–3)

But Laodamia wants her husband wholly back, not just a ghostly presence:

> Forth sprang the impassioned Queen her Lord to grasp;
> Again that consummation she essayed...
> (ll.25–6)

In response to this, Protesilaus insists that, 'Spectre though I be, / I am not sent to scare thee or deceive; / But in reward of thy fidelity' (ll.38–40). It seems that the purpose of his return is primarily to lecture Laodamia on the fact that history cannot be undone, and that she must resist the emotional and irrational consequences of her grief, accepting her husband's death:

> Be taught, O faithful Consort, to control
> Rebellious passion: for the Gods approve
> The depth, and not the tumult, of the soul;
> A fervent, not ungovernable, love.
> Thy transports moderate; and meekly mourn
> When I depart, for brief is my sojourn...
> (ll.73–8)

To this he adds reassuring words about his own fate:

> He spake of love, such love as Spirits feel
> In worlds whose course is equable and pure;
> No fears to beat away – no strife to heal –
> The past unsighed for, and the future sure;
> Spake of heroic arts in graver mood
> Revived, with finer harmony pursued;
>
> Of all that is most beauteous – imaged there
> In happier beauty; more pellucid streams,
> An ampler ether, a diviner air,
> And fields invested with purpureal gleams;
> Climes which the sun, who sheds the brightest day
> Earth knows, is all unworthy to survey.
> (ll.97–108)

But Laodamia is unable to control her emotions when Protesilaus departs. The poem gives the impression that she dies of grief; there is no mention of suicide. Readers of the version published in 1815 were then offered the following conclusion:

> Ah, judge her gently who so deeply loved!
> Her, who, in reason's spite, yet without crime,
> Was in a trance of passion thus removed;
> Delivered from the galling yoke of time
> And these frail elements – to gather flowers
> Of blissful quiet 'mid unfading bowers.

At some point before 1827 Wordsworth revisited the poem, and found its conclusion unsatisfactory. He reverted to Virgil's account, and Laodamia was made to pay the full price for her inability to control her passion:

> By no weak pity might the Gods be moved;
> She who thus perished not without the crime
> Of Lovers that in Reason's spite have loved,
> Was doomed to wander in a grosser climb
> Apart from happy Ghosts – that gather flowers
> Of blissful quiet 'mid unfading bowers.[18]

Wordsworth wrote to his nephew, John Wordsworth, to justify the change. He had realised that as it stood, the mission of Protesilaus was rendered pointless: 'He exhorts her to moderate her passion', he fails, and 'no punishment follows'. But then, as if still uneasy with the sentence he has now handed down, he asks John to compare the two passages 'and give me *your* opinion'. Later versions do perhaps suggest a slightly less severe judgement, but her banishment 'from happy Ghosts – that gather flowers / Of blissful quiet 'mid unfading bowers' remains.

The most obvious contrast between the poetry of Wordsworth's so-called 'great period' and 'Laodamia' is the use of a framing device taken from classical mythology. The poetry at once becomes a more formal, austere reflection on the loss of spontaneity which 'Effusion' (from *Memorials of a Tour of Scotland, 1814*) sought to express with more immediacy. 'Laodamia' opens with an impassioned outburst from the heroine:

> With sacrifice before the rising morn
> Vows have I made with fruitless hope inspired;
> And from the infernal Gods, 'mid shades forlorn
> Of night, my slaughtered Lord have I required:
> Celestial pity I again implore; –
> Restore him to my sight – great Jove, restore!
>
> (ll.1–6)

In one sense it is immediate and dramatic. There is no preliminary introduction or explanation; yet this is clearly not Laodamia's appeal to the Gods. The impact is muted as we realise that it is an account of what she has previously done. We find her at the point where her emotional energy is draining away (comparable in this respect to the way Pope represents Eloisa in his *Eloisa to Abelard* of 1717). The story-telling is then subtly tailored to create a continuing ebb and flow of emotion: she is revived by a new hope, then within one line 'terror' is followed by 'joy' ('O terror! what hath she perceived? – O joy!'). The contest between emotion and reason shoulders its way energetically through the poem, but because the outcome is never in doubt (as it is, for example, when the poet of *Lyrical Ballads* exclaims, '"O mercy!" to myself I cried, / "If Lucy should be dead!"'), the drama lies in the extent to which the emotions of Laodamia are brought to life. They are indeed evident, but they remain embedded in a rhetoric that pulls always towards stately utterance rather than emotional abandonment.

Laodamia's defence of love is characteristically muted by the delayed appearance of the word itself in the following stanza, not to mention the final reference to its home in 'feeble woman's breast':

> The Gods to us are merciful – and they
> Yet further may relent: for mightier far
> Than strength of nerve and sinew, or the sway
> Of magic potent over sun and star,
> Is love, though oft to agony distrest,
> And though his favourite seat be feeble woman's breast.
>
> (ll.85–90)

It is interesting to compare Laodamia's eventual fate with that of the murderer in the 'Salisbury Plain' poem that Wordsworth had begun to write in 1793–4. Originally, *Salisbury Plain* was a vehicle for the poet's Godwinian radicalism, and as *Adventures on Salisbury Plain*, revised through 1795–99, it remained (still in manuscript) an outspoken indictment of social injustice. The poem does not condone murder, but it portrays the murderer as one driven to the act by an uncaring, materialistic State. The murderer eventually hands himself over to the law, driven by his conscience, and while Wordsworth does not pardon the crime or question the death sentence, he does question the right of the State to stand in judgement over this man. The representatives of the law in England in the late 1790s are emphatically not to be compared with the Gods in 'Laodamia', 'the just Gods whom no weak pity moved'. This is made very clear not by the judgement, but by the way it is carried out:

> They left him hung on high in iron case,
> And dissolute men, unthinking and untaught,
> Planted their festive booths beneath his face;
> And to that spot, which idle thousands sought,
> Women and children were by fathers brought;
> And now some kindred sufferer driven, perchance,
> That way when into storm the sky is wrought,
> Upon his swinging corpse his eye may glance
> And drop, as he once dropp'd, in miserable trance.[19]

This, as the previous stanza claims, is justice 'violated'.

In the published version of the poem which appeared in 1842 under the title of *Guilt and Sorrow*, there remains no escaping the consequences of murder before the law. The man is executed. But two significant changes were made. The man is no longer a disciple of Reason, but a repentant Christian who cries out ' "My trust, Saviour! Is in thy name!" ', and the humiliation of the corpse is removed:

> His fate was pitied. Him in iron case
> (Reader, forgive the intolerable thought)
> They hung not: – no one on *his* form or face
> Could gaze, as on a show by idlers sought...[20]

In the revisions that went into the published *Guilt and Sorrow*, Wordsworth had tended throughout to deflect what was originally a critique of the political establishment into the realms of domestic melodrama; a revision not entirely dissimilar to the way Mary Shelley had refashioned *Frankenstein* (first published in 1818) for the later 1831 popular edition. The genesis of Wordsworth's story was such that (like *Frankenstein*) it could never be wholly depoliticised; but the thundering attack on old corruption that had brought the original 1793–4 manuscript to a close was replaced by an emphasis on the individual's guilt, and on the stern duty, but also the magnanimity of the State. For readers unaware of the earlier version of the poem, Wordsworth's decision to castigate himself for even thinking it could have been otherwise '(Reader, forgive the intolerable thought)', must have seemed a somewhat perverse way to conclude the poem. We see, of course, that he was dealing with an earlier version of himself; we can appreciate that in the later version of the poem his forgiving instincts are channelled towards the State, which he now views far more favourably than before, and towards the murderer in so far as his Christian faith will guarantee him a passage to Heaven.

In *Sonnets Upon The Punishment Of Death*, first published in 1841, Wordsworth developed his case further by urging readers not to allow their understandable sympathy for the fate of a murderer to blind them to due consideration of the sympathy and right to justice owing to the innocent victim. Dealing with bereavement, as he understood only too well, required a firm will and a rigid control over the temptation to indulge in morbid excess. Reflecting, as he clearly continued to do through these years, on the justice of the death penalty, added a general issue of principle in crime and punishment to the way he viewed Laodamia's failure to abide by the dictates of the Gods.

Here we have two texts, the one (*Salisbury Plain*) emanating from a radical political agenda prior to the 'great period' of the late 1790s and early 80s, the other ('Laodamia') of a significantly later date, reflecting on the dangers of emotional excess and the merits of reason in the trials that beset us around loss and bereavement. In both cases there is a will to mitigate a harsh law of natural justice, and in each case there comes a recognition both of the inevitability of suffering and deprivation as part of human existence, and the rightness of a stern legal code. While in both cases we appreciate that there is a debate going on, in the later poetry we can see a tendency to attempt closure that is not to be found in the early work. Compared, for example, to Lucy Gray, the fate of Laodamia and the murderer of *Guilt and Sorrow* are devoid of any comparable power to engage the reader's sympathies.

Lucy Gray is lost in a storm; her parents search for her and eventually have to accept that she is dead. They do what Laodamia cannot bear to do – they recognise the validity of the Christian promise that was eventually written in to the 'Salisbury Plain' manuscript: 'And now they homeward turn'd, and cry'd / "In Heaven we all shall meet!"'. But this poem does not end there. The poet continues the tale, in the process offering the reader – if not the parents – precisely the kind of open-ended conclusion that Laodamia has first to die for, and then to be punished for beyond the grave:

> They follow'd from the snowy bank
> The foot-marks, one by one,
> Into the middle of the plank
> – And further there were none.
>
> Yet some maintain that to this day
> She is a living Child,
> That you may see sweet Lucy Gray
> Upon the lonesome Wild.
>
> O'er rough and smooth she trips along,
> And never looks behind;
> And sings a solitary song
> That whistles in the wind.
> (*LB*, 172, 53–64)

There can be no suggestion that Wordsworth resisted closure to this extent in the later poetry; but if we return to the sonnet sequence, *Upon the Punishment of Death*, even in this most polemical of exercises, there remains evidence of an engagement with his former poetic self that brings a light (if only a sombre one) into an otherwise gloomy rehearsal of the need for an ultimate deterrent.

The sonnets were written in 1839–40 (*PW* 2, 135–41). The first one of the sequence describes a place that from its beauty might be expected to 'soothe in human breasts the sense of ill', but it is called 'Weeping Hill'. The 'Wordsworthian' effect of natural beauty on the soul is thus challenged. This is the place where convicted criminals have their first sight of what for many of them is to be their place of execution, Lancaster Gaol. The second sonnet argues (as previously mentioned) that, though we may feel pity for the criminal 'by Nature's law', we should be on our guard not to forget the victim:

> But O, restrain compassion, if its course,
> As oft befalls, prevent or turn aside
> Judgments and aims and acts whose higher source
> Is sympathy with the unforwarned, who died
> Blameless – with them that shuddered o'er his grave,
> And all who from the law firm safety crave.
> (ll.9–14)

What might well be taken as a characteristic Wordsworthian trope, the restorative power of nature, is relegated to a secondary role. In its place comes 'Duty', a concept reinforced by the form of the sonnet and the solemnity of the rhetoric employed. The poems exist to counter the argument for abolition that may spring from a mistaken idea of 'Nature's law' (perhaps even a mistaken reading of Wordsworth's poems), and in the final sonnet ('Apology') the poet explains that he is using the poetic medium, a means of expression informed by 'Imagination', in order to underwrite 'reason' and 'Truth':

> Imagination works with bolder hope
> The cause of grateful reason to sustain;
> And, serving Truth, the heart more strongly beats
> Against all barriers which his labour meets
> In lofty place, or humble Life's domain.
> (Sonnet XIV, ll.4–8)

This clearly denotes a profound shift from earlier poetry that appealed to the power of nature to give life and form to abstract ideas of justice and religion. Wordsworth uses the form of poetry here primarily to construct an argument, rather than to summon up the mysterious aura that may be found in natural forms. There is thus a distinction to be drawn between this work and the 'spots of time' passages in *The Prelude* (stealing the boat, skating or crossing the Alps), and the bleak moorland in 'Resolution and Independence'. A sense of the power of an abstract landscape remains, however, but it now exists as much in the form of a potential threat to a society that needs to maintain the rule of law within a Christian context, as a source of personal and social enrichment. We only have to recall the closing lines of 'The Old Cumberland Beggar', published in 1800, to appreciate the extent to which Wordsworth's views had changed. Composed between 1796 and 1798, the poem concludes: 'As in the eye of Nature he has liv'd, / So in the eye of Nature let him die' (*LB*, 234, 188–9). The beggar, of course, is no murderer, but in Sonnet XI of *Punishment of Death* the inference is that God is now understood to fulfil the role previously assigned to nature not just in relation to crime and punishment, but in universal terms:

> Hence thoughtful Mercy, Mercy sage and pure,
> Sanctions the forfeiture that Law demands,
> Leaving the final issue in *His* hands
> Whose goodness knows no change, whose love is sure,
> Who sees, foresees; who cannot judge amiss,
> And wafts at will the contrite soul to bliss.
> (ll.9–14)

This is a very different sentiment from that expressed in Book II of the 1805 *Prelude*, where nature leads the 'spirit of religious love' by the hand, not the other way round as is clearly the case in the Sonnets:

> 'Twere long to tell
> What spring and autumn, and the winter snows,
> And what the summer shade, what day and night,
> The evening and the morning, what my dreams
> And what my waking thoughts, supplied to nurse
> That spirit of religious love in which
> I walked with Nature.
>
> (*Prelude* II, 84, 371–7)

V

In *Wordsworth's Poems of Travel, 1819–42* (1999) John Wyatt argues that in the Preface, and more specifically in the 'Essay Supplementary to the Preface' to the Collected Edition of 1815, Wordsworth begins to signal the direction his later work is to take. It becomes apparent almost immediately that his preoccupations are with poetic form and tradition, and with his own process of categorisation. The primary impulse behind the 'Essay Supplementary to the Preface' is to mount a riposte to Francis Jeffrey's criticism of his work. Jeffrey had made much of Wordsworth's eccentric religious views, and in response the 'Essay' develops a particular focus on the relationship between religion and poetry. It soon becomes clear that the poet of 'Nature' in *Lyrical Ballads* and *Poems in Two Volumes* has become a poet in pursuit of 'knowledge', weighing the relative merits of all the things that produce great poetry in the poet: 'to create taste is to call forth and bestow power, of which knowledge is the effect; and *there* lies the true difficulty' (*Prose Works* 3, 82, 778–80). He has become the poet of 'Laodamia', a poet concerned to realign the relationships between religion and poetry, between reason, passion, and faith:

> In all this may be perceived the affinity between religion and poetry; between religion – making up the deficiencies of reason by faith; and poetry – passionate for the instruction of reason; between religion – whose element is infinitude, and whose ultimate trust is the supreme of things, submitting herself to circumscription, and reconciled to substitutions; and poetry – ethereal and transcendent, yet incapable to sustain her existence without sensuous incarnation.
>
> (*Prose Works* 3, 65, 136–43)

Informing this conviction is a sense of historical process from which Wordsworth conveniently extracts the notion of a poetry whose lasting value may be measured by the scarcity of its readers at any given time:

> wherever the instinctive wisdom of antiquity and her heroic passions uniting, in the heart of the poet, with the meditative wisdom of later ages, have produced that accord of sublimated humanity, which is at once a history of the remote past and a prophetic enunciation of the remotest future, *there*, the poet must reconcile himself for a season to few and scattered hearers.   (ll.818–23)

This conviction directs his own work towards a more formal style, and towards an increasing tendency to work within a culturally historicised framework. This is nowhere more evident than the long three-part sonnet sequence, *Ecclesiastical Sketches*, written for the most part in 1821, first published in 1822, then published in 1837 as *Ecclesiastical Sonnets*. We find it also in the poetry brought together as 'Memorials' of his continental tours in 1820 and 1837. *Ecclesiastical Sketches* were, like the *Punishment of Death* sonnet sequence, written in response to a specific moment, in this case it was the imminence of Catholic emancipation. Despite what has already been suggested about the way they are characteristic of the later poetry, Alan G. Hill has chosen to emphasise the continuity of thought that runs from 'Tintern Abbey' through *The Excursion* and on into these later sonnets. This is a reminder of how carefully the lines of distinction between Wordsworth's early and late work need to be drawn. Much the same awareness marks Jonathan Wordsworth's evaluation (in *The Borders of Vision*, 1982) of the way the poet's religious beliefs influenced the evolution of his poetry.

Hill illustrates how the development of an established church in England over the centuries came to represent for Wordsworth not only 'spiritual and doctrinal realities, but also ideals of family and community life sanctified by the national struggle for liberty over the centuries since the coming of the Romans to Britain'.[21] He reads the later Wordsworth as a poet continuing to engage with the preoccupations of the early work, despite the poet's own insistence that 'no subject but a religious one can answer the demands of my soul'.[22] 'In spite of the title of his sonnet sequence,' Hill writes, 'the poet always returns in the end to natural and human priorities. He does not write as an "ecclesiastic", but for everyman.'[23] Anne L. Rylestone makes a similar case:

While the subject of the series is Church history, its content manifests itself overwhelmingly in images of the natural world. ... More significant than the sheer number of images is the poet's linking of the soul to nature...and of the voice of Christ to the voice of streams. ...The Church takes nature into itself while it is also absorbed into the natural context as an institution, architectural element, and symbol of humanity's striving toward the divine.[24]

Rylestone insists that enthusiasts of the early Wordsworth do not need to look far before they recognise the poet cherished by the Arnoldian school of criticism. She works hard to remove as much of the barrier between early and late poetry as possible:

The power of sensual aspects of the natural scene that in Wordsworth's poetry traditionally prompt association and memory, moving to enlightened states of mind, is now transferred to the Church.[25]

By way of illustration, she quotes from Part III, sonnet 43:

These lofty pillars, spread that branching roof
Self-poised, and scooped into ten thousand cells,
Where light and shade repose, where music dwells
Lingering – and wandering on as loth to die;
Like thoughts whose very sweetness yieldeth proof
That they were born for immortality.
                              (*PW* 3, 405, 9–14)

While the argument is a compelling one, it cannot remove the historical/religious frame that Wordsworth has firmly placed around the sequence, or remove the formal element resident in the sonnet form. Hill and Rylestone do, however, remind us that what is new in Wordsworth here is certainly more complex and interesting than may have been appreciated by readers and critics in the earlier part of the twentieth century.

The sonnet sequence *The River Duddon* of 1820 (*PW* 3, 244–61), the collection that marked a turn in Wordsworth's fortunes where his public was concerned, is equally framed by a historical sense (reinforced by prose work included in the volume) that sets private memories in the context of a formal, public history:

What aspect bore the Man who roved or fled,
First of his tribe, to this dark dell – who first

In this pellucid Current slaked his thirst?
What hopes came with him? what designs were spread
Along his path? His unprotected bed
What dream encompassed?
                    (Sonnet VIII, ll.1–6)

Whence that low voice? – A whisper from the heart,
That told of days long past, when here I roved
With friends and kindred tenderly beloved ...
                    (Sonnet XXI, ll.1–3)

The Duddon volume contained, in addition to the sonnet sequence, a prose description of the geographical location of the river, a prose memoir of the Rev. Robert Walker (referred to in the sonnets), Wordsworth's *Topographical Description of the Country of the Lakes* (first published in 1810), and other poems, including *Vaudracour and Julia* extracted (and excised) from *The Prelude* manuscript of 1805. Wordsworth was making his way forward by joining new work to work already done, by combining poetry and prose, and by establishing religion and history as the monitory framework for such compilations. This is to be contrasted with an earlier time when, it seemed, his writing had been subject to nothing more specific than 'the spontaneous overflow of powerful feelings' (*LB*, 744).

Anne Rylestone argues that the *Duddon* sequence 'actually perpetuates *The Prelude's* impetus toward the integrated experience of material and spiritual realms'.[26] An alternative reading recognises the concoction of this volume as a symptom of Wordsworth's realisation that with the passing of the 'visionary gleam', a strategy had to be developed that would sustain his commitment to poetry. This strategy is made tangible through the construction of an historical frame that does indeed propose an integration of the material and the spiritual realms, while it also results in the editorial construction of a volume such as the *Duddon* anthology. Here we have a falling-off from *The Prelude* rather than a more positive outcome.

John Wyatt, also concerned to address the issue of how Wordsworth managed to sustain his creative impulse, directs his discussion of Wordsworth's later work in a particularly fruitful direction. He argues that for Wordsworth, a poet whose entire output reflects a restless life of constant travel, travelling in his latter years became a primary source of creative reinvigoration. He investigates the way in which travelling, particularly on the continent, helped to inform the construction of a historical narrative within which Wordsworth could place himself and his art. In 1820, Wordsworth retraced the route he had taken as an undergraduate in 1792 across France, through Switzerland into Italy, taking with him this time Mary and Dorothy; they were away for five months. In 1823 he travelled to the Netherlands, to Germany in 1828, and in 1837 (aged 67) he undertook a six-month Odyssey with Henry Crabb Robinson travelling through France and Italy to Rome.

In *Memorials of a Tour on the Continent, 1820*, published in 1822, the Simplon Pass is described in a sonnet (XXIX) as the location of a discarded triumphal column, intended by Napoleon for Milan. This makes the Simplon a place where very specific images of death and pain occur:

> The Soul transported sees, from hint of thine,
> Crimes which the great Avenger's hand provoke,
> Hears combats whistling o'er the ensanguined heath:
> What groans! What shrieks! What quietness in death!
> (*PW* 3, 189, 11–14)

The Simplon Pass was the point at which Wordsworth and Robert Jones had crossed the Alps in 1790, before descending through the Vale of Gondo. The poem that follows this sonnet, 'Stanzas, Composed in the Simplon Pass' (XXX), could hardly contrast more with *The Prelude* Book VI, and the same is to be said for its companion piece written for *Memorials of a Tour in Italy, 1837* (published 1842), 'At Vallombrosa'. Both poems are written in anapaests, the three-syllable metre frequently associated with the poet in his most provocatively 'simple' guise of earlier years. In a poem like 'The Two Thieves' from *Lyrical Ballads*, and even more so in 'The Childless Father', the galloping tendency of the three-syllable foot challenges a latent seriousness of content. This dynamic is completely missing in the later poetry. Wordsworth seems to be reaching for a lyrical music of wistfulness, a melancholy slow waltz rather than a doggerel gallop.

The 1820 Simplon Pass poem is about wishing he were somewhere else:

> The beauty of Florence, the grandeur of Rome,
> Could I leave them unseen, and not yield to regret?

> With a hope (and no more) for a season to come,
> Which ne'er may discharge the magnificent debt?
> (*PW* 3, 189, 9–12)

'At Vallombrosa' (XVIII from the 1837 collection) begins by quoting the 1820 Simplon Pass poem, 'Vallombrosa – I longed in thy shadiest wood / To slumber, reclined on the moss-covered floor!', announcing that he now has his wish (*PW* 3, 23–5, 1–2). The 'Simplon Pass' poem, therefore, turns out to be about something other than the Pass, while 'At Vallombrosa' is in fact a tribute to Milton. 'Vallombrosa' is also a poem in which, despite the trivialising tendency of its rolling metre, Wordsworth reflects seriously on change, on the prospect of death suggested by Autumn at Vallombrosa, and on what remains constant. The final two stanzas contemplate a loosening of ties with 'Forms that must perish', and attempts to focus on the afterlife, when 'the writer of age' increasingly clarifies his priorities:

> Vallombrosa! Of thee I first heard in the page
> Of that holiest of Bards, and the name for my mind
> Had a musical charm, which the winter of age
> And the changes it brings had no power to unbind.
> And now, ye Miltonian shades! Under you
> I repose, nor am forced from sweet fancy to part,
> While your leaves I behold and the brooks they will strew,
> And the realised vision is clasped to my heart.
>
> Even so, and unblamed, we rejoice as we may
> In Forms that must perish, frail objects of sense;
> Unblamed – if the Soul be intent on the day
> When the Being of Beings shall summon her hence.
> For he and he only with wisdom is blest
> Who, gathering true pleasures wherever they grow,
> Looks up in all places, for joy or for rest,
> To the Fountain whence Time and Eternity flow.
> (ll.25–40)

Wordsworth's later poetry without doubt accorded to the changing taste of his nineteenth-century readership. Wyatt considers Wordsworth's travelling not as an attempt to escape from the world in the way that we might expect from a poet of the 'Romantic' era. Wordsworth's travelling is undertaken in the name of education and improvement, and the historical perspective that emerges was bound up with a general reassessment of the Romantic generation that had tended to internalise landscape, frequently imbuing it with radical political inferences no longer acceptable in the post-war era. A return to the Simplon Pass as the young poet had experienced it was not possible. The poetry from his Scottish journey in 1814 had made the situation clear: Ossian was no more, and the poet was threatened with the prospect of becoming little more than a sight-seer. Wyatt's defence of the later poetry is grounded in a similar claim to that made in various ways by Johnston, Manning and Rylestone, heirs to the critical approaches of Hartman and Jonathan Wordsworth. He suggests that the changes we find in the later work are not the result of Wordsworth trying to resolve the problems he encounters as he writes on; flux and uncertainty continue to sit at the centre of his creative drive; but the terms of reference, even the rationale of the poetry itself, have had necessarily to change fundamentally with the passing of time. The question remains, however, as to how far such claims may justify an extended and detailed study of the later work.

10

Conclusion: Critical Issues Then and Now

> I have one request to make of my Reader, which is, that in judging these Poems he would decide by his own feelings genuinely, and not by reflection upon what will probably be the judgment of others. How common is it to hear a person say, 'I myself do not object to this style of composition or this or that expression, but to such and such classes of people it will appear mean or ludicrous.' This mode of criticism so destructive of all sound unadulterated judgment is almost universal: I have therefore to request that the Reader would abide independently by his own feelings, and that if he finds himself affected he would not suffer such conjectures to interfere with his pleasure. (Preface to *Lyrical Ballads*, LB, 759)

I

In this chapter I shall consider why there has been such a marked change in Wordsworth's fortunes in the course of the second half of the twentieth century. At the same time I shall be reviewing Wordsworth criticism in our own time; the latter needs the former to make sense of it. In many respects, the 1960s and early 70s was an inauspicious time to be excited by Wordsworth; there were plenty of other Romantics on offer who seemed more in tune with what was understood to be the spirit of both their own time, and with the preoccupations of post-second-World-War America and Europe. Not least among these was William Blake. New voices were also being discovered; one of the most exciting of these was John Clare (1793–1864), whose genuine 'peasant' simplicity seemed directly to challenge the more self-conscious, assumed simplicity of the

223

university-educated Wordsworth. In 1979 Routledge published Marilyn Butler's *Peacock Displayed*, a study of the life and work of the satirist and member of the Shelley/Byron circle, Thomas Love Peacock (1785–1866). This book was a reminder of how the whole process of canonisation had for some time been rigorously interrogated, along with larger questions about the status of single academic 'disciplines' such as English and History. In her first chapter, Butler developed what was becoming a characteristically historicised approach to the study of literature, moving forward from the lead given by E. P. Thompson and David Erdman to explore the intricacies of a reader/public relationship in what was seen as a technologically, politically and demographically transitional period following the relative stability of the earlier eighteenth century.[1] It was not a good time to be a canonical poet, least of all one who had changed his radical political tune 'for a handful of silver', as Robert Browning, and many others before and since, understood Wordsworth to have done.

Although it is unlikely that major Wordsworth scholars at this time felt seriously threatened or intimidated, there is clear evidence to suggest that there was indeed a widespread conviction that Romantic Studies in general were on the back foot. In 1973, a book of essays based on papers given at a Yale symposium on Romanticism in 1970–71 was published: *Romanticism: Vistas, Instances, Continuities*. It was edited by David Thorburn and Geoffrey Hartman, and included essays by Harold Bloom, Victor Brombert, Cleanth Brooks, Peter Brooks, M. G. Cooke, Paul de Man, Frederick Pottle, Roger Shattuck, and W. K. Wimsatt. In their Preface Thorburn and Hartman wrote:

> Though the War on Romanticism is far from over (the claim of 'countercultural' writers to be neo-Romantic is fostering new skirmishings and suspicions), it is time to acknowledge that Babbitt's 'Rousseau' is as defunct as Eliot's 'Shelley' or Yvor Winters's 'Emerson'. By the shock of juxtaposition – by bringing together, for example, Emerson and Nietzsche, or more expectedly, Wordsworth and Proust – or by a closer, though far from dispassionate, reading of Romantic precursors, new perspectives are born that did not seem attainable a generation ago.[2]

It was war, then, and soon after those words had been written, one of the most powerful weapons to be devised by Wordsworthians on behalf of their cause made its appearance. The first volumes of *The Cornell Wordsworth* began to be published, starting with *The Salisbury Plain Poems of William Wordsworth* in 1975. 'This series', we were told, inaugurated 'a fresh approach to Wordsworth scholarship'. It would present for the first time 'full and accurate texts of Wordsworth's long poems, together with all variant readings from original drafts down to the final printing in the poet's lifetime, or the first posthumous printing'. Before long the series was extended to include the poet's entire output.

I imagine that only the most optimistic of Wordsworth scholars in the 1960s and early 70s could have been tempted to predict the full extent to which the poet's star was to rise in the course of the late 1980s and on into the 90s, though the likely boost provided by the anniversary of the French Revolution was being planned for well in advance. Before considering what has happened in more recent decades, however, it will be helpful to be reminded briefly of the way Wordsworth was initially received when his first published poems began to appear.

II

Wordsworth's reputation was founded on a critical controversy over the poetic quality and political content of his work. Looking back it is possible to see him being reinvented in a haphazard and unpredictable way: *Lyrical Ballads* are read by Wordsworth's contemporaries as a collection of promising new poetry, but before long, they are attacked as the offspring of a nest of dangerous Jacobin 'Lake Poets'; the 1807 *Poems*, initially dismissed as for the most part work of puerile simplicity, subsequently become gems of distilled poetic genius; and *The Excursion* is written off as a tedious disaster, only to rise from the ashes as an inspirational work for Victorian intellectuals besieged by honest doubt and a sense of moral and religious decay. Canning (of the *Anti-Jacobin*) and Jeffrey find Wordsworth a subversive radical, Frederick William Faber thinks he has found a high church Tory, Arnold (side-stepping religion) finds an exquisite lyricist, while Read's Wordsworth is a proto-surrealist.

A résumé of this kind (set against the more detailed exploration of critical issues provided in previous chapters) shows the way in which the study of Wordsworth has from the first been predicated on a controversy over quality, and over where and how to locate the political and religious themes that inform the work. This may not seem to be a situation so very different from that which attends the critical debate around the majority of English Romantic writers and artists. If we think of Blake or Shelley, for example, as poets who failed to find a mass readership because they held firm to principles that were guaranteed to alienate the majority of review-ers and many readers, Wordsworth's commitment to 'simplicity' might well seem comparable. Critical analysis of the Romantics in the twentieth century, however, has come to distinguish between Blake's single-minded commitment to vision, Shelley's unwavering radical atheism, and Wordsworth's crisis of confidence when it came to the function of language as the poet's medium. This can be illustrated by comparing Shelley's *Defence of Poetry* (1821) or his Preface to *Prometheus Unbound* (1819), both single-mindedly didactic statements, to a late-twentieth-century reading of Words-worth's Preface to *Lyrical Ballads*. In 1980, D. D. Devlin ques-tioned the seeming confidence of the Preface, suggesting that to critics of his generation it exposed many anxieties: 'Whom did Wordsworth want to speak to, and to whom did he think he had succeeded in speaking? What should be the poet's relationship with his readers?'[3] Devlin was in fact looking to redirect our attention to Wordsworth's three *Essays Upon Epitaphs* of 1810, where he could illustrate the poet writing openly about the anxieties that informed his poetic practice. *Wordsworth and the Poetry of Epitaphs* (1980) looks like a narrowly focused, specialist study, but in fact it en-dorses a significant general shift taking place in Wordsworth stud-ies that was bringing the poet's work into an ever more harmonious relationship with late-twentieth-century literary critical preoccupa-tions in all areas. Hartman was in the vanguard, suggesting in the mid 1960s that Wordsworth believed 'that the very spirit presiding over his poetry is ephemeral', while two years after Devlin's *Poetry of Epitaphs* Jonathan Wordsworth comments that 'Wordsworth is writing poetry of deliberate imprecision'.[4]

Hartman, Devlin, Jonathan Wordsworth and others were instru-mental in the resurrection of a poet likely to engage the late-twen-tieth-century mind, but the battle was not to be that easily won. There remained powerful voices that threatened to compromise the Wordsworth revival. The literary heroes of E. P. Thompson's pan-theon in *The Making of the English Working Class* (1963) included Thomas Paine, Blake, Cobbett, Richard Carlile and Daniel Eaton. Wordsworth's fate here was to be compared to those whom Thompson had observed deserting the Left in the late 1950s, the apostates of his own day: 'There commenced, for an intellectual generation [and Wordsworth is named as an example], that pattern of revolutionary disenchantment which foreshadows the shoddier patterns of our own century.'[5]

There were many other scholars besides Thompson working on the relationship between Romanticism and political and social history through the 1960s. Amanda M. Ellis published *Rebels and Conservatives: Dorothy and William Wordsworth and their Circle* in 1967. This was aimed as much at the general reader as at the scholar, and it explained in liberal humanist terms why it was that Wordsworth travelled the political road he did. Ellis claimed to have 'examined all extant material on or about the Wordsworths and their circle in this country and in England', but there is not a single reference to Thompson, and he does not appear in the bibliography; nor for that matter does an earlier influential critic, F. M. Todd, who wrote *Politics and the Poet: A Study of Wordsworth* in 1957. In the year after Ellis's book appeared, Carl Woodring published *Politics in English Romantic Poetry*, where he reflected on Wordsworth's capacity to move from 'romantic revolt' to romantic 'fascism'.[6]

There was, therefore, a range of views and of styles to choose from, and it was to Wordsworth's benefit that this work found its place within the larger context of a debate that gathered momentum through the 1970s around the study of history and the practice of 'theory'. In this respect, Thompson's intervention here was once more a significant one with the publication of his essay, 'The Poverty of Theory' in 1978 (in *The Poverty of Theory and Other Essays*, Merlin Press). Wordsworth's engagement with 'history' ensured him plenty of exposure as tempers in History Departments up and down the land became increasingly frayed. In the process a revised version of the Wordsworth already rediscovered by literary critics began to emerge. Wordsworth the Romantic poet had, of course, undergone a major reconstruction well before Todd, Thompson and Woodring. He had been redefined through the work of Legouis, Read, Beatty (*William Wordsworth: his Doctrine and Art in their Historical Relations*, Wisconsin, 1922), and (within the context of textual research) through the work of Ernest de Selincourt, Helen Darbishire and others. But he was for all that still essentially a literary figure. It was the job of critics through the 1970s and into the 80s formally to introduce the inconclusive, anxious Wordsworth, the Wordsworth described by John Lucas in

1990 as 'never entirely sure . . . how to be a poet', to his historically located self.[7] At its most provocative this is the Wordsworth described by Peter J. Manning in 1985 as 'the squire of Rydal Mount', a man 'fulfilling a destiny predicted by his beginnings in that fine, comfortably bourgeois house in Cockermouth – a destiny expected by his relatives, achieved by his brothers Christopher and Richard, and denied John only by his early death'.[8]

Criticism informed by historicism, psychoanalysis, biographical and textual research, by the cross-fertilisation of the many theoretical positions proposed and constantly redesigned for criticism that began to take place in the 1980s, eventually delivered our most recently redesigned Wordsworth; it is a criticism that attempts to engage with as complete a recreation of the poet as possible, textually and biographically, yet a criticism that, being 'postmodern', admits to the impossibility of ever finally being able to 'know' anything for certain, and seeks to make a virtue of the prospect. As the reconstructed poet of doubt and uncertainty, Wordsworth was clearly likely to attract those interested in what has come to be known as our 'postmodern' condition. A postmodernist might be expected to warm to G. Kim Blank's reading of 'Tintern Abbey' and perhaps return to the poet with heightened expectations. In *Wordsworth's Influence on Shelley* (1988), Blank describes Wordsworth as a poet who 'appears to be obsessed with not being where he is but where he was, *even when he is there* . . . [He] handles his absence or dislocation through a subtle yet powerful rhetoric, although the logic of the experience borders on tautology.'[9]

There remain a number of additional factors that might help to explain a contemporary critical climate that places Wordsworth at the heart of current studies in Romanticism in Britain; they all in various ways relate to the reconstructed poet of 'absence or dislocation'. There is the way in which the broader debate around Romanticism has evolved; there is the progress of textual criticism, examples of which are the Cornell project, Owen and Smyser's three-volume *Prose Works of William Wordsworth* (Oxford, 1974), and allied studies which include Devlin on Wordsworth's *Epitaphs*, the reprinting in 1980 of Nowell C. Smith's *Wordsworth's Literary Criticism*, edited by Howard Mills (Bristol), and Jared Curtis's edition of *The Fenwick Notes of William Wordsworth* (Bristol, 1993); there is the progress of biographical research in Wordsworth studies; there is the rise to prominence, in the last ten years in particular, of environmental issues coupled with debates on the consequences of new technologies, a development which has had a profound knock-on effect on many aspects of literary criticism, its conduct and its content; and finally, there has been the appearance through the 1980s of an influential group of critics who adopted a new historicist approach, defining and refining it as they went along, claiming a distinctive and original voice among Words-worth scholars, and generating a good deal of critical heat and eye-catching headlines in the process.

This suggests a daunting agenda, and there is certainly not room to do it full justice within the confines of this chapter. I shall, however, consider each of the five items mentioned above to some degree, beginning with the first: the part played on Wordsworth criticism by the broader debate that has been taking place around the concept of a Romantic Movement.

III

H. G. Schenk's *The Mind of the European Romantics* (1966) sig-nalled a major direction the debate on Romanticism was taking at the time of its publication. Romanticism was here given a European context, and, as Isaiah Berlin stated in his Preface, English writers had been characteristically slow to respond to the European per-spective, and had taken little interest in 'Intellectual history' as a major concern. Schenk's second chapter, 'Progress and Disenchant-ment', discussed the complex process by which belief in 'progress' was undermined. Here again we can discern a perception of Ro-manticism, and of Wordsworth's rediscovered voice within it, that would appeal to critics of the 1980s and 90s; the 'clash between the rational belief in absolute standards and the Romantic concepts of relativity or singularity' that Schenk investigates were to become a major concern for new historicists.[10] Quite specifically, Schenk's reference to the significance in this respect of Giambattista Vico's work, identified as an important influence on Coleridge, establishes a continuity of purpose with a book already considered in previous chapters, Alan Bewell's *Wordsworth and Enlightenment: Nature, Man, and Society in the Experimental Poetry* (Yale University Press, 1989). Bewell embraced the European context in a study that now takes its place at the heart of a late-twentieth-century interdisciplinary critical initiative that had Wordsworth at its centre, and Vico as a primary source for a full understanding of the 'experimental poetry'. Bewell explained that his context was eighteenth-century anthropology, and that the field of study thus proposed might include eighteenth-century ethnology, geology, environmental theory, biblical studies, theology, the genesis of myths, the supernatural, and the idea of death. Isaiah Berlin would have been proud of him, and from this vigorous engagement with a Wordsworth placed in a European, multi-disciplinary context, there emerged a number of studies of Wordsworth rooted in a Euro-centred philosophical rather than a literary or historical method; for example, David P. Haney's *William Wordsworth and the Hermeneutics of Incarnation* (Pennsylvania State University Press, 1993), Mark Edmundson's *Towards Reading Freud: Self-Creation in Milton, Wordsworth, Emerson and Sigmund Freud* (Princeton University Press, 1990), and Amala M. Hanke's *Spatio-temporal Consciousness in English and German Romanticism: A Comparative Study of Novalis, Blake, Wordsworth and Eichendorff* (Peter Lang, 1981). Edmundson acknowledges his debt to Saussure, de Man and Derrida, while Haney recognises the influence on his work of Gadamer, Charles Taylor, Emmanuel Livinas and Stanley Cavell, hardly the staple diet of previous literary critics in pursuit of William Wordsworth.

Examples of more literary, but still essentially cross-disciplinary studies engaging with Wordsworth in the broader context of Romanticism are Susan J. Wolfson's *The Questioning Presence: Wordsworth, Keats, and the Interrogative Mode in Romantic Poetry* (1986), G. Kim Blank's *Wordsworth's Influence on Shelley* (1988), John Lucas's *England and Englishness* (1990), Alan Richardson's *Literature, Education and Romanticism* (1994) and Tim Fulford's *Romanticism and Masculinity: Gender, Politics and Poetics in the Writings of Burke, Coleridge, Cobbett, Wordsworth, De Quincey, and Hazlitt* (1999). All set Wordsworth's poetry in the context of a debate concerned to explore what Wolfson describes as 'the complex nature of English Romanticism and . . . the difficulty – if not the futility – of submitting its several texts to univocal definition'.[11] Her Introduction to *The Questioning Presence* remains a helpful summary of the various positions taken up by M. H. Abrams, de Man, Simpson, Anne Mellor, Tilottama Rajan, Jerome J. McGann and others; while her own thesis, an investigation of English Romanticism and the 'Interrogative Mode', enables her to forge alliances between poets of the period in ways that throw the 'obstinate questionings' of Wordsworth into sharp relief. In an intriguing chapter (already referred to in this book) on *The Excursion*, Wolfson charts in detail the disintegration of the poet as narrator and controlling presence. In consequence, 'We find tales that resist the interpretations put upon them, questions unanswered or answered inadequately, and answers that seem less to answer than to raise new questions about the intelligence from which they issue.'[12]

Two recent examples of books which discuss Wordsworth in the broader context of the Romantic Movement are Lucy Newlyn's *Reading, Writing, and Romanticism: The Anxiety of Reception* (Oxford, 2000), and Richard Cronin's *The Politics of Romantic Poetry: In Search of the Pure Commonwealth* (Palgrave, 2001). While Newlyn continues with the familiar process of decentring the writer, exploring (as her title indicates) the complexities of the relationships between readers, writers, and critics in their various manifestations within what has become only a provisionally located 'Romantic Period', Cronin's book constitutes a challenge to this trend. *The Politics of Romantic Poetry* is concerned to point out that, widely read as we may be, our current Romantic canon does not reflect the appearance of the literary landscape from the vantage point of the 1790s. The most popular poem of that decade, Cronin reminds us, was Erasmus Darwin's *The Botanic Garden* of 1791. Having thus challenged what might be the assumption of his readers with respect to the identity of Romanticism, Cronin moves on to colonise this disputed territory with an argument that attacks the use of a contextual approach designed all too often to explain texts by politicising them.

He suggests that such a form of criticism will tend to judge the merits of any given text in relation to their liberal or radical sympathies. Not entirely fairly (but equally not without some effect), he suggests that critics indulging in this activity rarely if ever show the political commitment they demand from the writers they find wanting. Wordsworth, for him, is very much a case in point, and he suggests that new historicists such as Jerome McGann and Marjorie Levinson are particularly to blame for losing sight of what the true 'politics' of Romantic poetry are, that is to say, primarily a matter of aesthetics rather than radical social and economic programmes of reform. Cronin, however, shares with critics like Butler, McGann, Nicholas Roe and Lucy Newlyn an approach which refuses to be bound by rigid distinctions when it comes to labelling work as 'major' or 'minor', and views the concept of a Romantic Movement as a problematic proposal always in need of careful qualification.

The revolt of the creative imagination against reason may continue to be the norm in accounts of Romanticism offered by books and exhibitions currently around us, but the credibility of such narrowly defined narratives has long since been eroded in criticism of this multi-disciplinary kind. Indicative of this process is Jeremy Adler's review of the early writings of Friedrich von Hardenberg, otherwise known as 'Novalis' (*Times Literary Supplement*, 13 October 2000, pp. 3–4). Here we have a writer whose early death from tuberculosis 'ensured that his pen-name – Novalis – became synonymous with the Romantic myth'. Since 1960 his reputation as a high priest of the imagination, one who, in the manner of a true Romantic, banished the cultural preoccupations of the Enlightenment, has become the subject of intense revisionary scholarship. With the editing and publication of new material, Adler writes:

> We must now replace the image of the inspired but fragmented genius by that of the assiduous early craftsman. ... The biggest surprise, perhaps, is his predilection for the classics, notably Horace ... and there are also versions of Homer and Virgil ...

One is tempted to say that we should not really be that surprised. The transformation of Romanticism into a complex cultural phenomenon which presents us with no clearly drawn boundaries, should prepare us for endless shocks and surprises when we come to look again at the people within the 'movement' we thought we knew well. In this respect it is easy to appreciate that in our own time Wordsworth and Romanticism have had a mutually beneficial relationship. There is manifestly a parallel between Novalis and Wordsworth in the way textual scholarship has functioned to redirect our critical thinking. Of the Novalis volumes under review, Adler writes, 'By painstakingly dating and commentating on every jotting, the editors have dispensed with the Romantic dreamer...' Waves of textual and biographical critics have reconstructed Wordsworth in the same manner, giving us Jonathan Wordsworth's oxymoronic poet of 'deliberate imprecision'.

IV

The second and third critical issues may be considered far more briefly, because a good deal of space has already been allowed to them in previous chapters. They are the growth of textual criticism, and the way biographical criticism has evolved.

The consequences for Wordsworth studies of the exposure given to the intimate textual history of his poetry are profound. While the retrieval, and (notably in Percy Shelley's case) the deciphering of manuscripts, is a consistent point in our critical engagement with most writers, Wordsworth does here seem to present us with a singular case, not least because of the extent of his personal involvement with the later representations of his work through a series of continually revised Collected Editions. Ernest de Selincourt pioneered a scholarly activity that is now a major area of work across the Academy. A crude but telling way of measuring the impact of this activity is to compare what in the mid-1960s constituted the last word in critical editions of *Lyrical Ballads* with what we have now. In 1963 Methuen published a scholarly edition of the *Ballads* edited by R. L. Brett and A. R. Jones. My 'new and revised impression' of 1965 runs to 345 pages. The Cornell *Lyrical Ballads* of 1992, edited by James Butler and Karen Green, has 829 pages. There is no reason to suppose that future editions will not continue to expand.

This proliferation of textual material has provided insights into the life and work of Wordsworth that have transformed our perception of him in most respects. It has also, of course, fuelled debates about how precisely such material should be presented and then used. What, at one level, may be conducted as an objective discussion about editorial procedure, may also move easily into a discussion of far more intimate, personal issues. Here we find ourselves concerned with the third, biographical critical issue.

At his death, Wordsworth left behind him – slowly ticking away – a biographical time bomb of which his notebook drafts and other unpublished matter form only one part. Arguing about Romanticism as a generic term, and the plethora of textual scholarship now available, have both contributed significantly to an explanation of why Wordsworth studies have steadily revived since the 1950s, and continue to expand. However, the discovery of a new Wordsworth, 'Poet – Lover – Rebel – Spy' as Kenneth Johnston summed it up in 1998, points us towards a third reason for the current buoyancy of Wordsworth studies that has been every bit as influential as the other two. What seems to be the British reading public's insatiable appetite for biography must rank very high in any list of reasons why Wordsworth has maintained the position he continues to enjoy in the Romantic rankings. We saw that from the first he was never one to fit in comfortably with what was expected of him, and he has continued to surprise us. A recent example was the debunking of Johnston's spy theory by Michael Durey, prompting a 'Poet – Lover – Rebel' revised edition from a largely unrepentant Johnston in 2000. At the beginning of the twenty-first century, running through virtually all the contemporary critical material on Wordsworth – though by no means always visible – is a response to the writing and rewriting of the poet's personality. A recent contributor to this literature is Juliet Barker, whose *Wordsworth: A Life* was published by Viking in 2000. One of Barker's main claims to originality is her concern to reveal more of Wordsworth as a family man, and to relate this aspect of his life to his poetry. To this end she includes previously unpublished diary and journal entries, and also builds a case for a more generous appreciation of the later poetry, in particular *The Excursion*.

V

The final two critical issues, the appearance of so-called eco-criticism alongside a response to new technologies, and the impact of new historicism, will be allowed more space. This is partly because, to do them anything like justice, it is necessary to return to a consideration of the literary criticism that immediately precedes their appearance. I shall begin, therefore, by looking at some more examples of critical writing on Wordsworth that cover the period from the 1950s to the appearance of the new historicists in the 1980s. It is interesting to see how the critical lines of communication seem to have evolved through the 30 or so years in question; attempting to establish the continuities and discontinuities involved remains the most effective way of understanding the contemporary critical issues at stake in environmental and new historicist work.

In the 1950s and early 1960s New Criticism still dominated. Discussion tended to centre on the poem as the self-sufficient unit for analysis, and to move beyond that was to look, not to ephemeral incidents relating to this world, but towards a unifying experience sought on a higher plain of consciousness. Writing in 1954, F. W. Bateson registered a New Critical urge towards the recognition of organic experience when he perceived 'the impelling need Wordsworth felt to integrate the more subjective or inward-looking aspects of his personality'.[13] Bateson, it should be said, was problematising the issue, but his position was fundamentally the same as that professed by David Ferry, who in 1959 was recommending students to read Wordsworth's poems not 'as evaluations of this world', but 'as symbols of man's relations to the eternal'.[14] Both men imply that we need the critic as a priestly intermediary to set us on the right course. Above all, we are brought back repeatedly to the primacy of the poetry.

In the early 1970s, Frederick A. Pottle reviewed the influence of New Criticism on Wordsworth studies and suggested that while the likes of Ransom, Leavis, Brooks and Empson were prepared to be respectful, they were inevitably prevented by their critical principles from being much more:

> Surely it is very hard to see how Wordsworth's poetry meets New Critical specifications in any obvious sense or in any large degree. Donne is still the type of poet of the New Criticism, and Wordsworth's poetry was consciously opposed to the Metaphysical mode. ...Though he is not wholly without irony and paradox, as Brooks has demonstrated, his poetry at large...offers lean hunting in that species of game. He scorns all the density, the obliquity and indirection treasured by the moderns: he not only tells you straight out how you are to take his poems, he keeps on telling you.[15]

We have already considered how the critical climate was steadily changing, not least as a result of the way Wordsworth studies and studies in Romanticism were jointly progressing. James Twitchell in an essay of 1983 on Wordsworth and the painter Joseph Wright of Derby, suggests a way of understanding how the New Criticism was gradually reinventing itself in the presence of Hartman and the new initiatives he reflected in linguistic, structural and reader-based theories. With reference to Wordsworth's experience of 'a sense sublime / Of something far more deeply interfused' described in 'Tintern Abbey' (ll.95–6), Twitchell suggests that 'we are not the least bit sure how much of the experience really depends on an external world at all'. Citing Hartman, Heffernan, Weiskel and Wlecke, he argues that the following summary conclusion is possible: 'Thanks largely to Wordsworth, the sublime was becoming a psychological event capable of moral significance; it was being transformed back to the sacred.'[16]

While there is clearly much that has happened to influence critical approaches to Wordsworth since Bateson and Ferry, there is no difficulty in recognising in Twitchell's comments an enduring theme from the 1940s: Wordsworth's poems function as 'symbols of man's relations to the eternal'. In 1982 we find David Pirie still probing the contradictions in Wordsworth that had so exercised Bateson. Pirie subtitled his book 'The Poetry of Grandeur and of Tenderness', and early in the Introduction he writes:

> Wordsworth aims to expand our admiration for the grandeur of an impersonal universe until we learn to define ourselves as inseparable from all the myriad forms of life without which we literally would not exist. Yet he also means to concentrate our minds upon a tenderness which only human beings seem to feel, and which may sometimes compel us to ignore everything except those few people whom time, strength or skill allow us to love intensely.[17]

Pirie's book has already been the subject of discussion (see Chapter 3). It may be taken to epitomise (along with Frances Ferguson's *Wordsworth: Language as Counter-Spirit* in the previous decade) the way in which New Critical influences were absorbed into a critical initiative incorporating later theoretical, biographical and textual work. The great poet who promises to transport the reader to a higher state of sensibility, towards an experience equivalent to spiritual revelation, is now also recognised as flawed:

> Wordsworth thus strains language beyond its normal limits. Under such tension, even the works written in his prime sometimes buckle into clumsiness. At points they even collapse into admitted defeat: then Wordsworth chooses to rail at the 'sad incompetence of human speech' rather than conspire with it and allow words to say less than he feels. (*The Prelude* [1850], VI, 593)[18]

In 1991 Brian G. Caraher's *Wordsworth's 'Slumber' and the Problematics of Reading* (Pennsylvania State University Press) developed a blend of philosophical and psychoanalytical reading techniques to produce a critique of Wordsworth according to what was termed 'literary pragmatics'. This seems to be an age away from New Criticism, yet even here it is possible to recognise the reference to a common epicentre, the tension between 'this world' and the 'eternal' (Ferry), between 'human speech' and what the poet 'feels' (Pirie), between 'imaginative construction and temporal unfolding' (Caraher): 'the activity of reading Wordsworth's poetry can lead critical readers into a recognition of the poetry's cognitive and performative fusion of imaginative construction and temporal unfolding'.[19] As well as suggesting a degree of continuity with the past, this also marks out a dramatic advance on what in the 1960s had become something of a rearguard action in defence of Wordsworth's wholeness of vision, what we have already seen Bernard Groom insisting on as 'the fundamental unity of [Wordsworth's] poetry'.[20]

This brings us to the final two developments I want to consider as centrally important in establishing the critical agenda for Wordsworth studies in the late twentieth century. Two critical initiatives emerged in the course of the 1980s in literary studies, both of which had the effect of changing significantly the tone of the critical debate around Wordsworth, and both of which raised the profile of Wordsworth studies within the broader context of studies in Romanticism. New historicism is by far the best known of these. Less often identified on this side of the Atlantic, but no less important, was the appearance of a phenomenon variously referred to as 'eco' or 'green' criticism.

In the course of the 1980s environmental issues became increasingly a matter of international debate, and of political moment in Britain. In the circumstances, Wordsworth (among others) was on offer in the way William Blake had previously been for a generation campaigning for nuclear disarmament. No co-ordinated critical or theoretical camp was formed beneath this banner, but as the issues took on substance and found adherents across university and college campuses, so the academic issues incorporated within the study of the Romantic Movement, the Industrial Revolution, and Wordsworth's poetry, began to show distinct signs of greening. Memories of lively arguments sparked off by F. R. Leavis's public debate with C. P. Snow following the latter's 1959 Rede Lecture on 'The Two Cultures and the Scientific Revolution' were revived, and syllabuses in schools and universities began predictably to twitch in response to environmental passions and technophobia.

Jonathan Bate was one of the first to see the opening and map out the territory with *Romantic Ecology: Wordsworth and the Environmental Tradition*, published in 1991 by Routledge. 'I acknowledge', Bate wrote in his Introduction, 'that a re-reading of a nineteenth-century poet is not actually going to have any effect on any government's policies concerning "green" issues...' But he went on to insist that it was 'valuable and important to make claims for the historical continuity of a tradition of environmental consciousness; Wordsworth by no means initiated that tradition, but he has been a vital influence upon it'.[21]

In the following year, Nicholas Roe published *The Politics of Nature: Wordsworth and Some Contemporaries* (Macmillan Press – now Palgrave Macmillan). Roe aimed to register the inadequacies of new historicism, but the blurb extended that agenda considerably:

> Provocative and timely, *The Politics of Nature* offers a challenging reappraisal of historical criticism in the Romantic field. Arguing that some aspects of new historicism have amounted to a 'cultural default' by the academy at a time of socio-political crisis, Nicholas Roe defines a new relevance for literary studies in the 1990s. In particular, he identifies our present condition with the 'greedy and unsocial selfishness' that, for John Thelwall, succeeded the collapse of the revolution in the mid-1790s. Nicholas Roe contends that the enlightened responses of this earlier generation have much to offer our own post-revolutionary age. While acknowledging the relevance of environmental issues to the 1990s, the author eschews generalisations about 'red' and 'green' politics. He looks instead to a new, radical humanism – the politics of nature – to initiate a future for the world of all of us.

Heady stuff, and laid out in that form it is hardly surprising to find that Roe's book, while forming a valuable addition to the critical canon, fails to deliver the entire package; and it seems to have proved to be too difficult an act to follow for any radical humanist Wordsworth scholar, no matter how strongly motivated.

The fact remains, however, that in the context of Romanticism there has been a significant development through the 1990s of work that is committed to raising awareness in the reader about environmental issues as they continue to impinge on our world with the threat of increasingly serious consequences. Such work has tended to focus initially on Wordsworth as a pedestrian traveller, as one who responded to those who were forced into travelling because they had no stake in a settled home. *Wordsworth's Vagrant Muse: Poetry, Poverty and Power* by Gary Harrison was published in 1994 (Wayne State University Press); the following year Celeste Langan published *Romantic Vagrancy: Wordsworth and the Simulation of Freedom* (Cambridge). Both of these books might be seen as promoting 'radical humanism'; neither of them engages directly with green political issues. The final paragraph of Langan's 'Methodological preamble' illustrates well how the environmental agenda is clearly implied where not explicitly stated. She has already referred to the distinction made by Marx between a 'peasant' world and that of modernity, insisting that it turned 'on a conflict between "the rights of agricultural property" and *absolute* property rights'. The Marxist reference conjures up images of a natural world being progressively destroyed by aggressive industrialisation in the course of the nineteenth century. Langan then seeks to free the Marxist perspective from its historical location by quoting Halpern on Renaissance culture, suggesting that what he has to say may be taken as a general truth. Marx on 'capital' is relevant to 'the postmodern subject' in respect of all its difficulties:

> In *The Poetics of Primitive Accumulation*, a study of Renaissance culture, Richard Halpern has also suggested that the vagrant is both the hallucinatory double of capital and 'a precocious and nightmarishly exaggerated image of modernity'. I believe this 'anticipatory' aspect of the vagrant, a figure of what 'will have been' the condition of the postmodern subject, is a consequence of the vagrant's formal imitation of an abstract concept: negative liberty. In the same way, I will argue, the Romantic poem's formal reduction of freedom of expression to a 'common' metre, the equalized lines of iambic pentameter, or the ventriloquized epitaph disables our tendency to regard even the most rambling story as a narrative of progress. In this sense, it is peculiarly 'postmodern', for Romanticism denies us a belief that modernity 'occurs,' except as a retrospective illusion.[22]

If neither Harrison nor Langan appeal overtly to 'green' politics, they are both, like Robin Jarvis in *Romantic Writing and Pedestrian Travel* (1997), concerned to explore a 'radically levelling culture of pedestrianism'. 'Only now, as we near the end of the twentieth century,' Jarvis concludes, 'have conditions been re-established in which walking has become, for some, a political act.'[23] Work of this order is reasserting the significance of our physical engagement with the landscape, reanimating ideas of the responsibilities we have towards the places in which we are; and it insists on the fact that our relationship to such places is incontrovertibly political. It also reanimates the notion of our potential status as rebels if we care about such things. It is with this point in mind that Roe's foray into environmental criticism is best understood; it provides him with the frame he requires to critique what new historicists have done with Wordsworth.

In an intriguing book published in 1998, *Romantic Geography: Wordsworth and Anglo-European Spaces* (Macmillan Press – now Palgrave Macmillan), Michael Wiley applies a postmodern geographical interest in spatial theory to a reading of selected canonical Wordsworth texts. Again, this is not a self-consciously 'green' exercise in literary criticism, but it exhibits throughout a sensitivity to environmental issues, and makes a convincing case for the relevance of contemporary spacial theory for the study of literature. Wiley's work is an example of the kind of interdisciplinary project that studies in Romanticism have engendered of late, and that have reanimated and frequently politicised the study of Wordsworth. It is all a far cry from the poem as inviolable object for critical study. One of the most interesting events in the recent history of eco-criticism has been the appearance of another book by Jonathan Bate, *The Song of the Earth* (Picador, 2001). Bate considers a wide range of Romantic and post-Romantic poetry, offering us in the process yet another visit to Wordsworth's 'Tintern Abbey'. Compared to American critics in this field (such as Cheryll Glotfelty) Bate's focus remains aesthetic rather than political; but impressive and stimulating as his practice of 'Ecopoetics' generally is, he can appear perversely indecisive when it comes to recognising the political issues that inevitably demand attention in the course of the book.

VI

It is time now to consider the fifth and final critical issue on this list: new historicism. Nicholas Roe's dissatisfaction with new historicism has been registered above. Bate, while acknowledging in *Romantic Ideology* the debt criticism owes to this approach for the way it has challenged 'the hegemony which idealizing, imagination-privileging critics like Geoffrey Hartman and Harold Bloom held over Romantic studies in the United States for twenty years', is equally critical of the final outcome. McGann's location of Romanticism as ideology, he insists, 'is splendidly true in some respects and deeply false in others'.[24] If there is one thing, however, that the majority of the twentieth-century critical approaches considered in this book have in common, it is the fact that they have to some degree been influenced by the evolution of clinical psychoanalysis. Where this is true of criticism dating from the 1980s and 90s, it will tend to mean that (whether the author likes it or not), such criticism may be deemed to fall within the ubiquitous critical shadow of new historicism. It is this specific style of analysis that has led to one of the major complaints about new historicism within the Wordsworth critical establishment. As we have already seen, new historicists such as Levinson, Liu and Simpson, make a point of addressing not just the poem as it appears on the page, but the 'absences' that they are able to deduce from the texts before them. We have already noted Thomas McFarland's attack on such work in his *William Wordsworth: Intensity and Achievement* (1992).

In his Introduction to *Wordsworth's Historical Imagination* (1987) David Simpson's engagement with the issue of absence is considerably more muted than that of Marjorie Levinson, McFarland's chief target. His perception of displacement is less a matter of absence than concealment:

> Close inspection of the poet's language seems to me, however, to make clear that it very seldom manages to repress efficiently the traces of whatever most threatens its ideal or other-worldly aspirations. We can admit that there is in many poems an attempt to establish an alternative (displaced) consolation beyond the empirical-historical; but the language of such attempts very often contains the terms of its own undermining.[25]

Simpson traces the origins of new historicism to what he calls 'materialist literary criticism', and he mentions in particular Raymond Williams's *Marxism and Literature* of 1977. He describes his own approach as resistant to, or wary of, an overly theorised commitment, preferring to apply psychoanalytical techniques to aid the project of historicising the text.[26] As a 'moment' in late-twentieth-century Wordsworth critical studies, it is not difficult (with hindsight) to see how the strands of critical enquiry that encircle the study of Romanticism lead towards a formulation of this kind for the study of Wordsworth. Alongside the appropriation of psychoanalysis, there is a revived interest in Marxist materialism: we observed its importance in Langan, it is there in Harrison, it appears (courtesy of Raymond Williams) in Simpson, and it is very important in the thesis of an immediate precursor to Simpson, John Turner's *Wordsworth: Play and Politics* (Macmillan Press – now Palgrave Macmillan, 1986), an intriguing exploration of the interplay between politically focused literary criticism and psychoanalysis.

The impact of new historicism on Romantic studies, and in particular on Wordsworth, has been considered in some detail in the course of previous chapters. An abridged genealogy of the movement should begin with Jerome J. McGann's *The Romantic Ideology* of 1983, followed by Marjorie Levinson's *Wordsworth's*

Great Period Poems of 1986, David Simpson's *Wordsworth's Historical Imagination* of 1987, and Alan Liu's monumental *Wordsworth: the Sense of History* of 1989. Understandably controversial from the start, no critical 'school' or 'movement', apart from the Cornell project, has done more since the biographical and textual work of the early twentieth century to breath new life into Wordsworth studies in England. What the Cornell editors have achieved, in conjunction with the progenitors of new historicism, is to redefine the perameters of what it means to study Wordsworth and his 'Romantic' context (for one thing, it has helped to hang a set of inverted commas around the term Romantic in this sentence).

At the end of *Wordsworth: the Sense of History* Alan Liu attempts to summarise his methodology and its difficulties through an imagined dialogue with himself. The result may seem coy, and he accuses himself (disingenuously) of being disingenuous, but it remains a useful exercise:

> *Yet it is your very belief we find disturbing. You have said that literature is historical in origin, and you have amassed historical context from whatever sources were available to you or that you have had time to accomplish in order to make yourself credible. And on the whole, you believe that you have succeeded, that armies of context allow you to translate yourself from literature into history, from present into past, from yourself into someone other...*
>
> *And now we come to the heart of your deception. Can you honestly say that what you mean by history is distinguishable from what your poet meant by imagination? Can you even say that history, for you, is different from autobiography?*

I do not know what you mean.

> *Do not be disingenuous. Critic, we criticize you in the way that recidivists were 'criticized' in that other revolution of culture you would rather not think about in that land of your parents' origin. We criticize you for being the romanticizer of your own elsewhereness. Has not Wordsworth's sense of history, emergent from the French Revolution, merely served as the medium for your own sense of history, emergent from a different revolution – a history and a world for which you have no other means of expression?*[27]

As his accuser closes in for the kill, it sounds as though Wordsworth's 'displacements' are in reality a projection of Liu's own displacement activity (726 pages worth). Or are they? Liu defends his position in this imaginary tribunal, and if you want to play, you must read on for yourself.

We surely all recognise well enough by now this process of intellectual game-playing generically referred to as 'postmodernism'. But given that Liu's strategy here seems to me to be painfully contrived, and not a little old-fashioned, we should also begin to consider whether the new historicist initiative might be running out of steam. Should that prove to be the case, what might replace it? If we are to believe Simon Jarvis, new historicism has most certainly had its day. He is prepared to suggest that for a critic in Liu's mould the determination to maintain a 'resistance to reductiveness' has resulted in sterile 'reductively anti-reductive' criticism. Here is how Jarvis begins his review (in *The Times Literary Supplement*, October 2000) of Catherine Gallagher and Stephen Greenblatt's *Practicing New Historicism* (University of Chicago Press, 2000):

> Critical movements which were once new get old, but they haunt the places where their honour died. They are condemned to remain forever 'new'. Despite the longevity of 'new historicism', its most subtle practitioners have been cautious about defining it. The fluidity has been important both to the intellectual, and to the institutional, achievements of the new historicists; but it is hard now to recall the sense of mingled relief and excitement with which one read early efforts in this line of work. Their resistance to reductiveness of all kinds; their tenacity in teasing out, rather than crushing, the peculiar historical flavour of an anecdote; their insinuation of extra-literary texts into the world inhabited by the great monuments: all these characteristic excellences now feel as though they have become the inert badges of an army of critics reductively anti-reductive, and eccentric by rote. In particular, new historicism can now retrospectively be understood as a crucial instrument in damagingly disconnecting literary theory from philosophy; and, thus, in clearing the way for jubilant anti-intellectualisms 'after' theory: the 'new' empiricism and the 'new' formalism.

As this book has attempted to suggest, old critical theories/schools/approaches/orthodoxies never die; rather, they fade away while at the same time being reborn in some alternative form in conjunction with other equally retreaded sets of ideas. Behind the process lies a number of constantly recycled sets of opposing forces of many different kinds. In the realm of studies in Romanticism, these opposing forces invariably seem to include Reason and Imagination, History and Literature, Cultural Studies and single disciplines, Public and Private, Thought and Feeling, Radical and Reactionary, Mind and Body, the Country and the City.

In the mid 1990s, G. Kim Blank, posing (quite figuratively so in the photograph on the dust jacket) as a 'maverick' among literary critics (the term for him used by Jean Hall, and quoted on the dust-jacket), summed up the critical issues that were jostling him for attention as he set about writing *Wordsworth and Feeling: The Poetry of an Adult Child* (1995). It is a passage that attempts to summarise the critical story to the end of the last millennium:

> When I read and study poetry these days, I feel that my response, my positioning, is uncertain – and maybe even paradoxical. It is partly the two-hand problem: the rhetorical versus the referential, the sliding of the signified under the signifier. Can we *extract* from language – more particularly, radically self-conscious written language – the actual feelings and meanings of another person from another culture and another time? And whose story is history: that of the victors or the victims? Whose meaning counts: that of the actors or the audiences, the coders or the decoders, the authors or the readers? To borrow Freud's syntax: Where the Author is, the reader shall be. Are producers of messages at one with consumers of meaning? Are we chameleon interpreters, capable of empathetically filling the body of any other, even a sparrow poet picking about in the gravel; or are we egotistically sublime readers, remaking the world in our own autobiographical or idealized image? Does language have its own independent reality? Should we respond to a text with our critical intellect or with our emotions? Can we even separate these two, or privilege one over the other? These are, in many ways, old questions, but they are also questions that will not go away with the birth or burial of a new theory of language, reading, or criticism.[28]

Blank's response in the course of this book is to lean heavily for his approach on psychoanalysis, to revisit with particular care the literary, historical and biographical evidence that surrounds the poet's childhood, and to appeal to his reader to reflect deeply on their own experiences in an attempt to explore the way in which Wordsworth first identifies, and then attempts to reconcile, the divisions in his psyche that haunt his poetry:

> When Wordsworth discovered something about his own inner healing, he also touched something within all of us. And so, in the end, we return to where this story began, with the universal that springs forth from the personal, to the child within all of us.[29]

Blank's resistance to any one guiding theoretical principle may be accounted 'modern'; in another sense, of course, his reference to 'the universal' born from 'the personal' is reminiscent of a much earlier-nineteenth and early-twentieth-century tradition of criticism. His investigation of the place of the child in Wordsworth's poetry, and of the child in Wordsworth himself, is hardly original. What Blank does that clearly is relatively unusual is to try and recapture a sense of Wordsworth as a singular person, rather than set an image of him up to be used as a case study for some theoretical or ideological position. Despite the somewhat pretentious foregrounding of Blank that takes place on the periphery of this book – he appears as a long-haired, leather-clad 'maverick' type of new-age academic straddling the chair he sits on – within the text itself the author is for the most part far less intrusive than is, for example, Alan Liu in *Wordsworth: the Sense of History*. I have quoted from the Introduction, and from the final paragraph. In the main body of the book room is made for the poet as subject to materialise. The critic, no less manipulative than he or she is ever likely to be, remains for the most part hidden from view.

Blank is at pains to avoid the more traditional tropes of biography, as well as the more familiar applications of psychoanalysis associated with reader response or gender criticism. With particular reference to the poet's childhood, he seeks to understand more about what caused Wordsworth to write in the way he did. The motive for this is firmly concentrated on the desire to understand more fully the poems themselves. He wishes to unlock the innermost secrets of the poetry because he knows they have been of benefit to him, and in the future may continue to be so; and he believes he may help us to benefit from them in the same way. Wordsworth himself, it seems, had had similar thoughts:

> Oh dearest, dearest boy! My heart
> For better lore would seldom yearn,
> Could I but teach the hundredth part
> Of what from thee I learn.
> ('Anecdote for Fathers', *LB*, 73, 57–60)

Notes

INTRODUCTION

1. Jerome J. McGann, *The Romantic Ideology: A Critical Investigation* (Chicago and London: University of Chicago Press, 1983), p. 90.

2. Ralph Pite, Review of *Wordsworth: A Life*, by Juliet Barker (Viking, 2000), in *The Times Higher Education Supplement*, 24 August 2001, p. 24.

CHAPTER 1: THE EARLY YEARS: POLITICS AND POETRY

1. *LB*, p. 743, ll.65–73; *The Edinburgh Review*, No.1, 25 October 1802, p. 63.

2. *The Letters of Mary Wollstonecraft Shelley*, ed. Betty T. Bennett, 3 vols (Baltimore and London: Johns Hopkins University Press, 1995), p. 65.

3. Quotations in this paragraph are from 'Ode: Intimations of Immortality' in *Poems 1807*, 277, 205; and 'Tintern Abbey' in *LB*, 118, 71–3.

4. See John Williams (ed.), 'Introduction', *Wordsworth: Contemporary Critical Essays*, New Casebook (London: Macmillan Press – now Palgrave Macmillan, 1993), pp. 1–32.

5. Kenneth R. Johnston, *The Hidden Wordsworth: Poet, Lover, Rebel, Spy* (New York and London: W. W. Norton, 1998).

6. John F. Danby, *The Simple Wordsworth* (London: Routledge and Kegan Paul, 1960), pp. 18, 33.

7. M. H. Abrams, 'On Political Readings of *Lyrical Ballads*', in *Doing Things with Texts* (New York and London: W. W. Norton, 1989), p. 379.

8. E. de Selincourt (ed.), *The Letters of William and Dorothy Wordsworth: The Early Years, 1787–1805*, 2nd edn, revised by Chester L. Shaver (Oxford: Clarendon Press, 1967), p. 3.

9. Nicholas Rowe, *The Politics of Nature* (London: Macmillan Press – now Palgrave Macmillan, 1992), pp. 17–35.

10. *Monthly Literary Recreations III*, July 1807, in *Romantic Bards and British Reviewers*, ed. John O. Hayden (London: Routledge and Kegan Paul, 1971), p. 10.

11. Robert Mayo, 'The Contemporaneity of the *Lyrical Ballads*', *PMLA*, 69 (1954), 486–522. See also Paul D. Sheats, 'The *Lyrical Ballads*', in *English Romantic Poets*, ed. M. H. Abrams (Oxford: Oxford University Press, 1975), pp. 133–48.

12. Johnston, *The Hidden Wordsworth*, p. 77.

13. Geoffrey H. Hartman, 'Wordsworth Revisited', in *The Unremarkable Wordsworth* (London: Methuen, 1987), p. 3.

14. John Williams, *Wordsworth: Romantic Poetry and Revolution Politics* (Manchester: Manchester University Press, 1989), pp. 30–1.

15. John Williams, *William Wordsworth: A Literary Life* (London: Macmillan Press – now Palgrave Macmillan, 1986), pp. 25–37. See Caroline Robbins, *The Eighteenth Century Commonwealthman* (New York: Atheneum, 1968).

16. Nicholas Roe, *Wordsworth and Coleridge: The Radical Years* (Oxford: Clarendon Press, 1988), pp. 192–8.

17. *An Evening Walk*, ed. James Averill (Ithaca, NY and London: Cornell University Press, 1984), pp. 32–4, ll.37–48.

18. Thomas R. Edwards, *Imagination and Power: A Study of Poetry on Public Themes* (London: Chatto and Windus, 1971), p. 119.

19. John Sitter, *Literary Loneliness in Mid-Eighteenth Century England* (Ithaca, NY and London: Cornell University Press, 1982). *British Literature: 1640–1789*, ed. Robert Demaria Jnr (London: Blackwell, 1996).

20. John Williams, *William Wordsworth, A Literary Life*, pp. 35, 55.

21. *Descriptive Sketches*, ed. Eric Birdsall (Ithaca, NY and London: Cornell University Press, 1984), p. 118, ll.810–11.

22. Thomas Paine, *Rights of Man*, ed. Henry Collins (Harmondsworth: Penguin Books, 1969), p. 64.

23. *The Salisbury Plain Poems of William Wordsworth*, ed. Stephen Gill (Ithaca, NY and Hassocks: Cornell University Press, 1975), p. 22, ll.61–3.

24. *The Borderers*, ed. Robert Osborn (Ithaca, NY and London: Cornell University Press, 1982), p. 62.

CHAPTER 2: NEW DIRECTIONS: *THE RUINED COTTAGE*

1. For further information and sources, see Butler and Green's Introduction to *LB*, pp. 3–5.

2. See Kenneth R. Johnston, *The Hidden Wordsworth: Poet, Lover, Rebel, Spy* (New York and London: Norton, 1998), pp. 526–31; and Nicholas Roe, *Wordsworth and Coleridge: The Radical Years* (Oxford: Clarendon Press, 1988), pp. 257–62.

3. Details of the textual evolution of *The Ruined Cottage* are to be found in *Ruined Cottage*, pp. 7–14.

4. John Williams, *Wordsworth: Romantic Poetry and Revolution Politics* (Manchester: Manchester University Press, 1989), pp. 29–31.

5. Johnston, *The Hidden Wordsworth*, pp. 513 and 901.

6. *The Salisbury Plain Poems of William Wordsworth*, ed. Stephen Gill (Hassocks: Cornell University Press, 1975), p. 38, ll.541–5.

7. Johnston, *The Hidden Wordsworth*, p. 524.

8. 'The Baker's Cart' is reproduced in *Ruined Cottage*, p. 463–5.

9. Jonathan Wordsworth, *The Music of Humanity* (London: Nelson, 1969).

10. F. R. Leavis, *Revaluations: Tradition and Revolution in English Poetry* (London: Chatto and Windus, 1936), p. 179. See *Ruined Cottage*, p. ix.

11. Geoffrey Hartman, *Wordsworth's Poetry* (London and Cambridge, MA: Harvard University Press, 1987), p. 140.

12. William H. Galperin, *Revision and Authority in Wordsworth: The Interpretation of a Career* (Philadelphia: University of Pennsylvania Press, 1989), p. 72.

13. David B. Pirie, *William Wordsworth: The Poetry of Grandeur and of Tenderness* (London: Methuen, 1982), p. 70.

14. *The Letters of William and Dorothy Wordsworth: The Early Years, 1787–1805*, ed. E. de Selincourt, revised by Chester L. Shaver (Oxford: Clarendon Press, 1967), p. 212.

15. Stephen Maxfield Parrish, 'Dramatic Technique in the *Lyrical Ballads*', in *Wordsworth: Lyrical Ballads*, ed. Alun R. Jones and William Tydeman (London: Macmillan Press – now Palgrave Macmillan, 1972), p. 130.

CHAPTER 3: NEW DIRECTIONS: *LYRICAL BALLADS*

1. Bernard Groom, *The Unity of Wordsworth's Poetry* (London: Macmillan Press – now Palgrave Macmillan, 1966), p. 30.

2. Stephen Maxwell Parrish, 'Dramatic Technique in the *Lyrical Ballads*', in *Wordsworth: Lyrical Ballads*, ed. Alun R. Jones and Williams Tydeman (London: Macmillan Press – now Palgrave Macmillan, 1972), p. 130.

3. Ibid., p. 132.

4. David B. Pirie, *William Wordsworth: The Poetry of Grandeur and Tenderness* (London: Methuen, 1982), p . 69.

5. Marjorie Levinson, *Wordsworth's Great Period Poems* (Cambridge: Cambridge University Press, 1986), p. 12.

6. Ibid., p. 5.

7. Thomas McFarland, *William Wordsworth: Intensity and Achievement* (Oxford: Clarendon Press, 1992), p. 5.

8. Ibid., pp. 10, 12.

9. Marilyn Butler, *Romantics, Rebels, and Reactionaries: English Literature and its Background 1760–1830* (Oxford: Oxford University Press, 1982), pp. 59 and 61.

10. William Hazlitt, *The Spirit of the Age* in *The Complete Works of William Hazlitt*, ed. P. P. Howe (New York: AMS Press, 1967), vol. XI, p. 132.

11. John Williams, *Wordsworth: Romantic Poetry and Revolution Politics* (Manchester: Manchester University Press, 1989), pp. 9–18.

12. David P. Haney, *William Wordsworth and the Hermeneutics of Incarnation* (Pennsylvania: Pennsylvania University Press, 1993), p. 91.

13. Roger Sales, 'William Wordsworth and the Real Estate', in *Wordsworth: Contemporary Critical Essays*, ed. John Williams (London: Macmillan Press – now Palgrave Macmillan, 1993), p. 96

14. John Lucas, *England and Englishness* (London: Hogarth Press, 1990), p. 106.

15. *The Letters of William and Dorothy Wordsworth: The Early Years, 1787–1805*, ed. E. de Selincourt, revised by Chester L. Shaver (Oxford: Clarendon Press, 1967), p. 314.

16. John Lucas, *England*, p. 104.

17. Kenneth R. Johnston, *The Hidden Wordsworth: Poet, Lover, Rebel, Spy* (New York and London: W. W. Norton, 1998), p. 701.

18. *The Letters of William and Dorothy Wordsworth: The Early Years*, p. 313.

CHAPTER 4: PUTTING THE POETRY IN ORDER: *POEMS IN TWO VOLUMES* (1807)

1. See Kenneth R. Johnston, *Wordsworth and The Recluse* (New Haven, CT and London: Yale University Press, 1984), p. xvii.

2. John Powell Ward, *The English Line* (London: Macmillan Press – now Palgrave Macmillan, 1991), p. 34.

3. Ibid., p. 35.

4. Mary Jacobus, *Romanticism, Writing, and Sexual Difference: Essays on The Prelude* (Oxford: Clarendon Press, 1989), p. 69.

5. *Poems in Two Volumes* was arranged in the following way: Volume 1, 'The Orchard Pathway' (this title was cancelled before publication), 'Poems Composed During A Tour, Chiefly On Foot', 'Miscellaneous Sonnets', 'Sonnets Dedicated To Liberty'. Volume 2, 'Poems Written During A Tour In Scotland', 'Moods Of My Own Mind', 'The Blind Highland Boy; With Other Poems'. *Poems 1807*, pp. 59–62.

6. Frances Ferguson, *Wordsworth: Language as Counter-Spirit* (New Haven, CT and London: Yale University Press, 1977), p. 94.

7. Ibid., p. 95.

8. Ibid., p. 95.

9. D. D. Devlin, *Wordsworth and the Poetry of Epitaphs* (London: Macmillan Press – now Palgrave Macmillan, 1980).

10. Geoffrey H. Hartman, 'Wordsworth Revisited', in *The Unremarkable Wordsworth* (London: Methuen, 1987), p. 3.

11. Marjorie Levinson, *Wordsworth's Great Period Poems* (Cambridge: Cambridge University Press, 1986). Alan Liu, *Wordsworth: The Sense of History* (Stanford, CA: Stanford University Press, 1989). David Simpson, *Wordsworth's Historical Imagination: The Poetry of Displacement* (London: Methuen, 1987).

12. Levinson, *Wordsworth's Great Period Poems*, p. 12.

13. Alan Bewell, *Wordsworth and the Enlightenment* (New Haven, CT and London: Yale University Press, 1989), pp. 222–31.

14. Francis Jeffrey, *The Edinburgh Review*, XI (October 1807), 214–31, quoted in *Romantic Bards and British Reviewers*, ed. J. O. Hayden (London: Routledge and Kegan Paul, 1971), p. 23.

15. Ibid., p. 15.

16. *The Letters of William and Dorothy Wordsworth: The Middle Years*, ed. E. de Selincourt, 2nd edn, Vol. I, 1806–11, revised by Mary Moorman (Oxford: Clarendon Press, 1969), p. 7.

17. Jonathan Wordsworth, *William Wordsworth: The Borders of Vision* (Oxford: Clarendon Press, 1982), p. 201.

18. Liu, *Wordsworth: The Sense of History*, pp. 1–31, and 469–87.

19. Frances Ferguson, *Wordsworth: Language as Counter-Spirit*, p. 98.

20. Levinson, *Wordsworth's Great Period Poems*, p. 5.

CHAPTER 5: THREE NARRATIVE POEMS: *PETER BELL* (1798/1819), *BENJAMIN THE WAGGONER* (1806/1819), *THE WHITE DOE OF RYLSTONE* (1807/1815)

1. *Champion*, 25 June 1815, pp. 205–6, quoted John O. Hayden, *Romantic Bards and British Reviewers* (London: Routledge and Kegan Paul, 1971), p. 66.

2. John Turner, *Wordsworth: Play and Politics* (London: Macmillan Press – now Palgrave Macmillan, 1986), p. 151. J. H. Alexander, *Reading Wordsworth* (London: Routledge and Kegan Paul, 1987).

3. Alan Bewell, *Wordsworth and the Enlightenment: Nature, Man, and Society in the Experimental Poetry* (New Haven, CT and London: Yale University Press, 1989), p. 96.

4. Bernard Groom, *The Unity of Wordsworth's Poetry* (London: Macmillan Press – now Palgrave Macmillan, 1966), pp. 128 and 130. See also Mary Jacobus, *Tradition and Experiment in Wordsworth's 'Lyrical Ballads', 1798* (Oxford: Clarendon Press, 1976), and Thomas McFarland, *Romanticism and the Forms of Ruin: Wordsworth, Coleridge and Modalities of Fragmentation* (Princeton, NJ: Princeton University Press, 1981).

5. John Williams, *William Wordsworth: A Literary Life* (London: Macmillan Press – now Palgrave Macmillan, 1986), pp. 80–5.

6. William Hazlitt, *The Complete Works*, ed. P. P. Howe (New York: AMS Press, 1967), vol. XVII, p. 118.

7. John Wyatt, *Wordsworth's Poems of Travel, 1819–42: 'Such Sweet Wayfaring'* (London: Macmillan Press – now Palgrave Macmillan, 1999), p. 28.

8. Ibid., p. 29.

9. Crabb Robinson and Pearson are quoted in *The Waggoner*, pp. 21–2, and 27–30.

10. *The Letters of William and Dorothy Wordsworth: The Middle Years*, ed. E. de Selincourt, 2nd edn, Vol. II, 1812–1820, revised by Mary Moorman (Oxford: Clarendon Press, 1969), p. 547.

11. Donald Reiman, 'Benjamin the Waggoner by William Wordsworth, ed. Paul F. Betz', *Studies in Romanticism*, 21, 3 (Autumn 1982), 505.

12. *The White Doe of Rylstone by William Wordsworth: A Critical Edition*, ed. Alice Pattee Comparetti (New York and Oxford: Cornell University Press, 1940).

13. John Williams, '*The White Doe of Rylstone*: An Exercise in Autobiographical Displacement', in *Writing the Lives of Writers*, ed. Warwick Gould and Thomas F. Staley (London: Macmillan Press – now Palgrave Macmillan, 1998), pp. 125–33.

14. Peter J. Manning, *Reading Romantics: Text and Context* (New York and Oxford: Oxford University Press, 1990), pp. 165–215.

15. Comparetti, *The White Doe of Rylstone*, p. 21.

16. Groom, *The Unity of Wordsworth's Poetry*, p. 139.

17. Geoffrey Hartman, *Wordsworth's Poetry 1787–1814* (Cambridge MA and London: Harvard University Press, 1964), p. 324.

18. Ibid., pp. 325–6.

CHAPTER 6: THE POEM AND THE POET IN EXILE: ISSUES OF TEXTUAL IDENTITY: *THE PRELUDE (1)*

1. Susan J. Wolfson, *The Questioning Presence: Wordsworth, Keats, and the Interrogative Mode in Romantic Poetry* (Ithaca, NY and London: Cornell University Press, 1986), p. 135.

2. John Sitter, *Literary Loneliness in Mid-Eighteenth Century England* (Ithaca, NY and London: Cornell University Press, 1982), pp. 157, 161–2.

3. John Barrell and Harriet Guest, 'The uses of contradiction: Pope's "Epistle to Bathurst"', in *Poetry, Language and Politics* (Manchester: Manchester University Press, 1988), pp. 79, 80, 89.

4. Ibid., pp. 97–8.

5. W. H. Pater, 'Wordsworth' (1874), in *Wordsworth: The Prelude*, ed. W. J. Harvey and Richard Gravil (London: Macmillan Press – now Palgrave Macmillan, 1972), pp. 67–8.

6. E. A. Horsman, 'The Design of Wordsworth's *Prelude*', in *Wordsworth's Mind and Art*, ed. A. W. Thomson (Edinburgh: Oliver & Boyd, 1969), p. 95.

7. Bernard Groom, *The Unity of Wordsworth's Poetry* (London: Macmillan Press – now Palgrave Macmillan, 1966), p. 66.

8. Ashton Nichols, *The Revolutionary 'I': Wordsworth and the Politics of Self-Presentation* (London: Macmillan Press – now Palgrave Macmillan, 1998), p. xi.

9. H. W. Garrod, *Wordsworth: Lectures and Essays*, 2nd edn 1927 (Oxford: Oxford University Press, 1970), pp. 59, 190.

10. Nicholas Roe, *The Politics of Nature* (London: Macmillan Press – now Palgrave Macmillan, 1992), p. 109.

11. Nichols, *The Revolutionary 'I'*, pp. xii–xiii.

12. Garrod, *Wordsworth*, pp. 188–9.

13. Roe, *The Politics of Nature*, p. 101.

14. David Simpson, *Wordsworth's Historical Imagination: The Poetry of Displacement* (New York and London: Methuen, 1987), p. 120.

15. *Theory in Practice: The Prelude*, ed. Nigel Wood (Buckingham and Philadelphia: Open University Press, 1993), pp. 3–4.

16. Ibid., p. 11.

17. The source is Virgil's *Georgics* Book II, translated by John Dryden in the 1690s as: 'O happy, if he knew his happy state, / The swain, who, free from business and debate, / Receives his easy food from nature's hand, / And just returns of cultivated land!' (ll.639–42).

18. Roe, *The Politics of Nature*, p. 103.

19. Stephen Gill, *William Wordsworth: A Life* (Oxford: Clarendon Press, 1989), p. 174. Simpson, *Wordsworth's Historical Imagination*, p. 114.

20. John Donne, 'Twicknam Garden', *Complete Poetry and Selected Prose*, ed. John Hayward (London: Nonesuch, 1941), p. 20.

21. Simpson, *Wordsworth's Historical Imagination*, p. 120.

22. Ibid., p. 129.

23. Geoffrey H. Hartman, *Wordsworth's Poetry* (Cambridge MA and London: Harvard University Press, 1971), p. 218.

24. Geoffrey H. Hartman, 'Words, Wish, Worth', in *The Unremarkable Wordsworth* (London: Methuen, 1987), pp. 104–5, 108. The Gospel According to John, Chapter 1, v.i.

25. Hartman, ibid., p. 103.

26. Ibid., p. 102.

CHAPTER 7: TWO CONSCIOUSNESSES: *THE PRELUDE (2)*

1. Ross Woodman, 'Wordsworth's Crazed Bedouin: *The Prelude* and the Fate of Madness', in *Studies in Romanticism*, 27 (Spring 1988), 3–29.

2. Ibid., p. 12.

3. Geoffrey H. Hartman, 'Wordsworth Revisited', in *The Unremarkable Wordsworth* (London: Methuen, 1987), p. 6.

4. William H. Galperin, *Revision and Authority in Wordsworth: The Interpretation of a Career* (Philadelphia: University of Pennsylvania Press, 1989), p. 166.

5. Alan Liu, *Wordsworth: The Sense of History* (Stanford, CA: Stanford University Press, 1989), p. 363.

6. Ibid., pp. 387, 360.

7. Keith Hanley, 'Crossings Out: The Problem of Textual Passage in *The Prelude*', in *Romantic Revisions*, ed. Robert Brinkley and Keith Hanley (Cambridge: Cambridge University Press, 1992), pp. 124, 116.

8. Liu, *Wordsworth*, p. 4.

9. Ibid., p. 23.

10. Ibid., pp. 19, 385, 387.

11. Ibid., p. 388.

12. Celeste Langan, *Romantic Vagrancy: Wordsworth and the Simulation of Freedom* (Cambridge: Cambridge University Press, 1995), p. 200.

13. Gary Harrison, *Wordsworth's Vagrant Muse: Poetry, Property and Power* (Detroit: Wayne State University Press, 1994), p. 126.

14. Gayatri Chakravorti Spivak, 'Sex and History in *The Prelude* (1805): Books IX–XIII' in *Post-Structuralist Readings of English Poetry*, ed. Richard Machin and Christopher Norris (Cambridge: Cambridge University Press, 1987), pp. 193, 194–5.

15. Ibid., p. 206

16. Hartman, *The Unremarkable Wordsworth*, p. 102.

17. Spivak, 'Sex and History in *The Prelude*', p. 207.

18. Mary Jacobus, ' "Splitting the Race of Man in Twain": Prostitution, Personification, and *The Prelude*', in *Romanticism, Writing, and Sexual Difference: Essays on The Prelude* (Oxford: Oxford University Press, 1989), p. 206.

19. John Barrell, *Poetry, Language and Politics* (Manchester: Manchester University Press, 1988), pp. 137–67; L. Kramer, in *English Literary History*, 54 (1987), 619–37.

20. Jacobus, '"Splitting the Race of Man in Twain"', p. 210.

21. Ibid., p. 213.

22. Ibid., p. 216.

23. Ibid., pp. 221–3.

24. Ibid., p. 217.

25. Spivak, 'Sex and History in *The Prelude*', p. 221.

26. Hartman, *The Unremarkable Wordsworth*, p. 104, 103.

27. Garrod, *Wordsworth*, p. 102.

28. Galperin, *Revision and Authority*, p. 188.

CHAPTER 8: A CHOICE OF TEXTS, A CHOICE OF WORDSWORTHS: READING *THE EXCURSION* OVER TWO CENTURIES

1. William Hazlitt, 'Mr. Wordsworth', in *The Spirit of the Age*, in *The Complete Works*, ed. P. P. Howe (New York: AMS, 1967), VII, p. 91.

2. Charles Lamb, *Quarterly Review*, XII (October 1814), 100–11, in John O. Hayden, *Romantic Bards and British Reviewers* (London: Routledge and Kegan Paul, 1971), p. 59.

3. William Hazlitt, *Examiner*, 21 August, October 1814, in *William Wordsworth: A Critical Anthology*, ed. Graham McMaster (Harmondsworth: Penguin Books, 1972), pp. 114–20.

4. Josiah Conder, *Eclectic Review* (January 1815). Ibid., pp. 121–2.

5. *The Collected Letters of Samuel Taylor Coleridge*, ed. Earl Leslie Griggs (Oxford: Clarendon Press, 1956–71), I, p. 527.

6. Kenneth R. Johnston, *Wordsworth and The Recluse* (New Haven, CT and London: Norton, 1984), p. xii.

7. Ibid., p. xiii.

8. Haydon, *Romantic Bards*, p. 53.

9. Ibid., p. 54.

10. Ibid., p. 55.

11. McMaster, *William Wordsworth*, p. 116.

12. Ibid.

13. Ibid.

14. Z. S. Fink, 'Wordsworth and the English Republican Tradition', *Journal of English and Germanic Philology*, 47 (1948), 107–26. 'Dion and Wordsworth's Political Thought', *Studies in Philology* (July 1953), 510–14; Caroline Robbins, *The Eighteenth Century Commonwealthman* (New York) 1959.

15. J. Crofts, 'Wordsworth and the Seventeenth Century' (Folcroft Library Editions, 1974), pp. 1–18.

16. Haydon, *Romantic Bards*, pp. 55, 57.

17. Ibid., pp. 57–8.

18. James Montgomery, *Eclectic Review*, 2nd Series, 3 (January 1815), 13–39.

19. Ibid., p. 61.

20. Ibid., pp. 41, 42, 45.

21. Ibid., p. 25.

22. Ibid., p. 52.

23. *Quarterly Review* (July 1816), 574.

24. Kenneth R. Johnston, *Wordsworth and the Recluse*, p. xvi.

25. Stephen Gill, *Wordsworth and the Victorians* (Oxford: Clarendon Press, 1998), pp. 43–4.

26. Ibid., p. 19.

27. Ibid., pp. 2–4.

28. *Quarterly Review*, XXXVIII (July & October 1828), 314–15.

29. Coventry Patmore, 'The Unknown Eros' (London: Bell and Sons, 1915), p. 269, ll.40–3.

30. Arthur Hugh Clough, 'I dreamed a dream', in *Selected Poems* (Harmondsworth: Penguin Books, 1991), p. 88, ll.80–4.

31. Edward Bulwer-Lytton, *Paul Clifford* (London: Milner and Co., 1890), p. 97.

32. Oliver Goldsmith, 'The Deserted Village' in *Gray, Collins & Goldsmith: The Complete Poems*, ed. Roger Lonsdale (London: Longman, 1969), p. 676, ll.10–12.

33. Matthew Arnold, *Essays in Criticism: Second Series*, 'Wordsworth', in *Matthew Arnold Selected Prose* (Harmondsworth: Penguin Books, 1970), p. 381.

34. Ibid., pp. 379–82, 383.

35. Leslie Stephen, 'Wordsworth's Ethics', in *Hours in a Library* (1879), in McMaster, *Wordsworth*, p. 216.

36. George Eliot, *Adam Bede* (Harmondsworth: Penguin Books, 1980), p. 515.

37. Ibid., p. 515.

38. Arthur Hugh Clough, *O qui me – !*, *Selected Poems*, p. 209 ll.1–4.

39. Edith C. Batho, *The Later Wordsworth* (New York: Russell and Russell, 1963), p. 131.

40. Gordon Kent Thomas, *Wordsworth's Dirge and Promise: Napoleon, Wellington, and the Convention of Cintra* (Lincoln: University of Nebraska Press, 1971), p. 153.

41. Paul Hamilton, *Wordsworth* (Brighton: Harvester Press, 1986), pp. 144–8.

42. Kenneth R. Johnston, *Wordsworth and The Recluse*, pp. 273–4.

43. Peter J. Manning, *Reading Romantics* (Oxford: Oxford University Press, 1990), p. 273.

44. David Simpson, *Wordsworth's Historical Imagination* (New York and London: Methuen, 1897), p. 186.

45. Ibid., p. 211.

46. Matthew Arnold, *Essays in Criticism*, p. 382.

CHAPTER 9: MAKING THE BEST OF IT: THE LATER POETRY

1. Frances Ferguson, *Language as Counter-Spirit* (New Haven, CT and London: Yale University Press, 1977), pp. 36, 241.

2. Matthew Arnold, 'Essays in Criticism: Second Series' (1888), 'The Study of Poetry', in *Matthew Arnold: Selected Prose*, ed. P. J. Keating (Harmondsworth: Penguin Books, 1970), p. 372.

3. Geoffrey H. Hartman, *Wordsworth's Poetry 1787–1814* (Cambridge, MA and London: Harvard University Press, 1987), p. 330.

4. Peter J. Manning, *Reading Romantics: Text and Context* (Oxford: Oxford University Press, 1990), p. 291.

5. Ibid., p. 295.

6. Stephen Gill, *William Wordsworth: A Life* (Oxford: Clarendon Press, 1989), p. 335 passim.

7. Herbert Read, *Wordsworth* (London: Faber and Faber, 1949), p. 13.

8. Ibid., p. 34.

9. Ibid., p. 20.

10. Ibid., p. 72.

11. Ibid.

12. Ibid., p. 118

13. Ibid., pp. 118–19.

14. Ibid., pp. 135–6.

15. Hartman, *Wordsworth's Poetry*, p. xiv.

16. Jonathan Wordsworth, *The Borders of Vision* (Oxford: Clarendon Press, 1982), pp. 187–8, 370.

17. Read, *Wordsworth*, p. 146.

18. The text of the redrafted stanzas, along with a summary of the debate that accompanied them, is included in the Notes to the single volume *Wordsworth: Poetical Works*, ed. Thomas Hutchinson, and revised by Ernest de Selincourt (Oxford: Oxford University Press, first published in that edition 1936).

19. *Adventures on Salisbury* Plain, in The *Salisbury Plain Poems of William Wordsworth*, ed. Stephen Gill (Ithaca, NY and Hassocks: Cornell University Press, 1975), p. 154, ll.820–8.

20. Ibid., pp. 281–3, ll.657–67.

21. Alan G. Hill, *Tennyson, Wordsworth and the 'Forms' of Religion* (Lincoln: Tennyson Society Monograph, 1997), p. 19.

22. *The Letters of William and Dorothy Wordsworth: The Middle Years,* ed. E. de Selincourt, 2nd edn, Vol. 2, 1806–1811, revised by Mary Moorman (Oxford: Clarendon Press, 1969), p. 268.

23. Hill, *Tennyson, Wordsworth and the 'Forms' of Religion*, p. 19.

24. Anne L. Rylestone, *Prophetic Memory in Wordsworth's Ecclesiastical Sonnets* (Carbondale and Edwardsville: Southern Illinois University Press, 1991), p. 52.

25. Ibid., p. 97.

26. Ibid., p. 11.

CHAPTER 10: CONCLUSION: CRITICAL ISSUES THEN AND NOW

1. E. P. Thompson, *The Making of the English Working Class* (London: Gollancz, 1965); David V. Erdman, *Blake: Prophet Against Empire* (Princeton, NJ: Princeton University Press, 1954).

2. *Romanticism: Vistas, Instances, Continuities*, ed. David Thorburn and Geoffrey Hartman (Ithaca, NY and London, 1973), pp. 7–8.

3. D. D. Devlin, *Wordsworth and the Poetry of Epitaphs* (London: Macmillan Press – now Palgrave Macmillan, 1980), pp. 3–4.

4. Geoffrey H. Hartman, 'Inscriptions and Romantic Nature Poetry', in *The Unremarkable Wordsworth* (London: Methuen, 1987), p. 43. Jonathan Wordsworth, *William Wordsworth: The Borders of Vision* (Oxford: Clarendon Press, 1982), p. 17.

5. Thompson, *The Making of the English Working Class*, p. 176.

6. Amanda M. Ellis, *Rebels and Conservatives: Dorothy and William Wordsworth and their Circle* (Bloomington and London: Indiana University Press, 1967), p. xiii. F. M. Todd, *Politics and the Poet: A Study of Wordsworth* (London: Macmillan Press – now Palgrave Macmillan, 1957). Carl Woodring, *Politics in English Romantic Poetry* (Cambridge, MA: Harvard University Press, 1970), pp. 24–48.

7. John Lucas, *England and Englishness* (London: Hogarth Press, 1990), p. 90.

8. Peter J. Manning, 'Wordsworth at St. Bees', in *Reading Romantic: Text and Context* (New York and Oxford: Oxford University Press, 1990), p. 291.

9. G. Kim Blank, *Wordsworth's Influence on Shelley* (London: Macmillan Press – now Palgrave Macmillan, 1988), p. 163.

10. H. G. Schenk, *The Mind of the European Romantics* (Oxford: Oxford University Press, 1979), p. 9.

11. Susan J. Wolfson, *The Questioning Presence* (Ithaca, NY and London: Cornell University Press, 1986), p. 17.

12. Ibid., p. 96.

13. F. W. Bateson, *Wordsworth: A Reinterpretation* (London, 1954), in *William Wordsworth: A Critical Anthology*, ed. Graham McMaster (Harmondsworth: Penguin Books, 1972), p. 374.

14. David Ferry, *The Limits of Mortality: An Essay on Wordsworth's Major Poems*, in McMaster, *Wordsworth*, p. 433.

15. Frederick A. Pottle, 'Wordsworth in the Present Day', in *Romanticism: Vistas, Instances, Continuities*, ed. David Thorburn and Geoffrey Hartman, pp. 117–18.

16. James B. Twitchell, *Romantic Horizons: Aspects of the Sublime in English Poetry and Painting, 1770–1850* (Colombia: University of Missouri Press, 1983), pp. 60–1.

17. David B. Pirie, *William Wordsworth: The Poetry of Grandeur and of Tenderness* (London: Methuen, 1982), p. 1.

18. Ibid., p. 11.

19. Brian G. Caraher, *Wordsworth's 'Slumber' and the Problematics of Reading* (London: Pennsylvania State University Press, 1991), p. 7.

20. Bernard Groom, *The Unity of Wordsworth's Poetry* (London and New York: Macmillan Press – now Palgrave Macmillan, 1966), p. 1.

21. Jonathan Bate, *Romantic Ecology: Wordsworth and the Environmental Tradition* (London and New York: Routledge, 1991), p. 9.

22. Celeste Langan, *Romantic Vagrancy: Wordsworth and the Simulation of Freedom* (Cambridge: Cambridge University Press, 1995), p. 12.

23. Robin Jarvis, *Romantic Writing and Pedestrian Travel* (London: Macmillan Press – now Palgrave Macmillan, 1997), p. 215.

24. Bate, *Romantic Ecology*, p. 6.

25. David Simpson, *Wordsworth's Historical Imagination* (London: Methuen, 1987), p. 14.

26. Ibid., p. 17.

27. Alan Liu, *Wordsworth: the Sense of History* (Stanford, CA: Stanford University Press, 1989), pp. 500–1.

28. G. Kim Blank, *Wordsworth and Feeling: The Poetry of an Adult Child* (London: Associated University Presses, 1995), p. 17.

29. Ibid., p. 215.

Index